W9-AUE-520

Emerge

The Opening of the Human Heart to the Power of Love

Inspired by a True Event

by Susan M. Omilian JD

Butterfly Bliss Productions LLC
West Hartford, CT

Anne Marie,
You are
AN
angel
and a
thriver!

Su
9/2019

Butterfly Bliss Productions LLC
P.O. Box 330482, West Hartford, CT 06133
ButterflyBlissProductions.com
ThriverZone.com
SusanOmilian.com

This is a work of fiction. Names, characters, places, and incidents are the products of the author's imagination or are used fictitiously. Any resemblance to actual events, locales, or persons, living or dead, is entirely coincidental.

ISBN # 978-0-9985746-4-6 print book
ISBN # 978-0-9985746-2-2 e-book

Author photo by Cynthia Lang Photography
Cover and interior design by Anita Jones, Another Jones Graphics I AnotherJones.com

This book is available at quantity discounts for bulk purchase. Contact the publisher.

A portion of the proceeds of this book will be donated to services for women and children who have experienced abuse and violence.

Publisher's Cataloging-In-Publication Data
(Prepared by The Donohue Group, Inc.)

Names: Omilian, Susan M., author.

Title: Emerge : the opening of the human heart to the power of love / by Susan M. Omilian JD.

Description: West Hartford, CT : Butterfly Bliss Productions LLC, [2019] I Series: The best revenge series ; [2] I "Inspired by a true event."

Identifiers: ISBN 9780998574646 (print) I ISBN 9780998574622 (ebook)

Subjects: LCSH: Abused women--Psychology. I Homeless men--Fiction. I Birthfathers --Fiction. I Love--Fiction. I LCGFT: Domestic fiction. I Psychological fiction.

Classification: LCC PS3615.M55 E44 2019 (print) I LCC PS3615.M55 (ebook) I DDC 813/.6--dc23

Printed in the United States of America

"Emerge *is a good read and a great opportunity to learn. With Susan's unique insights into the impact of violence and abuse on women's lives from her personal and professional experience with victims and offenders alike, the characters come alive for the reader. They also learn how stigmatizing trauma can be for its victims.*"

— **Linda McMurray, LCSW, Domestic Violence Counselor**

"*Susan's fast-paced story,* Emerge, *highlights the changes that have been made on college campuses and what work can continue to be done to increase student safety regarding intimate partner violence and sexual assault. It is also an inspiring story of how victims of such violence can, with courage and determination, face the long-term psychological impacts on their lives and find hope in the future.*"

— **Michael Siembor, PhD, Licensed Psychologist, College Counseling Center**

"*I thoroughly enjoyed traveling with Lisette on her exciting journey to find unconditional, reliable love. I laughed, I cried, I was held in suspense as to what would happen next. Seeing things unfold for Lisette gives all of us who are searching for unconditional love a vision of how it can be found. This book was hard to put down!*"

— **Theresa Coughlin, Fiscal Manager of a Health Care Agency**

"Emerge *is a riveting story with superb character development and a well-paced plot. It shows how a traumatic experience can connect a diverse group of people and bind them for life on a path to growth and healing.*"

— **Adrienne Doughty, M.A., Energy Healer, Reiki Master**

"Emerge *is a perfect sequel to* Awaken. *I couldn't put it down! The characters, male and female alike, all 'emerge' to create a beautiful story.*"

— **Edith, a *My Avenging Angel Workshop*™ participant**

What People Are Saying About Susan's Books In *The Best Revenge Series*™

Awaken

"*Treat yourself to this moving story!* Awaken *is a fascinating extension of the cutting-edge, healing work Susan has done with her My Avenging Angel Workshops™ and workbook,* Entering the Thriver Zone. *Susan's novel captures the heart and soul of the important personal journey to thriving.*"

—**Kathryn Tull, M.A., LMFT, author, *The Next Bold Step***

Entering the Thriver Zone

"This workbook offers faith, courage and dignity to women who have survived the destructive and selfish actions of abusive men. Susan's message is 'Don't settle for anything less than a life that is better than ever.' She knows that women can do it and by the time a woman has worked her way through this excellent guidebook for healing, she will believe it, too."

— Lundy Bancroft, author, *Why Does He Do That?: Inside the Minds of Angry and Controlling Men* and *Daily Wisdom for Why Does He Do That?*

"Susan begins with a rare insight—that what makes a battered woman is not what the abuser has done to her but what he has kept her from doing for herself—and then takes her readers on a jubilant journey of self-realization. On the way, Susan helps them remake their world and get back in touch with their power and possibility."

— Evan Stark PhD, MSW, Professor and Author of *Coercive Control: How Men Entrap Women in Personal Life*

Staying in the Thriver Zone

"Susan has a gift of giving women who have been battered and beaten new hope and a way forward. This workbook is her best work yet, forging a clear path to a life of power and purpose for women who want to thrive in peace, love and joy!"

— Alyce LaViolette, MS, MFT, author, *It Could Happen to Anyone: Why Battered Women Stay*

"Susan's work is impressive. I use her workbooks in my practice, helping abuse survivors, young or old, move beyond survivor to thriver. Her materials can help all who have suffered trauma. I love how Susan's books incorporate a journey to healing without having my clients relive the trauma itself."

— Diana Barnes-Fox, MA, AMFT, ALPCC

For

Maggie

1980–1999

This is not your story.
But I hope this is the way you
would want this story told.

May the reading of this story be a healing journey
for those who have been
most devastated by your loss.
You were so loved!

My heart is moved by all that I cannot save;
so much has been destroyed.
I have to cast my lot with those who, age after age,
perversely with no extraordinary power,
reconstitute the world.

—Adrienne Rich

ACKNOWLEDGMENTS

Thanks to all those who have helped me tell this story and put it on the page so it can be of benefit to others.

Thanks to those who work tirelessly on college campuses every day to ensure the safety of all students and enforce the provisions of Title IX of the Education Amendments of 1972. That law requires that a woman cannot be discriminated on the basis of her sex in pursuit of her educational opportunities.

Thank you to Claudia Volkman for editing and Anita Jones of Another Jones Graphics for the book covers and interior design.

Special thanks to Sharon Castlen of Integrated Book Marketing for getting what I do and helping me get it out into the world.

Susan M. Omilian

Note from the Author

Readers of *Awaken*, the first book in *The Best Revenge Series*™, will remember that the inspiration for this story told in a series of three fictional books was a true event. On October 17, 1999, my niece Maggie, a nineteen-year-old college student, was shot and killed on campus by her ex-boyfriend who then killed himself.

As I wrote in *Awaken*, that story came to me by using one of the best tools that a fiction writer has: the "what if" method of finding the story. What if there was a young woman like Maggie who had been killed in a similar manner? What would happen to that person, her friends and family members? Would she ever rest in peace? How would they find a way to move forward without her?

With this book, *Emerge*, set ten years after the death of Lacey, my fictional main character, I continue to explore those intriguing questions as well as others. What could Lacey's friends do after such a horrific event to honor her and make the world safe for other women like her? What issues would they take on? What would they be able to accomplish in ten years? What about the next ten years?

While these are great "what if" questions to speculate about in a fictional story, it is true that because this book is being published in 2019, you, the reader, already know what actually happened in the real world during that twenty-year period from 1999 to 2019. We know, for example, that the #MeToo movement started in 2017 and spread so virally on social media in the United States and around the world that it immediately raised the awareness of how widespread and prevalent sexual assault, domestic violence, and sexual harassment still are in our society. It created greater empathy for the victims—mostly female—and a better understanding of the impact of these crimes on them physically, financially, and emotionally.

It is the impact of violence on women and girls that the fictional *Emerge* story describes in 2009, eight years before the #MeToo movement and before terms such as "trauma-informed care" and "survivor-centered services" entered the public discourse. In the story, several characters are in that healing process and their stories show how by surrounding yourself with people—family, friends, colleagues—who can give you unconditional love, the effects of the trauma experienced can be lessened. Lisette, one of the main characters in the novel, describes how she was looking for and found "reliable love," given without conditions or offered without anticipation of getting something in return. It is the kind of love we can get from others and we can also give ourselves because no matter what mistakes we've made, we are still worthy and deserving of such love. May you be inspired by Lisette's journey to find such love and use it to fuel your journey to manifest the life of your dreams.

Ever since I was a little girl, I dreamed of writing novels with intriguing characters and powerful plotlines that people would love. This series of books, first *Awaken*, now *Emerge*, and finally *Thrive*, is that dream fulfilled. True, I didn't wish for something so tragic and sad, such as the death of my niece Maggie, to be a way for me realize this dream. But good things can come from tragedy. After all, living well is the best revenge!

I will miss Maggie every day of my life, but I will also celebrate her life each day by living my best life. I hope this book will inspire you to do the same.

Susan M. Omilian

"*When I despair, I remember that all through history the ways of truth and love have always won. There have been tyrants, and murderers, and for a time they can seem invincible, but in the end, they always fall. Think of it—always.*"

— Mahatma Gandhi

CONTENTS

Living well is the best revenge.

— George Herbert

*There is no inner landscape in the invisible world of our souls
and hearts but is full of the most melodious and
nourishing and wild freedom.
And everyone should go there, to the wild place, where there are
no cages, where there are not tight rooms without windows
and without doors, everyone should go to the free clearance
places in their own hearts.*

— John O'Donohue

*We need love
as we need water.*

— Maya Angelou

August 25, 1979

From Marie's Diary

Today it's my nineteenth birthday, and I am starting this diary as a birthday present to myself. I want to write down everything so I won't forget because this is the story of my new life. I am going through what some people call a "transformation"—a big word, but it simply means that from this day forward, I will never be the same again.

Everything I write here is the absolute truth. So help me God! I don't know how it happened to me, but it did. I am after all just a girl who makes her living as an exotic dancer—I guess that's the polite word for it. I dance real sexy for men in bars and don't wear a lot of clothes when I do it. My favorite tune to dance to is "Bad Girls" by Donna Summer, so you know where I'm coming from. I don't know where to start this story, so I'll just begin by saying I'm in love with Brad and Brad's in love with me. Bradford Reginald Bufford. That's his full name. It's a great name to put a Mrs. in front of—Mrs. Bradford Reginald Bufford—and soon it'll be my name. I never knew that anything this good could happen to me. I am so happy!

How did I meet someone with such a great name like Bradford? Someone whose family has money and who fell in love with me? That's the most amazing part of the story. One afternoon last

April, I was sitting around with some of the girls I dance with at the bar watching the soaps before our shift started. Suddenly, a news flash breaks in, and we all groan because we hate to miss our shows. But this news guy was going on about a meltdown at the nuclear power plant in Harrisburg, Pennsylvania, at a place called Three Mile Island and how all this radioactive stuff got into the air and so I guess we all should've been listening to him. But then this other guy comes on from a local anti-nuke group—who turns out later to be Brad—and boy, he got our attention. Not by what he was saying but because of his gorgeous face, incredible body, and these amazing dark brown eyes. Me and the girls goofed around talking dirty about what it would be like to land someone like him when one of the girls broke in.

"Hey, forget it," she said. "None of us will ever get close to him. He's too rich, too white bread."

I didn't know what she meant by white bread, but her mouthing off felt like a dare, so I took her on.

I said, "I bet you I could get him to want to marry me and take me home to meet his folks. You know, the whole thing, babies and a big house in the suburbs."

All the girls laughed, but I was serious. I knew I could do it! Next thing I know, I'm making up a plan about how I can meet Brad.

I needed the right look. I fixed my hair differently, toned down my makeup, and found a second-hand shop in town where I got me some clothes that make me look like a college girl. Then I went to the office where Brad worked and asked for him. I told him how I saw him on television the other day about Three Mile Island and how that freaked me out. I wanted to help. I was worried that he might be all stuck up and not as good-looking in person, but when I saw him, he was even more gorgeous and *soooo* nice. He explained everything to me about what his group was doing, but I was hooked the moment he flashed those dark brown eyes at me. I had my own meltdown, you see. Just a joke, ha-ha. An anti-nuke joke. Get it?

Now that I know him better, I do think we could make it to-gether, have kids and all that. I'm serious about this. I love him, and he loves me. I've always wanted a daughter. I'd name her Lisa. I love that name! And our son would be Brad Jr. We'd be proud of our kids, and I'd give them the kind of love that I never got from my parents. Plus all the things I never had! We'd love them to the moon!

That's how Brad says he loves me—to the moon and back!

I am so happy. I did it. I am part of Brad's life now and forever. We are happy.

Nothing can stop us now.

December 24, 1990
From Lisa's Diary

It is Christmas Eve. I am ten years old. I don't write real good but Mommy says I should write in my diary when I feel lost or con-fused. I sure feel like that today.

My Mommy's name is Marie. She gave this diary to me on my birthday and showed me hers. She has kept it for a long time. Someday I can read it, she says, but not now. That's okay.

Mommy is real sick and in the hospital. Ralph is coming to get me soon to take me to see her there for Christmas. It is hard to see her so sick. When I go there, I sit with her and she smiles and holds my hand. But then she gets really tired and falls asleep.

Ralph is my dad. When he's mad at me, he says he's not. Mommy says he is joking. I don't care as long as Mommy is here. Mommy says that she loves me to the moon and back. It's a long way to the moon. She says that means she loves me a lot.

I wish she felt better. I don't want her to go away. Ralph told me if I was bad Mommy would go away. But I don't believe him. He is a liar. Mommy always told me telling a lie was bad. Ralph is bad. My mommy is good.

Mommy says she loves me no matter what and she'll never leave me. We will always be together.

Please don't leave me, Mommy. I'll miss you, Mommy. I love you.

I love you to the moon and back!

CHAPTER ONE

Wednesday, October 14, 2009

Before the Anniversary

Lisette wasn't thrilled about coming back to this place. After all, it was the college on the hill where ten years ago a crazy guy named Ari, a man with a gun, killed Lacey and then killed himself.

But she was there on a Wednesday, a few days before the tenth anniversary of that horrible day October 17, 1999. Besides not wanting to be reminded of all the trauma and drama of that time in her life, she never felt comfortable on a college campus. True, it was here that she found Sophie, Lacey's college roommate and best friend, who believed Lisette when she told her that Lacey's spirit had come into her body and she needed her help. It was a wild ride, but at least, Lacey was at peace now.

But Lisette's biggest fear of being on the campus again was more about how little schooling she had and how she couldn't read so good. Then too, she had been a stripper dancing under the stage name of Attila the Hunny the night Lacey died and when she first met Sophie at Lacey's funeral days later. Lisette felt stupid even being around college kids and couldn't understand why Sophie wanted her to come back and help her celebrate the tenth anniversary of Lacey's murder. To Lisette, it was more like something you'd want to forget or try to remember without feeling sad, but somehow Sophie saw it as a celebration. She was putting togeth-er a Tenth Anniversary Gala—that's what she called it—and she wanted Lisette to help her.

As crazy as it sounded, Lisette couldn't say no. When Sophie told her of her plan to gather all those who had helped her become so successful in her work—and her work *was* amaz-ing—so she could thank them personally, Lisette wasn't sure that she was one of the people to thank. She hadn't done that much. Sophie was the one who was so smart, so clever, and so brave. She knew how to get things done. Still Lisette was curi-ous about what she had accomplished and how everyone and everything was. She had heard so much about it from Sophie on the phone and in the letters she wrote her. She had to see it with her own eyes.

But riding up to the school in a taxi that afternoon wasn't ex-actly the best way to take it all in, Lisette realized later. She could see that the buildings on the campus looked the same, but the students...they looked so much younger than she remembered. Of course, she was ten years older now—almost 30—and not get-ting any younger. For someone in her line of work, staying and looking young was everything.

As the taxi drove through the campus and headed toward the large, open green space where the Student Center was located, Lisette wondered if Sophie or anyone else on the campus would actually recognize her now.

In the last ten years, she had gone through quite a transformation from Attila the Hunny, the stripper, to a successful businesswoman. Only Todd, her business manager and sometime boyfriend, knew how hard that change had been for her. But it wasn't the biggest change she had ever made in her life. True, in the last ten years, she had lent her stage name, Attila the Hunny, to a nationwide chain of strip joints, which Todd liked to call "upscale male entertainment venues." The business logo featured that pouty pose of her dressed up in her skimpy, white furry outfit she had worn for years on the stage—her Attila the Hunny getup. *Ha!* she thought. She got paid a lot of money now licensing her name and image for the clubs, but she had to admit, what she was doing wasn't so remarkable or exciting. Not compared to Sophie's work for sure!

But Todd thought she was wonderful and smart, and he needed her in the business. Sure, she worked with new girls hired for the Attila the Hunny clubs, but mostly Lisette lived off the royalties from the use of her name and image on that company logo. She imagined doing something more important and special, something for women who grew up hard like she had to help them be financially successful too. Couldn't she find a way to do that? Maybe that's why she came when Sophie called.

She wished Todd had come with her so he might understand what she really wanted to do, but he said he couldn't take the time away from the business. Still he encouraged her to go. "Have a good time," he said as he hugged and kissed her that morning. Then he held her for a moment as if he didn't really want her to go. "Come back and tell me what's going on with everyone. I want a full report on the place that was the inspiration for our Attila the Hunny franchise."

But that's what he didn't get, Lisette thought. Attila the Hunny was something that she had worked on for years, perfecting the act, the music she played, and the costumes she wore, but it was just a job. It was something her mother had done and she fell into to support herself. But being a stripper wasn't the only thing she wanted to do. Something else was calling her, but what was it?

That question haunted her most days, and today it was like a voice screaming in her head: "What are you doing? You need to make more of yourself! Look at what Sophie has done in honor of her best friend Lacey! What have you done? Nothing!"

Still Lisette knew she had come a long way in her life. After losing her mother, Marie, when she was only ten years old, she had escaped living with her father, Ralph, at sixteen. That's when she changed her name from "Lisa" to "Lisette," which she believed was a sexier, cooler name. Then, at nineteen years of age, she was dancing in town one night at the Pussycat's Meow as the headline stripper. That's when things really changed in her life.

The wild ride she took ten years ago started with finding Sophie here on the campus, working with her and her grandmother, Radiance, a shaman, to journey to the Upper World and help Lacey's spirit cross over. Lisette remembered how happy Lacey was to see her mother again, there on the other side, ready to help her over and enter paradise. That experience had changed Lisette's life. She went back home to Los Angeles, gave up dancing, and got into business. She liked the money and fame that came with lending her stripper name to clubs all over the globe, but something was missing. Sophie's letters and phone calls over the last ten years made Lisette realize that there was something back here, in this town, on this campus, that she needed to see and be inspired by. She needed to know what Sophie had done to transform what happened to Lacey into something good, something to help others. Maybe then she could find her way to do something like that too.

As the taxi stopped in front of the Student Center, Lisette got out and paid the driver. She had arrived this morning from LA, gone to her hotel from the airport, and after unpacking her bags, came here to meet Sophie for lunch. Sophie told her she'd meet her at the Student Center because her office on campus was right up the hill next to the chapel. She'd watch for her up there, await her text that she had arrived, then come down to meet her.

Lisette was excited to see Sophie and spend some time with her before all the festivities began over the weekend. But before walking toward the Student Center, she looked up the hill toward the chapel and was filled with amazement. What she saw she could never have imagined ten years ago. *My God!* Lisette marveled. Lacey would be so proud of all Sophie had accomplished! She had found her best revenge. But what about hers?

Would Lisette ever get there, too?

◈ ◈ ◈

Sitting in her office near the top of the hill in a building next to the chapel, Sophie looked down at the Student Center. She knew that soon Lisette would drive up in a taxi and she'd be there on this campus for the first time in ten years. That fact amazed Sophie not only because it had been that long since Lacey was gone, but also that she was still here on this campus, trying to make a difference. It was that hard.

She often wondered what Lacey would have done if she, Sophie, was the one who had been killed so violently, so senselessly and Lacey was the one who had survived. In the short time that Sophie knew her, Lacey was driven, single-minded and downright stubborn. Maybe she would have accomplished more than Sophie had so far, maybe not. But at least, Sophie was determined not to give up. Lacey was never a quitter.

Although she had graduated seven years ago from the college, Sophie had come back here after law school to take a part-time job at the school. She wanted to do the work she had vowed to do the night her best friend was shot and killed in a dorm room on the other side of campus. But this wasn't Sophie's only job. She also worked off campus at a nonprofit organization she had founded three years ago. She loved what she did. It gave her joy every day to be doing this work.

Today she was excited to see Lisette again. They had bonded for life ten years ago but she knew that the sight of Lisette would both delight and unnerve her. Sure, Lisette would still have her amazing physique and stunningly beautiful face. She wouldn't have changed a bit! But the sight of her would fill Sophie with a flood of memories and, for a moment perhaps, an overwhelming sense of sadness. Lisette had come back to town today, and they'd laugh and have lunch together like old friends. But Lacey, the one true friend in her life, would still be gone.

She still missed Lacey so much and all that they had planned to do together after they graduated college. They were going to go out and change the world, making it a better place for their children. Of course, the work they were going to do would be very glamorous and fulfilling and yet still leave time for a happy, successful relationship with the man of their dreams. Sophie would often laugh at their naiveté, about how their future would unfold and wonder if Lacey, wherever she was, shared her assessment.

The work she did now was here on this campus and it was hardly glamorous. It was satisfying and fulfilling except that she always felt as if she hadn't accomplished enough. There was so much more to do. At least today, she could show off to Lisette some of the work she had done to date on and off campus. Then later this weekend at the Tenth Anniversary Gala, everyone would see not only what had been accomplished to date, but also what her vision was for the future. The work had to continue and be expanded to ensure Lacey's legacy on this campus and beyond.

Sophie had to keep going. This was only the beginning, she told herself from the start. Get the guns, change the campus, save the victims, and heal the survivors.

She had to do it for Lacey. She had to do it for herself.

As Sophie waited for Lisette, she remembered that day ten years ago when she took the first step.

◈ ◈ ◈

Thursday, November 18, 1999

Sophie was pissed.

She had read in the police report after Lacey's murder last month about the gun store where Ari had bought the gun that killed Lacey, and she knew she had to do something about it. Isn't that what Lacey always said? "This is so unfair! We have to do something about it!"

But it wasn't going to be easy. She could see that she had no authority to tell this gun shop owner to do anything. But she thought maybe, just maybe, she could appeal to his heart. But then she wondered, do people who sell guns that kill other people have a heart? Or is it just all about making money?

She didn't know. All she knew was that she had to try. It was a whole month since Lacey's death and she had to do something!

Driving to the gun store, Sophie had her doubts. Maybe she should have had someone else come with her. She could have waited until Lisette was available. She was still in town, and it looked as if she and Erick might get together. But Lisette was busy today, and Sophie couldn't wait for another day.

Still it would've made more sense to have someone come with her. What if the guy in the gun store got pissed at her and tried to throw her out? She had no backup and he had all the guns. She didn't know anything about guns. Her mother and grandmother, Radiance, would never let her have toy guns when she was growing up. Her mother was a hippie, after all. She was into her peace marches and taking drugs, too many drugs. What made Sophie think she could talk about guns with this guy!

As she turned the corner onto the street where the gun store was located, she saw the word "GUNS" painted in large letters on the front of the building, with the name of the store "Guns Galore!" underneath it. Suddenly the glaring realization that this was the place Ari came to buy the gun that killed Lacey hit her. Maybe this wasn't the thing that should be occupying her focus and attention so soon after her best friend's death.

Then she heard Lacey's voice in her head again—"This is so unfair"—that Ari could just walk into this place and buy a gun.

Then again, "we have to do something about this," and Sophie knew she had to at least try to talk to the owner of this shop.

She got out of the car, grabbed her notebook, and headed through the front door into the store. As she did it, she gagged at the pungent smell—oil, grease, and the odor of metals. She saw counters, one after the other, of guns of all kinds, shapes, and sizes. *Amazing!* she thought. *Were there really so many choices out there?* Not to mention ammunition, all kinds of hats, targets, and clothing. She walked up and down the aisles until she came to a glass counter with a cash register on it. Behind it was a wall with all kinds of gadgets and products for the hunter, sportsman, and gun owner. Sophie almost felt for a moment that these gun owners were just like any other shoppers, and they would come here to get it all.

But then she saw a sign saying, *"God made man, but Samuel Colt made them equal,"* attributed to Colt Manufacturing. Of course, that was a reference to the guns like the Colt 45 manufactured by Colt. Suddenly Sophie felt as if she were in alien NRA territory where the National Rifle Association ruled, and nobody would care about what happened to Lacey. In her mind's eye she could see Lacey's face and the gun blast and how Ari killed her. Her heart jumped, and she felt nauseous. *This is too much,* she thought. *I can't do it.*

As she was about to turn around and escape this crazy world, a man emerged from a door behind the counter and called out to her.

"Can I help you, Miss? Is there something you're looking for today?"

Sophie turned slowly to see a man, tall and lean, with crisp blue eyes and long silver-streaked hair pulled back into a ponytail. She was startled not only by his gentle appearance, but also his mellow-sounding voice. He couldn't be the owner, she thought. That aggressive, hard person must be in the back room hiding out.

"No, no," Sophie stammered. "I just came to...to..."

He looked at her for a long moment, taking her in, maybe assessing why she was there, and then he asked her casually, "You must be a college student, right? I have a daughter about your age. Did you see her picture on our website?" He pointed to the wall behind him where there was a framed photo of a younger girl with soft blonde curls holding a gun up to her face and smiling. "That was taken a few years ago to be sure," he added with a smile. "But she's still loves her guns!"

His friendliness unnerved her. He talked so casually about his young daughter loving guns, and he acted like Sophie had come to shop for guns the way she might shop for shoes at Walmart.

Okay, she thought quickly, *I have to do this—for Lacey.*

She took a deep breath and began.

"Are you the owner of this store? I need to talk to the owner."

"Yeah, that's me. Jimmy Trager," he replied with a swagger.

"Um, okay. I wanted to...I need to ask you something." She paused for a moment, then blurted out, "Do you really own this place?"

"Yes," he said slowly, like he was trying to be patient with her, but he sighed and then his voice went deeper. "This is my business, been in my family for years. It belonged to my father before me, and my grandfather before him." Then his voice returned to a friendlier tone. "Who knows? Maybe I'll hand it down to my daughter, Trisha!"

"So how old is your daughter?"

"She'll be nineteen this month."

"Really?" Sophie said with surprise. His daughter wasn't any older than Sophie.

"Yeah," he continued. "She's all grown up and going to school out of state. She says she's a business major." Then he smiled. "Who knows, maybe she will turn this business into a gold mine.

Then I can retire and live off her hard work after all those years of her living off mine!"

All this chatter about his legacy of the family business to his daughter was overwhelming Sophie. She had to be brave and remember why she was here.

"Listen," she began, her voice as firm as she could muster with her knees shaking beneath her. "I'm here to let you know—" She stopped and corrected herself. "Actually, I'm here to demand to know why you sold a gun to this man." She pulled a folded page of a newspaper out of her notebook and flashed it in front of him. On the page was a photo of Ari with the article about Lacey's murder.

The man stared at the page but didn't speak.

"You remember him, right?" she demanded.

The man sighed, "Yes, he was here. He wanted to buy a gun, and I sold it to him. That's it."

"No," Sophie shot back. "That's not it. He killed my friend." She pulled up the newspaper article again and pointed to Lacey's photo on the other side of the fold. "See her face? He blew her face away with the gun that you sold him. Do you care that what you sell here kills people?"

She was getting agitated now. She could feel her face getting hot and her stomach turning from the anger she felt.

The man shook his head, and his voice softened when he spoke. "Listen, I'm sorry about your friend. I don't sell guns to hurt people, but I can't control how people use the products I sell. Sure, I remember this kid. He said he wanted to go hunting; it was hunting season."

"But according to this newspaper article," she said, waving the page in front of him again, "he gave you a college dormitory address and you didn't feel an obligation to contact the college about the gun. Do you know that our college has a zero-tolerance, no-guns-on-campus policy? It was just put into place this fall."

"No," he admitted. "Of course I didn't know about that policy. And I have no legal obligation to report to anyone at the college. The only thing I'm required by law to do is a simple background check on anyone who buys a hunting rifle. Usually it only takes a day. With a handgun, it takes longer, but he didn't want to buy a handgun."

"But that may be why he wanted a hunting rifle. Don't you see? He was a computer kid. He knew how to research guns and gun laws on the internet. He figured out that you'd ask him the least number of questions if he bought a hunting rifle. Particularly in hunting season and in goddamn NRA country here."

"Look," he said, leaning over the counter. "This is not my problem. Jesus, what do you want from me? I sell guns for a living." Then he repeated, "I can't control what people do with them." His voice was rising now, and it looking to Sophie as though he was reaching for one of the guns under the counter.

"Oh, great!" she cried. "What are you planning to do now? Kill me too with that gun you are reaching for? Solve your problem about me coming in here and accusing you of having no morals. That's what Ari did, don't you see that? Buy a gun, solve a problem. Makes it so simple!"

"All right," the man said, suddenly straightening up and grabbing the phone next to him on the counter. "I'm going to ask you to leave my store right now. If you don't choose to do that, I'll call the police. Do you understand?"

"Yes, I understand," she replied sarcastically. "Remember, I'm a college student, and I know how to do research on the internet too. I know the limits of your legal obligations. I was just hoping as a human being you would want to go a little further. Like help me do something about this."

"Do what? About what?"

"About the proliferation of guns on college campuses. Did you know that a study by Harvard School of Public Health just this past July found that over 3.5 percent—or 450,000 college students—currently keep a working firearm at college? That fact is shocking and scary to me!"

"Look, if your friend had a gun, she could have defended herself, and maybe she'd still be alive today."

"Great! You want our college campuses to be like the Wild West. Shoot-outs in dorm rooms, and if you don't like someone, or someone has broken up with you and you are an angry, controlling man, it's okay to shoot the girl. Maybe if she's lucky, she can shoot you back so you die before her. That's crazy!"

The man's face was bright red now, and he was shaking his finger in her face. "I'm asking you to leave right now, and I do mean NOW! Or I will call the cops."

"Fine," she shot back. "I'll be leaving your family-owned, 'I'm American and proud of it' business. But I'll be back. Don't think this is the end of this for me. I just thought—crazy thought!—I could come here and maybe find that you had a heart and wanted to help me stop someone else's best friend from being shot down like an animal." Sophie stuffed the newspaper article back in her notebook and turn to leave the store.

"By the way," she yelled over her shoulder as she walked out the door. "Samuel Colt...the hero that you idolize with your quote there. He was an asshole. He sold his guns to both the North and South during the Civil War, and the newspapers at the time labeled him as a Southern sympathizer and traitor to the Union. So much for making everyone equal."

Then she added, her heart pounding, "You know they ended the violence and hatred of slavery a century ago, despite Samuel Colt's double dealing. Let's see how long it takes people to turn on you, too, and I don't mean with a gun. Remember, we believe in liberty and justice for all. We don't need guns to make that happen."

She left the building, feeling momentarily victorious. But then she wondered what exactly she wanted from this guy? What could she do about the guns in light of Lacey's death? She didn't have a plan.

What she did know was that this smug, self-righteous excuse for a human being in there had made her really mad, and when she was that pissed, she didn't let go of anything.

This she wasn't going to let go of at all.

❖ ❖ ❖

As Lisette emerged from a taxi and stood for a moment before texting Sophie that she had arrive at the Student Center, she recalled the day ten years ago, a month after Lacey was killed.

That day, jumping out of her cab, Lisette had seen Sophie racing out of Guns Galore, heading for her car. She hadn't known Sophie that long, but she knew when Sophia was mad as hell about something. She looked as though steam was coming out both of her ears.

"Hey, Sophie!" Lisette yelled. "I thought you were going to wait for me before you went inside." Lisette gave her a look of disappointment.

Sophie grimaced. "Sorry! I didn't realize you had changed your plans and could be here. I should've waited for you. Maybe you could have charmed the guy better than I did." She opened her car door and threw her notebook and purse on the front seat.

Then she turned back to Lisette, her eyes looking wild again. "Do you know he wants to hand the business down to his daughter some day and keep it in the family? She's only nineteen years old, just like Lacey was! He doesn't get it!"

Lisette sighed. "Sophie, we may not be able to do anything about that."

"Oh yes we will, and we can," Sophie yelled back, her face flushed. "Just you wait and see. There are a lot of changes to be made here, and at the college too. We have to do something. We can't give up."

"I'm not saying give up, but maybe we should take a breather. I know I need one. With Lacey's death and the whole thing of getting her out of my body, it's too much." She paused and then added, with a catch in her throat, "I need to tell you something. Erick and I broke up this morning." She hesitated a second and then went on. "Actually, I should say that I broke up with him." Then she started to cry. "It was awful, Sophie. I said terrible things to him. He doesn't deserve it. I have to go. Leave town. Go back to Los Angeles."

Sophie came over to Lisette and put her arm around her shoulder. "Don't go. You and Erick can work this out. You've only know each other for a little while. You can work this out. You and Erick are so good together."

"There you go again, being so positive. How do you do that? I sure can't."

"What's the alternative? I'm not saying things are easy, but they can be good again."

Lisette sighed. "One thing is for sure, I need to get back to work. My agent, Mo, is furious with me about canceling a bunch of dates that were coming up, and I'm not sure I can go back on stage. Not after all that's happened with Lacey. Mo wants me to go back to the West Coast and talk to a guy he knows about some business deal he wants to propose. I've got to go and at least talk to him about it."

"What kind of deal?" Sophie asked. "You don't even know if you'll like it. Stay here and help me. We've got a lot of work to do."

"But you're still in school. You've got to finish your classes, and I need to make money for as long as I can in this business. I'm not getting any younger. That's all I can do right now."

Sophie went on, as if she could convince Lisette to stay. "I have a brilliant idea of how to make a difference on the campus, in this town, maybe even throughout this country. It's wild and crazy, but I know that if we start it now, we can get somewhere big in a few years. Make a difference. Really change things. It's what Lacey would want. "

Then Sophie took a deep breath and looked Lisette in the eye. "Lacey would be outraged by the way she died. So violent, so senselessly, so wrong. She would want us to do something about it. And we will. Please stay and help me."

Lisette stopped her. "You will do something, Sophie. I believe that you can, but I can't stay here. There's been too much pain and loss. I need to get away for a while, maybe longer. I don't know." Then she stopped and laughed. "I'm not as fierce and strong as you are. I just play Attila the Hunny on stage. I'm not the warrior type."

"I think you are," Sophie said softly. "But I know you've gone through a lot and maybe you need some time away from here. But you'll always have a place here. Always!" Then she laughed and said, "When you get that business deal nailed down and make a lot of money, you can give me a bunch for what I want to do. You can be a part of whatever I do. Trust me!"

Then Sophie hugged her and held her for a moment.

"One more thing," Sophie added. "Remember that quote—'Living well is the best revenge?' That's what we want, Lisette. Ari destroyed Lacey's body, but not her soul or her spirit. That will live on in us. She'd want us to live well, despite all that has happened to us, and help others to do so too. That will always be our best revenge!"

◈ ◈ ◈

Standing there on campus now ten years later, Lisette smiled. She could see how that quote had inspired Sophie's work for the last decade. But Lisette also remembered another date and time that had inspired Sophie on her journey to avenge what happened to Lacey and all of them on that campus.

Lisette still had a letter Sophie wrote to her about Sunday, June 20, 2002, which was graduation day at the college, two years after Lacey had been killed. Lisette loved what Sophie wrote to her about it. She kept the letter and read the last part of it often, almost from memory.

I also had to write you and tell you about graduation day last Sunday here on campus. I thought you should know how Lacey lives on today, as she will forever.

The day was amazing. Very full, very emotional. At times, I felt happy, I felt Lacey. I knew she was with us and she was okay. But then there were times that I missed her so much. I just wanted her to be there and show her around the school, so she could see what had changed, what still needed to be changed. She'd tell us how wonderful and dear we all were, and we'd be pleased and inspired to do more.

Lacey's father, Howard, and her brother, Jimmie, were there for the ceremony. They stood in the reviewing stands above us, but they looked glum. It was as if they were still in shock even though two years have passed since Lacey's death. I felt so bad for them.

A part of the day was very good for me. I loved putting up pictures of Lacey on the school bulletin board in the Student Center, even if the college administrators didn't like that. They have tried over the last two years not to speak of Lacey or show pictures of her on campus. I had to defy them about that on my last day at school. They'd know it was me. I've been an instigator on the campus ever since Lacey's death.

I'm the one who pushed to have the bench put up in Lacey's honor and who demanded every year since her death that there be a remembrance of her on October 17th, the anniversary of that horrible day. I'm the one who insisted that someone be hired to focus on violence against women issues on the campus, and although we only got a part-time employee for now, it's more than what we had before.

Four years ago, when I came to this school, I thought it would be a place that would feed and nourish me before I entered into the adult world. It would prepare me to face anything, to reach my goal of success and a life well lived. Unfortunately, Lacey's death taught me more about that than anything else that has happened to me on this campus. I've learned to be strong, passionate, and determined. I've also learned that sometimes you have to stand up and say what no one else will say—such as how this college didn't do enough to keep Lacey safe or alive. She was my dearest friend, pal, and confidant. She was the best person I have ever known. I miss her so much!

We honored her Sunday as part of our graduation ceremony. Sure, we still felt a sadness and a feeling of loss, but it was easy to imagine her all dressed up for graduation, happy, smiling, and bubbly. That was our Lacey, always a smile or a laugh and a joke, but serious, real serious, when you had a problem, there for us when we needed her. She could fix anything, including things that seemed impossible. If she couldn't fix it, she'd give you a big smile and say, "It's going to be all right, you'll see." And somehow, even in the most hopeless of situations, you would believe it because she told you so.

As for the graduation ceremony, I know that having Lacey receive her degree even though she died before she took all her courses might seem odd to some people. There are probably some who think it was creepy. But Lacey was a part of this class. She was still been on this campus with us every day, every minute since her death two years ago. We would talk about her sometimes as if she was still here, as if she would be coming through the door of her dorm room any minute. So why not believe that she was walking down the aisle to get her diploma with us too? Others in the history of Lacey's college have been granted degrees after they died in a car accident or from some disease. What makes Lacey's demise different was that she was murdered right here on this campus. Violence against women does exist here at this school and that point had to be made at graduation.

I know that some people don't want to hear about a dead person all the time. For the last two years, I have been accused of being obsessed, *stuck in a bad place, or just plain crazy! Even my family believes at times that I've gone off the deep end. Only my grandmother Ruth (you know her as Radiance the shaman) understands and supports me. Of course, she's a little crazy herself, so I'm not surprised that she gets it.*

What does Radiance get? That Lacey's death was not a coincidence or an aberration, as the president of our college likes to tell us whenever he can. He says that going to school at this kind of a college is like living in a bubble that shields us from the troubles and concerns of the outside world. Lacey's death burst that bubble for us, he said and that's why is it so hard. But I see the whole thing very differently. We live in the real world here on campus, and violence against women is a part of that reality here as it is at every school in this country. We have an opportunity to do something about it here, but we haven't done enough in the last two years to deal with it. What is wrong with us? Lacey is dead, and we still haven't gotten this right. How can anyone be safe if no one is safe?

Okay, so I'll probably always feel more bitter, resentful, and frustrated than most of the students about what happened to Lacey. But as we walked into the outside graduation area on the green on a beautiful Sunday afternoon in June, I wanted to make sure no one forgot about how and why Lacey was killed. Yes, I knew that there could be consequences to me if I was found to be the one who instigated this stunt, but could they really take a college degree away from a dead girl's roommate who loved her dearly? Besides it was a brilliant plan I had cooked up, and it worked perfectly!

I'll let a bit of the article from Monday's newspaper describe the rest of it for you, Lisette.

<u>Capitol City Enquirer—Monday, June 21, 2002</u>

Wearing white carnations and purple tags that read "End Violence Against Women" pins, the graduates of the college paid tribute to their classmate, Lacey Lockhart, who was murdered on the campus in October 1999 by her ex-boy-friend who then killed himself.

During the ceremony, Lacey's name was called in sequence, and when it was, there was a moment of silence. But there also was thunderous applause that lasted a full five minutes.

At the same time, an airplane appeared above the campus trailing a banner behind it that read "End Violence Against Women" on one side and on the other, "Lacey Lives ON." Officials at the college had no comment on the banner, nor did they speculate who might have ordered or paid for such a display.

When asked if the banner was an indictment of the college's failure to address the issue of violence against women on campus, Charles E. Williams Jr., the college's president, said, "We are working on a whole program on violence against women dedicated to keeping Lockhart's memory alive and stopping domestic violence against women." However, President Williams did not detail what reforms or changes have been made on the campus or what plans are being made to create change in the future.

Thank God, Lisette, that no one figured out it was me who did the skywriting banner. Wasn't that cool? Cost me a lot of my graduation money, but it was worth it. I owe Erick, your friend, a big favor. He made sure that my name wasn't on the order. By the way, Erick has been helping me on a few other things I have in the works after I graduate. He's a good guy.

All in all, graduation was quite the day. After the ceremony, I went back to Radiance's apartment and sat looking out the back window of her workroom, the place where you and Lacey came to help her cross over. I watched the rain pouring down, and I felt Lacey with me, talking to me in my ear, telling me that it was a good day and she loved every minute of it. Is that so crazy? Was it possible that she heard me? And that I could hear her?

Just in case she could, I said out loud, "Thanks, Lacey. It was a special day, and I had to make it big and bold." Suddenly the rain stopped, and everything seemed so clean and shining. The sun came out again, and as the rain was still dripping down, something magical happened in the sky.

A rainbow! Big and bold, high in the sky, and I knew.

Lacey was here with me. She was sending me a sign.

She was happy. And so was I.

Love you!

SOPHIE

CHAPTER TWO

Wednesday, October 14, 2009

In the Garden of Peace and Justice

Lisette caught sight of Sophie coming down the hill and heading toward the Student Center. They had exchanged texts so Sophie knew that Lisette was waiting for her. But now Sophie was waving frantically and running toward Lisette.

When the two women met, they grabbed each other, hugged for a long time, and then started talking.

"My God, Sophie! You look amazing! And look at this place!" Lisette point up the hill to the chapel and beyond. "How the hell did you do all this?"

Sophie smiled. "It is beautiful, isn't it?" she said proudly as she pointed up the hill. "The garden leads all the way up to the top and around the chapel. It's our 'peace garden.' That's what we call it. We brought a little peace and serenity to a campus devastated by death and destruction ten years ago. Now we have beautiful flowers, butterfly bushes, and a bubbling brook that leads to a fountain. All this reminds us, I hope, that while our bodies may be damaged and destroyed, some things—such as our spirit and souls—can't be."

Then with a sigh, she added, "Do you think Lacey would like this?"

"*Like* it? She'd *love* it!" Lisette answered. "Yes, I can feel her here—at peace. If that's what you wanted, Sophie, you got it!"

She hugged Sophie again and added, "Yes, you did!"

"Thanks!" Sophie said softly. "That means a lot to me. And we're so grateful for the money you gave us, the notoriety you lent to us. You have a national name, a brand, as they say in the internet world of today. It helped us get other money and help too."

"Don't remind me!" Lisette said, with embarrassment in her voice. "Attila the Hunny has all the fame, not me. I'm just—what did my lawyer call it?" She paused for a moment, then added, "I'm just the 'instrument.'"

"That's fine with me. And we have so much more to do. I'm going to be announcing some big new developments on Saturday concerning what we'll be taking on with my nonprofit organization, *Survivor Strong, Thriver Resilient!*"

"I love that name," Lisette said. "It sounds so positive and hopeful."

"Because we are so positive and hopeful, right?" Sophie grabbed her hand and led her back toward a car parked down the path from the garden. "I assume you have checked in at your hotel already. I want to take you somewhere later. I think you'll appreciate this. Do you remember that gun store where Ari bought the gun that killed Lacey?"

"You mean the one you went to after she was killed, and the owner almost called the cops on you?"

"Yeah," Sophie replied. "But it got more intense after that. I called a press conference a few days later to try and shame him about not reporting to the college that Ari bought a rifle at his shop ten days before he shot and killed Lacey. I called for a boycott of his shop, and people responded. Then he sued me personally for trying to take away his customers' Second Amendment rights to buy a gun. Something crazy like that. Of course, he didn't win that lawsuit. That's one thing I learned in law school: anyone has the right to sue you for anything, but that doesn't mean that they are going to win!"

Lisette laughed. "You sure gave him a run for his money, I'd say!"

"I'd say I gave him a lot more trouble than that. Guess where my office for my nonprofit organization is now?"

"No," Lisette said, drawing out the word. "Is the address you gave me same as where the gun store was?"

Sophie smiled wickedly at her. "One and the same! I rent the place now. And his daughter Trisha is one of our angel investors. She liquidated the business, sold the building, and now teaches marital arts self-defense classes for women. So there *is* justice in this world!" Then she paused and added more soberly, "At least there is *some* justice in this world."

"Sounds like my meeting with Wiley this morning. We get our justice where we can!"

Sophie smiled at her broadly. "So, you bought that old Pussy-cat Club? That must have been so satisfying for you."

"Yeah, Wiley almost pooped his pants when he saw me walk into his club again, this time to close the deal. That's the business I told you I came to town a few days early to do. The Pussycat's Meow, that horrible strip club where I was dancing as Attila the Hunny right after Lacey was killed, is no more. Mostly we bought it for the building, which we'll gut and then fix up right. We run a clean business and take care of our employees. It's all about good management, quality employees, and great dancers. Not to defend the entire sex-entertainment industry to someone like you, Sophie, but…"

"Another time, Lisette, and we'll have it out on that issue. Right now, I want you to come inside the Student Center and meet some of the students who have been working on the anniversary events here on campus and for the Saturday night gala at the hotel. I told them you were around here when Lacey was killed. They don't know about the part where Lacey's spirit was inside you for a time. But they are interested in you as a female entrepreneur and how you grew your business. In fact, several of them visited one of your clubs as a class assignment. I'm sure that they will raise all those human rights issues with you!"

"Oh great!" Lisette moaned, but she was excited to meet with the students. She did have one more question for Sophie.

"I was wondering if Erick is still around," she asked, her face set in a frown.

"Sounds like you don't want to see him. Is that a problem?" Sophie asked carefully. "He'll be part of our activities, including the Tenth Anniversary Gala on Saturday night. He's done so much for us. You know he helped plan and design the gardens. He's really good at it." Then she stammered, "I mean, he didn't say anything about not wanting to see you. But I didn't ask. Should I have asked?"

"It's okay," Lisette said slowly, trying not to show her distress. "I can see him. I'm not upset. I was just wondering if…"

Sophie jumped in. "…he's seeing anyone? But I thought you had a boyfriend. Todd, isn't that his name? Are you two still to-gether?"

"We are. We are," Lisette said quickly. "We're on and off, mostly off. I mean, he's my business manager and a damn good one, so I don't want to screw anything up. Neither of us own the company, but we both have a stake in it. So we're casual, like they say. Kind of together."

"Sorry, I don't mean to pry. I just don't want you or Erick to be uncomfortable on Saturday night. There will be enough to be sad about. Lacey won't be with us for still another important occasion, and we'll all feel bad about that. But we have things to celebrate, changes we've made at the college and in the community. And we'll have something new to announce. That's the part that Erick will be there for."

"Really? I didn't know Erick was into this kind of thing."

"You mean feminism and preventing violence against women?"

"No, no, I'm sure he is for all that. Just wondering…" Her voice trailed off.

Sophie jumped in. "You'll have plenty of time to talk to him about all that. We'll have some preliminary events and meetings. I've got a schedule for you here."

Sophie pulled a page out of her bag and scanned it.

Then she added, "I don't think there is any specific event that you'll be together at, but something could be arranged."

She handed the page to Lisette and asked her, "You are attending the lunch tomorrow at the hotel, right? I'll be meeting with you and the other angel investors at the lunch, and the board will have a dinner Friday night. You don't have to attend that dinner. But I'm sure you'll see Erick on Saturday for the Tenth Anniversary Gala. It will be black tie and evening gown. I hope you brought something spectacular to wear that will knock him out. I don't know how you keep your amazing figure!"

"I guess I can wait until Saturday to see him. He probably doesn't think of me much anymore so…" Lisette's voice trailed off again, but her thoughts were racing. She wondered if Erick thought about her as much as she thought about him.

Now that they were both back in this same time and space, she had to admit Erick was quite a guy.

Why did she ever let him go?

❖ ❖ ❖

Lisette.

That was about the fifteenth time she came into Erick's thoughts today. Maybe it was because Sophie had told him that

Lisette would be in town for the activities planned for the coming week to mark the tenth anniversary of Lacey's death.

He kept thinking about all the good times he had shared with Lisette, and he wondered if she had changed since he had seen her last. She was a beautiful woman and probably still was. He'd seen the ads for her strip clubs on television and in magazines. Her business was doing well. Maybe she thought of him too sometimes.

He always wondered what really had happened between the two of them ten years ago when they broke up after only a month together. But he couldn't think about Lisette much more right now. It was almost time to train his last clients of the day, an older couple named Gerald and Shirley. He liked his job, but some days he just didn't have the energy to put up with one more person. Today it would be Gerald, whining about how hard Erick was pushing him with the day's exercise routine.

Working as a personal trainer seemed as though it would be right up his alley when his scholarship money dried up and he gave up on his long-term dream of becoming a psychologist. As a bouncer at the Pussycat Dance Club while going to school part time, he had kept himself in shape, and the gym was always felt like his second home. Then, when he realized he could transfer the credits he had already earned toward a degree in Exercise Science, he took a job at this gym.

He quickly realized that it wasn't the job of his dreams; he'd never make a lot of money at it, and the hours were crazy. That created havoc in his life, and at the time, it added to the wreckage of his life after Lisette broke up with him and left town.

Lisette! Once again he found himself thinking of her.

He remembered how difficult a time it was for him when she left so abruptly and without a whole lot of explanation. As hard as it was for him, he thought about how it must have been even harder for Lisette. There had been so many changes in her life at that time—maybe it was too much for her to stay and try to work things out with him.

Instead the breakup was fast and precise. She screamed at him, accused him of cheating on her—which he wasn't—and basically told him she didn't want to be with him anymore. She wouldn't explain it, but he tried to understand. She had suffered a lot of trauma as a kid, her mother dying so young and going to live with her father who, from what little Erick knew, was not a very nice guy. And Erick knew from the classes he had taken in psychology that such trauma can have an impact on a person's emotional life, their ability to cope, and their capacity to have healthy relationships. So, in a way Lisette's breakup with him didn't surprise him that much. Still it hurt. He really cared about Lisette and wanted to be in her life. He thought he could help her heal from her childhood trauma and they could have a good life together.

Most of all, he just missed her. Maybe that's why he got involved in some of the activities on the campus after Lacey's death. If he couldn't help Lisette, maybe he could help Sophie do her work helping other women heal after abuse. Besides, he loved helping with the planning and designing of the peace garden on campus. Sophie had an idea of what she wanted the garden to look like, but she was short on specifics. He did that part and loved it. He had to admit that staying involved with Sophie's work just might allow him to cross paths with Lisette again someday. Maybe they could work something out between the two of them. He knew it was a vague possibility, but he was willing to wait and see.

Now that he knew Lisette was coming to town, he was nervous and confused. Would she see his work with Sophie as just a way to worm back into her life or simply just to stay connected with her? He did want to support Sophie, but he didn't have the kind of money Lisette had to invest in her organization. When the owner of the gym where he worked wanted to sell a few years ago and offered him a good deal, Erick invested what he had, borrowed the rest, and took over as the owner. All he had to offer Sophie was his hard work on the garden, and he guessed Lisette would have to see it for what it was: a genuine interest in making some real changes on that campus.

Otherwise, he liked the work he was doing at his gym. He liked being in charge and doing the training, even though the hours were long. He hired a full-time fitness manager to cover the hours he wasn't there, and he worked on marketing ideas to build the membership. Being busy gave him less time to think about Lisette and no time to date other women. *And now it has been ten years, you jerk,* he told himself. *What harm could there be in seeing the girl who broke your heart?*

"Erick!" a voice called out from the other side of the gym.

Erick looked up to see his client, or at least one part of the pair that had booked the three o'clock afternoon session. Gerald and Shirley Backus were a long-time married couple who had started working out at the gym as their New Year's resolution last January. God knows how Shirley put up with Gerald outside the gym! He was bad enough to deal with in the gym. He was as ornery, nasty, and mean as they come, and he complained about every exercise Erick put them through and at times refused to do some of them. He'd stand there, looking mad at the world, while Shirley went on with whatever Erick asked her to do.

Now Erick saw Shirley standing over Gerald lying on the ground at her feet. Had Gerald fallen? Erick quickly raced toward them.

"What happened?" Erick gasped. Suddenly he noticed that Gerald had his hands gripped tightly around Shirley's leg and wouldn't let go.

She bent down and pounded on his hands, but his grip was strong, and she couldn't break it.

"He's having a fit," Shirley said, a level of mild frustration in her voice, as though she had put up with worse from Gerald in the past. "He's like a little kid. He doesn't want to get up and exercise, and he won't let go of my leg until I tell him we can go home. For some reason, he's being unreasonable today."

Erick wanted to laugh. Today? Gerald was always unreasonable and uncooperative. Erick thought Shirley was a saint to put up with him. He could hardly stand to deal with Gerald once a week for an hour of personal training.

"All right," Erick said authoritatively to Gerald. "That's enough. Let's get up and get this session going. The sooner you start, the quicker you'll be done.

"No," Gerald said emphatically. "Shirley knows why I'm not participating today. It's all her fault."

Shirley looked up at Erick and shrugged. "I'll be damned if I know what he's talking about."

Then Gerald started to rant. "Goddamn, stupid people. I don't have to do anything I don't want to. I have my rights. They can't take anything away from me."

Shirley looked down at Gerald. "Is this about those stupid guns? I can't believe you're still going on about that." She turned to Erick. "We were warming up on the StairMaster earlier and watching something on the overhead TV. He must have been watching Fox News. I swear those news people are going to be the death of me. They get him so riled up. It takes him days to calm down."

"But why is this your fault?"

Shirley snapped back. "It's because I made him take the guns he had out of the house. We have our grandkids over for a few weeks every year and I don't want those things around with them there. He's upset and he's taking it out on me at the gym, because he knows how much I enjoy coming here and working out with you. He couldn't care less if he exercised or not. He's punishing me."

Erick looked down at Gerald and then back at Shirley. "Is he ticklish?" he asked her quietly.

Shirley grinned and nodded. Erick reached down, grabbed Gerald about the rib cage and tickled him. Gerald reacted almost by reflex and let go of Shirley's leg. He put up his hands to protect himself from Erick's tickles.

"Jesus Christ!" Gerald yelled out as he leapt to his feet. "What the hell do you think you are doing? You can't touch me like that!"

"It got you up and ready to go, right?" Erick said with a laugh. "I'd say that was a good thing."

"I'd say that was an assault and I could report you for that."

"Now, Gerald," Shirley said calmly. "Let's forget all of this and just have a good session with Erick. Then we'll go home, and you can watch Fox News all you want."

For some crazy reason, that seemed to mollify Gerald, and Erick sighed with relief as he started the two of them on their first exercise. Gerald, of course, complained about how hard it was, but Shirley just kept talking to him in her high, sweet voice. For Erick, the hour went by quickly, distracting him from thinking about that evening and what he would do if Lisette showed up. Would they pick up from where they left off or was the way they parted so traumatizing that neither of them would ever want to go back?

What did he want? To be honest, he wasn't sure. He'd have to remember and consider his choices.

Was Lisette even thinking about him?

And what did she remember about their breakup?

❖ ❖ ❖

All that talk about Erick with Sophie left Lisette thinking about him and her last days in town ten years ago.

As she sat now in a taxi taking her to back to her hotel after having lunch with Sophie, Lisette tried to remember the good times she and Erick had had. But her thoughts were mostly about why she broke up with Erick in the first place.

She remembered how the negative voice in her head went on from almost the start of their relationship.

He doesn't really know who you are. When he finds out, he'll leave you. You feel safe with him now, but is it really safety that you want? You don't want to be hurt again. You don't want to feel that strongly about anyone because you'll get hurt by them someday. They'll leave you, disappoint you. It will hurt. You learned that lesson years ago with your mother. You loved her so much, and she had to go away. She said she was going away to God, that the cancer made her leave you. That wasn't her fault or yours, but it still hurt.

She knew she shouldn't have fallen so hard for Erick. He was a good man, a lovely man. He made her believe that it would all be okay if she just loved him and he loved her. So silly! How could she be so stupid! She was a fool to believe that, after all those years of pain and neglect with Ralph, the man who was her father, Erick could make it all go away. It would never go away, and she could never forgive Ralph. She could have shared some of her pain about this with Erick, but he was a man. He wouldn't understand. He would stick up for Ralph. She couldn't go there, although at times she wanted to. Of course, Erick would be like any other man and, at some point, treat her like dirt no matter how nice he was to her at the start. Why did she ever think that with Erick it would be different?

"Where were you last night?" Lisette had screamed at Erick the last night they were together. She had asked him four times, and his pathetic answer still didn't change. He was lying. She could tell.

"I told you. I was at the club. I was working the last show. It was late when I got to leave."

"Yeah, right! You expect me to believe you were there all night."

"I told you. The cops were called, and we had to stay to talk to the cop who was writing the report."

"Who? You and the new headliner? What's her name anyway? Starlight or Sapphire or one of those other stupid stripper names?" She tossed her hair and went on, enraged now. "Jesus, Erick do you think I'm stupid? I know what goes on in clubs like that. You asked me to leave the club, stop stripping when we got together. Yet you still work there. What is that about? It's okay for you, but not for me."

She paused for a breath, but barely, and went on before he could jump in and defend himself with more lies.

"You did it just to get rid of me, so you could have fun with all the girls. You thought I wouldn't figure it out. You thought I wouldn't know."

Full of rage, her face reddened and her body shook.

"You know that's not true," Erick said quickly. "You said you wanted to go back to school, and I agreed that was a good thing for you to do. You told me that stripping wasn't for you anymore. I agreed, but don't make it sound like this is all about what I wanted and that I manipulated you into something. Now you are living off your savings, but I can't. I need to work, so I'm out there every night late after a full day of school, busting my butt, and this is what you think is going on. Really, Lisette! Really!"

"Fuck you, Erick. You'll tell me whatever you think I want to hear. You're just like Ralph. He diddled all the girls who helped out at his bar, and when he wasn't doing that, he'd push me onto the men, getting his cut. He sold me like..."

Suddenly Lisette gasped and put her hand up to her face. What had she just said? Erick didn't know anything about that. She never told him. He wasn't supposed to know. No one knew. NO ONE!

But Erick jumped in quickly. "What? What are you talking about Ralph doing to you? He sold you? What! What does that mean?"

She was in too deep. She'd never worm her way out of this. She had to go. She had to go *now*!

Looking back on it now, she shuddered to think about what she had missed not being with Erick for the last ten years. What surprised Lisette the most about Erick...how gentle he was. He didn't want to fuck her or even have sex with her. He wanted to make love to her. Imagine that!

That was so different for her after the guy in the bar who paid her father to fuck her. With Erick she could do less pretending, be more real and maybe even find true love like in the fairy tales. Was Erick her Prince Charming? Was she like her favorite, Cinderella? Her rags had become riches. Was he a man who could love her even with all the bad things she had done in her life?

That was such bull, she thought. Of course, there was no happy ending. She had given up on that years ago...and when they broke up, she knew she'd never go back there. To those deep, scary feelings. What was that word Erick had used to explain it to her...*intimacy*? Yes! She didn't want intimacy. Too much trouble and work and too much possibility of being hurt—hurt really, really bad. She had had enough of that in her life. She was a strong independent woman. She didn't need a man. They were nothing but trouble, and she had had enough of that in her life. Her father, Ralph, that creep Ambrose, and even Erick. He got a little clingy at the end. Maybe even possessive. Too much of that was not good for her. She couldn't rely on anyone to have her back. How many times had she learned that in her life? A life lesson learned and applied every damn day. Yes, she could and would do this on her own.

Coming back to the present, she prided herself on having picked out her current boyfriend, Todd, because he knew what she wanted, and that's just what she got from him. No commitment, no trust, no future. Just today, and maybe tomorrow. What more could she plan for? She wasn't sure, but she knew she was not going back to Erick. Not ever!

But she still remembered the first time she and Erick talked, really talked. It was so nice. It was the night Lacey was killed and she was dancing at the Bare Bottom Dance Club, a wretched place where the college students stormed the stage. Erick had taken care of her, getting them off the stage and away from her. He also looked out for her when she was attacked on her way back to her dressing room by a guy with a knife.

Erick protected her that night, and then he was kind and funny and sweet when he walked her back to her hotel from the Club. That was the Erick she really loved, and that was her at her best.

It was one of their good times together, and she always wanted to remember it.

How could she forget!

◈ ◈ ◈

Early morning hours of October 18, 1999

It was two o'clock in the morning by the time Erick walked Lisette to her hotel room. Wrapped in her furry white coat, she felt the cool, fall of the October night against her flushed face and finally relaxed a little.

It was her idea to walk. She thought the exercise would do her good and, with Erick by her side, she wasn't afraid of being on the street in the middle of the night. Erick has suggested that they take a taxi. He said he was worried that she was too tired to walk after all that had just happened to her.

She liked that about Erick. He seemed to be thinking about her all the time. And she liked it when someone paid attention to her. He wasn't her type, though. He was a big guy, about six foot two with a barrel chest and strong arms. He also had soft blue eyes and a nice smile. With an earring in his left ear and his white-blond hair cut close to his head, he looked like a normal guy, not someone who busted heads at the Bare Bottom Dance Club.

They walked in silence for the first block or so.

"How are you doing?" he asked her as they crossed the street to another block. "I can still get us a cab."

"No," she said, giving him a quick smile. "I'm doing fine."

"You're awfully quiet."

"I have a lot to think about."

Erick was silent again for a while, like he was thinking too. Then he blurted out, "You know, things don't normally get out of control at the Bare Bottom. It's a pretty quiet place."

"Then I guess my act stirred it up a bit, huh?" Lisette said with a laugh.

"I'd say that you stirred things up a lot. You really are something up on that stage." He gave her a shy smile.

"So you liked my act?"

"What I saw of it so far, yeah."

"Well, that's all you're probably going to see. I'm not going back to the Bare Bottom. I've got to get my agent on it in the morning, but I've already decided."

"Don't leave just because of what happened tonight," Erick said. "You're what the club needs. A class act and a good draw for steady business."

"But I don't dance in front of crowds of goofy adolescent boys," she said firmly.

"The college kids can be a problem. You're right about that. But the usual crowd is more subdued. You know, more…more…" He paused, searching for a word.

"More likely to storm the stage," she sneered.

"No," he insisted. "You know what I mean. More middle-aged

men who come here to get their rocks off. Not hot-headed college types. I hate them too. I get nervous every time we have two-for-one drinks night." Then he looked at her seriously. "Students are more excitable than guys in suits. It makes sense since the psychology for coming to a strip show is so different for the two groups."

Lisette snickered. "So, you're into psychology and all that mumble-jumble, are you?"

"Actually," Erick said, with an embarrassed look on his face. "I'm a college student myself."

She stared at him in amazement.

"I'm studying to be a psychologist," he went on. "I only work as a bouncer part time."

She nodded slowly, then turned away from him, walking again in silence.

"You don't like college kids, do you?" he asked her carefully after a minute.

"I wouldn't say that. I just avoid them whenever I can."

Then she saw the hang-dog look on Erick's face and added with a sigh, "Look, it's not about you. But I don't want to discuss it, okay?"

Erick nodded, and they fell silent again until they arrived at the front door of Lisette's hotel. "I can get upstairs all right by myself," she muttered in a tight, tired voice.

"Maybe I should walk you to your room," he insisted. "That guy with the knife could've followed us here, you know." He looked around for a moment until his eyes settled back on Lisette. "I'm sorry I upset you about me being a college student. I should've told you sooner."

"You shouldn't feel sorry about anything," she said more easily now. Then she put her hand out to him and flashed him a smile. "Thanks for walking me home. And for pulling those guys off me tonight. You've been great."

He took her hand and held it for a moment. "It was my pleasure. Take care of yourself, okay? Maybe I'll see you around some time." Then he squeezed her fingers, held her eyes for a moment and added softly, "You really are something, you know that?"

She smiled back, this time almost shyly, and pulled her hand away. "Good luck with school. You're going to be great. I mean it. You're so easy to talk to."

"Thanks," he replied with a grin.

"I've got to go now," she said, lingering one moment more. "It's late."

"Yeah, me too. I've got to get up early tomorrow to study before class."

She looked at him standing there looking at her and wanted to say something more, but she didn't. Instead she turned and walked into the hotel lobby. She didn't know how long he stood there watching her because she wouldn't let herself turn around and look at him. She didn't want him to see her tears. Suddenly she felt so sad and lonely that she wanted to call him back, ask him to come up to her room and keep her company for a while.

But he had already done so much for her. Besides, it wasn't fair. He really wasn't her type. Somehow, she never fell for nice guys like him.

She didn't know why, but she never did.

CHAPTER THREE

Wednesday, October 14, 2009

Blamestorming

While the last ten years had been really bad for him, Ambrose had to say that today, October 14, 2009, was his lucky day. He started his usual morning routine casually reading the newspaper at the public library. Not much in there except...wait! What's this?

Lisette is back in town.

He felt like he just won the lottery and he hadn't even bought a ticket!

A flood of memories came back to Ambrose about how he and Lisette had left it ten years ago. He didn't think he'd ever see her again, not after she ran off and left him holding the bag. He had made that sweet offer to her that would position her in a new career as a performance artist. But he also wanted her to help him break the logjam with his son Mark, then ten years old, so he would agree to see his father again.

He had told her that he and Mark had been estranged ever since Betsy, Ambrose's wife and Mark's mother, as well as Mark's younger sister, Jeanine, had been killed in a car accident. Things had gotten so bad between them that Mark went to live with Abigail, his grandmother, who was Betsy's mom. His mother-in-law hated Ambrose!

She told Lisette that right to her face that day Abigail confronted Ambrose and Lisette on the steps of the public library. Her screaming match with him almost derailed Ambrose's chances then to woo Lisette to work with him. Abigail blamed him for the accident that killed her daughter and granddaughter who was sitting in the back seat with Mark when the crash occurred. Ambrose, sitting in the front passenger seat, came out of the accident physically unscathed, but still he was haunted to this day by how his family life and legal career tumbled into an abyss after the accident.

All he had left then was Mark, and he wanted to be a father to him. That's why ten years ago when Lisette was in town, he thought Lisette would want to help Mark. From what Ambrose knew of Lisette's life, he was sure she'd be willing to help out a kid who was damaged as she was when she was a child. He knew that under Mark's tough exterior, so like hers, he was wounded and vulnerable and needed a father. Lisette, a beautiful young woman closer in age to Mark, could get his son to listen to her about how his father wasn't such a bad guy. "Look what he has done for my life, Mark," she could say to him. "He's a great guy!" she could tell him, and Mark would believe her.

But she wouldn't even help him with Mark. That was infuriating enough for Ambrose, but then she left town without letting him help her turn her Attila the Hunny strip act into a political performance art show. He was sure it would catch fire or "go viral," as they say on the internet. Hell, with the help of social media now, anyone could get famous really fast.

Even ten years ago, he saw the possibility of a meteoric rise to fame for Lisette—comparable to what happened with Jane Fonda and her exercise video that skyrocketed to infamy by the early 1990s. He had "googled" it. In 1982 Fonda released her first exercise video, *Jane Fonda's Workout*, which became the highest-selling video of that time. It would be the first of twenty-two workout videos released by her over the next thirteen years, which would collectively sell over 17 million copies. But a better example to-day, Ambrose found, would be Susan Boyle, who earlier that year had gone viral by singing just one song on a TV talent show. Shit! Ambrose knew Lisette had so much more to offer than that sorry singer.

Still since he last saw her, he had to admit that Lisette hadn't done too badly for herself. In fact, her name was listed in the newspaper today, he realized, because she had given a huge dona-tion to an organization and was being recognized at an event here in town this weekend. So she was still Attila the Hunny, but now that name graced the outside of upscale strip clubs with locations around the country. Ambrose found a list of them on internet using one of the public computers at the library.

Whether she actually owned the clubs or just lent her name to them as part of licensing agreement, Ambrose didn't know. But as a lawyer himself, he knew that some high-powered attorneys had set up the deal of a lifetime for her. She wouldn't have to do much for the rest of her life but show up for the ceremonial grand open-ings of new clubs and smile a lot. With her slim build and big boobs, she was the image of the sexy women that were available to men who wouldn't be caught dead in a seedy strip joint. Like *Playboy* magazine years ago, Ambrose thought, these Attila the Hunny strip clubs made it respectable and fashionable for men to look at naked women. Jesus, Ambrose thought. What a scam!

Lisette had sure made the best of her retirement, transforming her career from dancing in the strip joints to making millions of dollars just on the value of her stage name. That's why he was even more pissed at her for dumping him ten years ago and leaving him in the lurch. They could have done something big together and both be swimming in money right now.

But why didn't that happen? Maybe, he thought, she had gotten in with the wrong crowd, including that crazy shaman lady, whatever her name was…something like "Radiation" or "Radiance." But it was more than that. Why did Lisette disappear suddenly, like a puff of smoke, with not even a word to him then or ever?

Now she's back in town flashing her money around, and she doesn't think there will be any pay back for what she did to him. He had had something to offer her, something he needed her help with, and she rejected it all.

It was all her fault and now there would be consequences! Sure, she was free to do whatever she like, Ambrose thought, but if she was back in town, he had a few ideas in mind to make her feel those consequences. For one thing, he still had the book he pilfered from Lisette's hotel room. He wasn't sure why he had kept it. It was, as he remembered it, a diary with a bunch of hand-written drivel in it by someone name Marie. Maybe Lisette had missed it, or maybe she didn't even notice it was gone, but now he was in an even better position to blackmail or extort something from her to exact his revenge.

As he headed out of the library, he had a certain destination in mind where he might have stashed the book. He had to find it, read through it, and see what treasures might be there. But he couldn't stop thinking about how this all started ten years ago. He had gone to see his son, Mark, at school to wish him a happy birthday, and the next day he met Lisette for the first time.

Ambrose believed that it wasn't so much a coincidence that he had met Lisette back then. Instead, he saw it as a collision of forces that brought him to today still lost and aggrieved. Being reminded of how he had been humiliated by Mark on the school playground was hard for him, but he allowed himself to go there just so he could wind himself up and let his wrath fuel him.

This was all Lisette's fault, and this time she wouldn't just walk away from him.

This time, he'd get her!

He would get his revenge!

◈ ◈ ◈

Early Tuesday, October 19, 1999

From the far end of an elementary school play yard, Ambrose stood alone, peering forlornly through the chain-link fence at the unruly gangs of children yelling and racing around the field during the lunchtime recess.

As he looked out on the noisy rabble, he gripped the fence with both his hands and rocked back and forth from his right foot to his left in his filthy, torn sneakers, the ones he'd found in the trash can behind the pizzeria two days ago. They weren't much better than his old ones, but at least they were both the same brand and color and they had laces. Mark was ten years old today, and at ten, he would notice if his old man had matching sneakers. Ambrose didn't want to embarrass his kid in front of his school friends.

That's why he had cleaned himself up today before coming. Besides the sneakers, he put on the clean white t-shirt he had traded a guy on the street for and combed his long hair back into a tight ponytail. He couldn't do much about his beard. He had lost his razor the last time he stayed at the shelter. Some asshole must have stolen it, but at least he took the time to wash his face and hands in the men's room at the public library before he caught the bus down to Mark's school.

That was the best he could do. He looked less like a bum, but he was a bum no matter what he did. There was no way to hide that from Mark. The kid wasn't stupid. He'd see him for what he was. He just hoped he'd be glad to see him. He had come for Mark's birthday, after all. Even gotten him a present. It wasn't much, but it was something to show Mark that he cared, even after all that had happened.

Maybe he should've come sooner to see him. *How long had it been?* Ambrose thought as he scratched his beard and squinted his eyes, trying to make out which boy was Mark in the group racing around the field. The last time he saw Mark, he was eight years old; he had been seven at the time of the accident. Today, he'd be ten. That was two years of growing to account for. Of course, he'd looked different. Ambrose knew how much a kid could sprout up even if he saw him every day. Until Mark was six, Ambrose had known everything that had ever happened to his son. Every joy, every sorrow, every skinned knee, and every damn Christmas present he ever got from Santa Claus.

But now, in the last three years, Ambrose had only seen Mark maybe three times—no, four, counting that time in the judge's chambers—but never up close, never to talk to him or spend time with him. Three years. That was a long time in the life of a kid. *Christ,* he thought, *any one of the kids running around on the field could be Mark.* He stared harder. If his son was out there, he had to be in that group of kids kicking around the soccer ball in the middle of the field. Mark would be athletic like that, Ambrose thought proudly. Wasn't that Mark, the kid with the red shirt on in the middle of that tussle to get the soccer ball? It could be. But then what about the kid in the green shirt right next to him? That could be him. Or was that kid too small and scrawny-looking to be his son?

"Jesus," Ambrose muttered in frustration. This was impossible. Mark could be any of these kids or none of them. Maybe he didn't even go to school here anymore.

Ambrose smacked his lips and swallowed hard. His mouth was dry, and his throat ached for a drink. He'd need one soon, very soon, because the aggravation of this was getting to him. And the memories too. They were coming back. About the accident and Betsy and Jeanine. The ones he didn't want to come back. Not now. Even the booze couldn't keep them from creeping back up on him.

Maybe he should wait until the boys got closer so Mark might see him. Even with his beard and long hair, he'd still be recognizable. A kid would always know his father. But would he be too scared to admit it? Who knows what stories his grandmother had told about him? Lies, most likely. Abigail had always hated him, and now she was poisoning his son against him.

The sounds of kids yelling as they came closer to him brought Ambrose back to the moment, and he looked up to see the tall, thin kid in the red shirt racing down the field, kicking the soccer ball in front of him with a swarm of boys close behind. His face had a wild expression on it, as though he was really enjoying himself, and for an instant, the kid looked up at him and Ambrose could have sworn that he smiled at him. It had to be Mark! He held his son's eyes for a moment and noticed how his face had lost its little boy look. But his eyes, his piercing blue eyes so much like his own, were the same, and for one long glorious moment, he almost burst with pride.

The kid in the red shirt was Mark, he was sure of it. And Mark had recognized him too. That meant he'd be coming over soon to say, "Hey, Dad. How's it going? Long time no see! You know how to play soccer, don't you? Why don't you come out here and give me and my friends a few pointers? Didn't you play soccer in college and were really good at it? I want everyone to meet you, Dad. Please."

Oh, how good that would be! Mark would see how much he loved him. He would whisk him back to the life they once had together, and it would be like before. The nightmare would be over. His son would be home with him again.

Ambrose was so sure about all of this that he called out to the kid wearing the red shirt and dark shorts.

"Hey, Mark! Over here! It's me."

But Ambrose's voice startled the boy, and he tripped, losing control of the ball. Ambrose yelled again. "Stop chasing the ball, and you won't fall all over it, son. Get out in front of it. Go for it. You can do it."

He watched Mark attack the ball as if on his command and take off with it, his friends screaming and squealing behind him as they all raced to the other end of the field.

"That's it!" Ambrose bellowed, rattling the fence with his hands and whistling. "That's the way to do it."

He's a good kid, Ambrose thought as he watched Mark from the distance. *He'd be a damn good soccer player one day. He just needs a little coaching. What was wrong with this stupid school anyway? Didn't they teach these kids anything? Too much emphasis on academics,* he thought. Boys need to be more physical. That was Ambrose's problem when he was a kid. Too much going on inside his head. Always on the outside looking in. But not his kid, he thought proudly as he watched the boy come running back toward him. His kid would be happy and well-adjusted, whatever that was. He just needed someone to teach him how to play soccer.

Ambrose could teach him. There had to be some way around the court case so he could see his son and teach him to play sports. If Ambrose put his mind to it, he could figure something out. After all, he had been a pretty good lawyer when he was practicing, and this could be a way for him to make everything up to Mark.

The crowd of boys came closer again and their squeals and shouts drowned out his thoughts.

"Keep it up, Mark," Ambrose yelled. "Stay in front of that ball. Move with it. Play hard."

Ambrose watched Mark steal the ball from one of the other boys and go sailing down the field toward him. Then he kicked the ball into the chain-link fence right in front of Ambrose for a goal.

"What a play!" Ambrose shouted excitedly as the boys all crowded around Mark, slapping his behind and falling down on the ground into a heap of sweaty, panting bodies.

He could almost touch Mark now if it wasn't for that damn fence, and Mark was looking up at him with a crooked smug smile on his face. Like he was the king of the world.

Ambrose had no doubt now. This was his son.

"Hey, Mark," he sputtered excitedly. "Happy Birthday to you, son. I brought you a present. Do you want to see it?"

Without waiting for an answer, Ambrose pulled a black object out of his pocket and held it up for Mark to see.

"Hey, look what I found for you. It's a remote control. You know, to a television set or something. You always like to play with these gizmos, right?" Ambrose fiddled with the buttons as he continued. "Remember that time you took the garage door opener and hid it from me? You said you took it so that you could beam someone up just like on *Star Trek*!" Ambrose guffawed and looked up again, expecting to see Mark laughing along with him. "I was so mad at you, but I had to laugh. I just couldn't help it."

Ambrose's voice trailed off when he realized that Mark was standing there gaping at him with his mouth wide open, recognizing him for sure but not saying a word. Then he stood up, turned, and made his way back to the ball.

"Don't go, Mark," Ambrose pleaded as he watched his son trot away.

"Hey, Mark," one of the boys near the fence yelled. "Do you know that guy? He keeps talking to you. He knows your name. He's calling you."

Mark glared at Ambrose so intently that he held his breath thinking that Mark was finally going to say something to him. Something important. Something meaningful. Something just because he was his dad even if the other boys had shamed him into doing it.

But instead Mark winced and shrugged his shoulders.

"That guy?" Mark's face was flushed, and his mouth set in a scowl. "How would I know a bum like that?"

Then Mark scooped by a handful of rocks from the ground and threw them over the fence at Ambrose.

"Get out of here, you bum," he screamed. "You're disgusting, and I hate you!"

Then Mark's friend grabbed rocks and handfuls of dirt too and flinging them over the fence at Ambrose.

"Get out of here, you old coot," they hollered. "Or we'll call our teacher. You some kind of pervert or what?"

The boys jeered and taunted Ambrose until the rocks they had sent flying over it hit their mark. Ambrose shielded his face with his hands.

"No, no," Ambrose wailed. "I know you know who I am. No matter what your grandmother says, I'm still your dad."

Suddenly a bell rang across the field and the boys stopped and ran back toward the school building.

"Come on," one of the boys yelled at Mark. "We'll be late."

But Mark stood frozen in front of the fence with a handful of dirt and stones still clenched in his fist. Ambrose took the opportunity to move closer.

"Mark, son," he said gently from the other side of the fence. "I came to wish you happy birthday. You don't like my present, do you? That's all right. Is there anything else you need? Something Abigail can't give you?"

Mark moved closer, and Ambrose was ecstatic. *It was working,* he thought. Mark was going to talk to him. Delighted, Ambrose broke into song.

"Happy birthday to you..." His voice cracked as the words came out of his mouth. "Happy birthday, dear Mark..."

But as he opened his mouth to belt out the last refrain, Mark threw what was in his hand through the fence and into his father's face.

"That's for you," he screeched. "Don't ever come here again, do you hear me?"

"Oh God!" Ambrose sputtered, as he choked and spit the dirt from his mouth. Then his face went beet red and he exploded, "You little bastard! What the hell do you think you're doing?" Ambrose thrust his body against the fence and beat his hands on the chain links. "If I get my hands on you," he continued. "You little…"

"Go ahead," Mark said, sneering at him, seemingly without fear. "Do something mean to me. I don't care. I'll tell Grandma, and she'll have you thrown in jail. That's what she told me. You hurt me again, and you won't see me or the light of day ever again."

Ambrose's eyes locked eyes on Mark's. He wouldn't do that, would he? Tell Abigail about today? How could he want him out of his life forever?

"No," Ambrose shouting, backtracking. "Don't you know that I love you? I didn't do anything wrong. It wasn't my fault."

"Nothing's ever your fault, is it?" Mark growled. "Well, it's not mine either. I didn't kill my mother!"

"Of course you didn't! It was an accident. It wasn't anyone's fault."

But by then, Mark was gone.

Ambrose yelled after him. "Don't go! We can talk this out. I know we can."

Mark didn't turn around, and Ambrose stood there alone until his son was a small speck on the other side of the schoolyard. "Good God!" he groaned, as he slunk away from the fence. What was he thinking, coming here? He had just made things worse. He had to get his son back. It was his only hope to be the man he wanted to be, to have everyone know him and his son. They'd say, "Look at Ambrose. What a man he is! He is the greatest father. He has a son."

Ambrose needed Mark in his life. He wanted to show him off and keep him on track. He knew he had high expectations for

Mark, but he wanted his son to make him proud. *Mark can't be off on his own,* Ambrose thought. *Without me in his life, Mark would never be good enough.*

Enraged, he took the remote control he was still holding and heaved it with all his might it into the air above him. He watched as it hit a steel pole of chain-link fencing and shattered into a hundred little pieces that came showering back down on him. "Christ," he bellowed. "This is all Mark's fault. I've done everything for him, and he is so ungrateful!"

Then Ambrose raised his arms to the sky. "My life is shit. All shit! Oh God, God! I need a drink."

He didn't want to be sober anymore. His son had outsmarted him and would probably tell his grandmother, Abigail, all about it. He hated it when he got caught. It didn't happen often. The last time was when he was twelve years old and his mother caught him burying his cat, Samson, in the backyard. Yes, he had killed the cat but what was the big deal! He'd never forgotten how she harped at him. When she told his school counselor about it, he had to go see a psychiatrist. But he got the best of that good doctor and remembering that now made him feel good.

Yes, he could think about that. How he went to see one of the disciples of Sigmund Freud and performed brilliantly. He'd hold that thought until he got to a liquor store and could buy a bottle. Then he'd figure how to get the best of Abigail and get his son back.

If he was brilliant then, he would be again.

He was sure of that.

◆ ◆ ◆

Hating himself now for remembering the humiliation of that day ten years ago with Mark, Ambrose moved quickly to another memory.

Now he reminded himself about how he had gotten the book

with the mad scribblings in it from Lisette's hotel room without her knowing it.

Ten years ago, it had never been his intention to steal the book or even think it had any value. But he had snuck into her hotel room twice back then. The first time, he remembered, was when he was desperate to talk to her about helping him with Mark, but she wasn't returning his calls or responding to the notes he left her under her door. That time, he told the maid in the hallway that Lisette was his wife and he had lost his hotel key. The maid let him in, but he fell asleep on the bed and when he woke up, Lisette still hadn't appeared. So he gave up and left more messages at the hotel for her.

The next day, when she still hadn't responded to him, he came back, even more desperate to see her than before. This time, he remembered how it happened.

He was so clever, so desperate and she was so unavailable. It was a perfect storm.

That's how he got the diary, and that would give him a clear path now to get his revenge on Lisette.

It was indeed a perfect storm!

◈ ◈ ◈

October 1999

Ambrose got off the elevator on the floor where Lisette's room was located.

As he rounded the corner of the hallway, he was ecstatic to see a maid right outside Lisette's room with her cleaning cart stacked up with dirty towels and bed linens. He watched the maid go back into the room again, but when she came out into the hallway, she headed into another room down the hall and disappeared.

With the door to Lisette's room still wide open, Ambrose quickly scurried down the hall, slipped into the room, and stepped inside the closet. He pushed aside the clothes hanging there, found a space to stand in and then pulled the clothes back in front of him. As he closed the closet door without a sound, he heard the maid come back into the room, spend a little more time in the bathroom, and then exit, closing and locking the door behind her.

Perfect, he thought. Now all he had to do was sit in the room and wait for Lisette to return. But this time he didn't want to fall asleep on the bed, so he took his jacket off, draped it over a chair and sat down in the chair facing the door so he'd be the first thing she'd see when she walked in. Then he waited...and waited. A few minutes went by, then ten, fifteen, twenty more, and still no Lisette. Should he be worried? He needed to be patient. He took a deep breath and looked around the room. There had to be a newspaper or something he could read while he waited. But all he saw were fashion magazines on the nightstand next to the bed, so out of desperation he grabbed one. As he did, he spotted a small, dark green book lying under it. It looked like the diary Lisette had told him she wrote in every night in her illiterate scrawl.

This he had to see, he thought with a chuckle. How does she do that? He opened it to a page in the middle and to his surprise, it was filled with precise, well-formed handwriting, hardly what he imagined. As he flipped through the pages, he saw that the entries weren't recent. In fact, they dated back almost twenty years.

This can't be Lisette's, he thought, *but whose is it? Why is it here?* He had to find out. He opened the book to the first inside page and read the inscription:

> *This private diary belongs to Marie Patterson. If you find it, don't be an asshole and read it. Return it to me or I'll smack you upside the head. (P.S. I mean it!!!)*

Marie? Who was Marie? Lisette never talked about any Marie.

Ambrose turned to the first handwritten entry in the diary and began to read:

August 25, 1979

It's my nineteenth birthday today, and I am starting this diary as a birthday present to myself. I want to write down everything so I won't forget, because this is the story of my new life. I am going through what some people call a "transformation," I think. From this day forward, I will never be the same again.

1979? Lisette told him she was nineteen years old. That meant she was born in 1980. This diary was written before she was born. What was Lisette's mother's name? She had told him that her mother was a stripper and her father's name was Ralph—but she didn't like to talk about him. Could Marie be her mother, and could this be her diary? Could she have kept a diary, too—like mother, like daughter?

What was the transformation Marie was talking about? Quickly Ambrose skimmed the page to the middle of the next paragraph and he got the gist of what Marie was talking about.

I'm in love with Brad and Brad's in love with me. Bradford Reginald Bufford. That's his full name. It's a great name to put a Mrs. In front of—Mrs. Bradford Reginald Bufford—and soon it will be my name. I never knew anything this good could happen to me. I am so happy!

❖ ❖ ❖

Now, ten years later, all Ambrose could remember about the diary was that it was filled with a lot of adolescent drivel about Marie meeting this guy named Brad, being in love with him and taking his name when they got married. Yet today, Ambrose couldn't even remember stupid Brad's last name.

He'd have to find the diary where he had probably left it in one of the piles he kept upstairs in a closet at the Community Center.

Over the years, he had stashed clothes, books, and other things there to hide them away. He needed to find the diary and read more of it. Who knew what he might find to exact his revenge on Lisette?

As he walked to the Community Center, he wondered why he hadn't read more of the diary that day in Lisette's hotel room ten years ago. But he had heard a noise at the door and he panicked. If it was Lisette, could he explain what he was doing in her room, much less reading the diary? So he closed the diary, jammed it in the pocket of his jacket, and pretended to read a magazine as the door to the room swung open.

It was the maid who he had seen out in the hall who entered, not Lisette.

Relieved but shaken at how he almost got caught in the room, Ambrose made up a story, which the maid bought and he left the room, thinking it was too risky to stay. He forgot about the diary in his pocket until later than night. While he intended to read more of it, he never did. *Today*, he thought, *things have changed.* Now what was in the diary had more possibility. Maybe there was something about Lisette and this Brad, whoever and wherever he was now. It could be something they would both pay him big bucks to keep hidden. With Lisette associated with a chain of Attila the Hunny strip clubs, Brad, whoever he was today, might not want to be associated with her. All kinds of scenarios that might profit Ambrose ran through his head.

But finding the diary was key. He had to know exactly what secrets it held. It was an opportunity of a lifetime, a better prospect for him than even before with Lisette.

Yes, today was his lucky day!

◈ ◈ ◈

Lost in thought, Ambrose suddenly looked up and saw that he was right across the street from the Community Center, a place he always gravitated back to.

He still did some work there for Pedro, the Center's director. He had first worked there after the car accident. Broke from funeral expenses for Betsy and Jeanine, he lost his focus and his job at a downtown law firm. Pedro, a former priest, felt sorry for him he guessed and listened sympathetically to his sob story. So he hired him to set up a legal aid clinic and Ambrose worked steadily there for a while until one day, he didn't show up and that was that. He had an explanation. People who have their kids taken away from them have a right to be upset, especially if they get shafted by the judge.

God, he hated that judge. Her name was emblazoned on his memory. It was all her fault. She only believed what Abigail told her. He hadn't hit Mark. He couldn't do that. There was no denying that Mark was a handful after the accident, but what kid wouldn't be? That didn't mean they had to take him away. Mark was all he had left, his only bright spot.

His whole world came crashing down with the judge's decision. Drunk and disgusting, Ambrose stopped coming to work at the clinic and left Pedro in a lurch. Somehow Pedro found someone to fill the job, but after that their relationship deteriorated and Ambrose didn't really care to mend it. After Mark was gone, he didn't even keep his attorney license current. Still when Pedro needed him, like when an attorney quit on him suddenly, Ambrose would do some paralegal work to keep the cases moving. Usually the job didn't last long but while it did, Ambrose had a little money coming in and access to the building during the day so he could keep his stuff stored upstairs in a closet. Of course tonight, he had no idea if his things were still in their hiding place. That's what he had to find out but if Pedro was there working late, he couldn't just walk in the front door and expect him to let him wander upstairs to look for the diary. No, that wouldn't work.

So as Ambrose looked over at the Community Center, he could see no lights were on inside and that meant the front door was probably locked. His plan was to walk across the street to the back of the building, climb through the basement window, which was always unlocked, and get what he needed upstairs without Pedro even knowing about it. It was worth the risk, he decided. No problem.

But by the time he made his way through the basement window, found his way through the cellar and up the stairs to the first floor of the Community Center, he was covered with spiderwebs and sweat poured off his brow. Quickly, he passed through the first-floor reception area, feeling that all he had to do was get up to the second floor and he'd be fine. But as he moved toward the stairs, he heard a jingling of keys outside the front door, and he jumped back.

"Shit!" he mumbled. Someone was coming in and it had to be Pedro. Quickly he looked for a place to hide. As he ducked into a storage closet beneath the stairs, the front door opened and he heard Pedro talking to someone.

"I'm telling you, it's no problem coming here like this. It's better to do this now. No prying eyes."

Do what? Where? How long? Ambrose thought, as he heard the sound of the light switches going on. *Who was Pedro talking to?* Then he heard another voice.

"But I hate taking you from your family at this hour, Padre," the voice replied. Ambrose thought it was some kind of joke that this guy called Pedro, an ex-priest, "Padre."

The male voice continued. "I do appreciate this. I've got nothing to hide, but it's not easy convincing anyone of that."

"Don't worry, Brad. This will all work out, you'll see," Pedro reassured him, but he sounded unconvinced. Ambrose could tell his heart wasn't in it. Who was this Brad—and what kind of trouble was he in that even Pedro wasn't sure he'd get out of it?

Brad went on. "You're the only one who can save me. I need those housing subsidy records to prove I'm innocent."

Pedro's voice came back more enthusiastically. "If that's all you need, I think I've got the files in my office going back to the time you worked in the program. If you know the dates you're looking for, this shouldn't take too long."

"Don't worry," Ambrose heard Brad say. "I'll stay here all night if I have to."

Great! Ambrose thought. So much for his plan for getting upstairs, getting his stuff and maybe even taking a shower. *Jesus! Couldn't they at least get back to Pedro's office soon*, he thought, *so I can get out of this damn, stuffy closet?*

Then he heard the men's footsteps cross in front of him and head down the hall.

"I can make us a pot of coffee," Pedro said, his voice fading.

Brad responded, but his voice was far away too and hard to hear. He waited until the voices completely faded, and then he bolted out of the closet. He knew how organized Pedro was, so going through the files might not take very long. He had to get up upstairs and back down again before Pedro and Brad finished. At least that way, he could walk out the front door rather than crawl out through the basement.

He took the stairs two at a time, and at the top, he tried the doorknob to the second-floor room. He twisted it and sighed with relief when it opened. This was going to be easier than he thought, but as he came into the room, dimly lit by a streetlight outside, everything that had ever happened to him there came back in a flash.

The hours he had spent working, eating, and sometimes sleeping there in the "loft," as he called it.

The final memories came first.

How he had humped Elena Marquez on the couch next to the

window. He didn't love the dark-haired woman from Columbia, but he craved the soft, adult comfort of her body. It was his kids, Mark and Jeanine, he missed. Without them, he felt an emptiness he couldn't fill. Soon Elena figured it out and went on her way.

Suddenly his thoughts were interrupted by the sound of voices downstairs. He moved closer to the door and from the top of the stairs he heard Pedro's voice.

"See, Brad. That didn't take very long. Let me know if you need anything else."

"I will," Brad replied. "I can't thank you enough. This means a lot to me and my wife."

"Say hello to Jenny," Pedro said. Then he continued more conversationally. "Do you think as governor she can survive this politically? Not every governor can ride out a scandal like this involving their husband."

"Jenny is tough. And she is a good governor; she really works at what she does and cares about the people, all the people, even the ones who are not so powerful."

"You better hope she is perceived that way. This scandal does involve those less-than-powerful people, and the press will eat you alive if you don't get this to settle down soon."

Brad laughed. "My name will be mud if I don't get this settled soon. I was born Bradford Reginald Bufford with no mud on it. I want to keep it that way!"

Suddenly Ambrose ears perked up. Did he really hear what he heard? That name, Bradford Reginald Bufford. Was *that* the name in Marie's diary all those years ago? Who was this guy that Pedro was talking to? He was married to the governor? Ambrose hadn't seen his face, at least not around the Community Center, and Pedro had never mentioned a Brad. It sounded like whatever business Pedro and this Brad had was in the past.

He had seen photos of the governor's husband in the papers,

but he didn't pay much attention. He had no reason to like or even vote for Jenny Jablonski as governor, or lieutenant governor before that. He did have a score to settle with her from years ago, but he had never found any way to settle it, given her prominent place in state government.

As the front door closed, Ambrose heard a cell phone ring downstairs. Pedro answered and said, "Hi, honey," and then paused. "I'm leaving right now. See you in a few minutes." Then he continued. "Yeah, Brad just left. He'll be okay, I think. Not sure Jenny will survive as governor, but that's politics for you. See you soon." After another pause, he said, "Yeah, love you too," and the call ended.

Ambrose's mind raced. If he was correct about the conversation he had just overheard, and if he remembered the name Brad from Marie's diary correctly, could the full name in the diary have been, Bradford Reginald Bufford? If so, things could get very interesting very soon. Ambrose's heart was pounding now with excitement.

When he was sure Pedro had left the building, he quickly started looking through drawers and closets where he had stashed his stuff, his mind racing.

What was the connection between Lisette and someone named Brad? Did the book he had of hers belong to Lisette's mother? Was there something in that diary that could give him a clearer idea of that connection?

How close a relationship was there back in the 1970s between Marie and Brad? Close enough to produce a baby? Close enough to—what?

Ambrose did want to speculate any further.

He thought only of getting back at Jenny Jablonski and Lisette all in the same sweeping motion. But mostly he thought about finding Mark again. He'd be almost twenty years old now. Mark might not remember or want to see him now, but what if he showed up with a pocket full of money? Lots of money. Maybe thousands of dollars, maybe millions? How much was Lisette's stake in her Attila the Hunny strip clubs? Better yet, if she was connected to Brad and Jenny, how much was it worth to them to keep that connection private?

If Pedro thought a federal scandal involving the governor's husband could bring her down, just think what a stripper in the family with her name plastered all over fancy strip joints could do to sink her political ambitions forever. Ambrose had read in the local paper that Jenny's name was being mentioned as possible candidate for vice president in the next national presidential election.

Wow! This was big! Suddenly he had to find the diary if it took him all night.

His life and his future depended on it.

This was big!

CHAPTER FOUR

Thursday, October 15, 2009

Playing Politics

Brad sat at the breakfast bar in the governor's mansion Thursday morning with a cup of coffee in his hand and read, maybe for fifth time—by then, he had lost count—the front-page headline of the *Capitol City Enquirer*: "Bufford Nears Indictment."

Each time he read that headline, it infuriated him, but still he read on, hoping he might have missed something in this newspaper article that would give him some hope that his whole life wasn't coming apart.

The Federal Bureau of Investigation (FBI) has nearly completed its probe into the business affairs of Bradford Reginald Bufford, a wealthy capitol city developer, and inside sources say that the U.S. Justice Department will indict the owner of several large housing developments and retail malls for fraudulent use of federal program dollars. Bufford had no comment yesterday as he rushed from meeting to meeting with officials presenting evidence he hoped would clear his name.

How could this be? he fumed silently. Was all the work he did last night at the community center with Pedro for nothing? Were they really that close to indicting him? Yesterday they said they'd welcome any other evidence that he could offer to prove his innocence. Were they lying to him?

"Jesus!" he swore under his breath. He needed this to go away as soon as possible for Jenny's sake, and to the press it was just a game. That's what upset him the most. He felt so guilty about dragging his wife into this mess, yet he couldn't do anything about it. He read further.

> Bufford's wife, Governor Jenny Jablonski, had no comment on this latest development in the investigation into her second husband's business affairs. Her press office has maintained that posture since the Justice Department investigation began several weeks ago, and Jablonski, a popular governor nearing the end of her first term, indicated through her campaign director, Everett Hall, that she fully expects to announce her candidacy for another term in the next few weeks despite her husband's financial troubles.

Wait a minute, Brad thought, as he read this last part of the story again. It said that Jenny had had no comment on the latest development in the FBI's investigation. If that was so, then the *Enquirer* must have called her yesterday afternoon and told her about the possibility of him being indicted. But she didn't say a word to him about it, not then or now.

How was that possible?

That shocked him; it really did. He had to take it in for a moment, reeling back and forth on his stool at the breakfast bar. His wife had known about the FBI indicting him on bogus charges, and she hadn't even tried to warn him about what would be on the front page of the paper this morning.

"Thanks a lot, Jenny," he growled under his breath, but he was feeling more hurt and confused than angry. Was this just one more way that Jenny was punishing him for the FBI's intrusion into their personal life?

How many times had he told her that he hadn't asked the FBI to dredge up this old accusation against him and breathe new life into them just as she was about to announce her reelection plans?

How could she be so petty? he wondered. That wasn't like Jenny at all. What he admired about her most was her integrity and how sure he was that she'd never compromise their relationship to save her political career. Otherwise he would never have asked her to marry him a few years ago. He had had enough women in his life who had hurt and betrayed him to know that he wanted another kind of life, and—up until a few weeks ago—that was exactly what he had with Jenny.

Not that either of them had any control over the media circus that accompanies FBI investigations. Even now, as he gazed out the kitchen window into the front yard of the mansion, he could see the reporters and camera people gathering down at the end of the driveway, just waiting there for him to show his face.

No way was he going run down that gauntlet. No, he'd sit here in the kitchen all day if he had to rather than give them any clue as to how he was dealing with all this. But defending himself to the media was nothing compared to dealing with Jenny. He wanted to give her the benefit of the doubt because he loved her more than any of the other women in his life, and she had never double-crossed him before. Not like the women who had told their stories to the FBI so that they could be distorted and manufactured into lies. Or Marie, the mother of all liars in his life. Her betrayal years ago hurt him the most.

He wanted to talk it out and make it right with Jenny, so when he heard footsteps coming down the stairs and into the dining room, he felt hopeful. She had come down to find him. She wanted to talk too. This nightmare would soon be over.

But from the sound of her short, quick steps, he could tell that Jenny was on the prowl and she was pissed. Any other day, he reasoned, a front-page headline above the fold about her and her brilliant political future would have been a good thing for Jenny. After all, she was the media darling, the first woman governor of the state and, by a poll he saw last month, the most popular governor in decades. All the political pundits had been twittering as her first term ended that, not only would she easily be reelected next November but also that surely she'd be on the short list of governors to be considered for vice president a few years from now. But Jenny wasn't stupid. She knew her bright political future could evaporate in a minute if headlines like those appearing in today's paper continued.

So what was this all about? Maybe she was angry and had given up on him. Suddenly she entered the kitchen, looking seemingly calm, with her glasses perched on her nose and reading from a sheaf of papers as she walked. Maybe she was waiting for him to make the first move and then she'd blow up in his face.

That was so unlike Jenny. She didn't have a passive-aggressive bone in her body. He always knew how she felt about everything. And if this article had been about anyone but the two of them, they'd be sitting at the breakfast bar right now enjoying themselves. They'd be pointing out how stupid these people looked, how silly the press had made them appear, and then together they would analyze and dissect how it would all play out politically.

That was what he loved about their marriage—how they could share their most difficult moments, particularly if one of them was on the front page of the newspaper that day. So why had Jenny completely shut down on him? He eyed her cautiously as she stood across the room from him by the coffeepot.

"I didn't expect to see you downstairs this morning," he said carefully.

She looked up at him and held his eyes for a second as if she might be interested in what he had said. Then her eyes went blank and she stared at him as if he was part of the furniture.

"And I thought you'd be at the office by now," she muttered.

"You know that's not going to be possible today," he shot back, but he held his voice steady, knowing each word was a test to see if he could engage her in a meaningful conversation. "There's no way I'd get out of the mansion alive, with the media camped out at the bottom of the driveway." Then he added purposefully, "Your 'no comment' in the papers this morning didn't help."

But instead of responding, Jenny turned away and poured herself a cup of coffee from the pot. Her continuing indifference was too much for him.

"Come on, Jenny," he said with as much exasperation and force in his voice as he dared. "I know you've seen the article in the *Enquirer*."

"Yes," she said, turning to face him now, her voice steady but flat. "Everett called me about it first thing this morning, and we've talked four times since. It's all over the internet and the TV morning political talk shows too."

Brad winced. He hadn't thought of that. The TV news reports were usually a day behind on stories like this that broke first in the *Enquirer*. But social media was much faster and politically deadlier. That meant whoever had leaked it knew how to launch a full, frontal attack on Jenny and take her by surprise.

He wanted to feel sorry for her, but it hurt that she had turned to Everett first and not to him. Not that Everett wasn't the man most responsible for getting Jenny elected governor four years ago. And he was also the one who had brought Brad into her campaign for lieutenant governor to help woo the business community to her side. That's how the two of them met.

"So Everett's going to be running both of our campaigns now?" Brad asked sarcastically. "You get reelected and I get crucified."

"No," Jenny snapped back, anger edging into her voice. "You deserve to be hung for what you've done to me."

"And what about what you did?" Brad came back indignantly. "You had no comment for the press, and you didn't even tell me I was going to get trashed in the paper this morning."

"How could I tell you when you were out to all hours of night?"

"What does that mean?" Brad exploded. He couldn't believe what she was accusing him of.

Jenny glared back at him. The gloves were off, and the fight was on.

"The way I feel about you right now," she sputtered, "you're lucky that's all I did for putting me through this...this..." she said, her voice cracking as she jabbed her finger in the direction of the newspaper in front of him, "this humiliation."

"You knew about this before you married me," he said forcefully, holding back nothing now. "I told you that these rumors about me had been floating around for years."

"I can ignore the rumors," she said. "It's the truth that hurts. You never told me how many women or how you met them and what you did to them."

"You really don't believe what those women told the FBI, do you?" he wailed. "That I forced them to have sex with me? I didn't rape them, for God's sake!"

"No, you took advantage of them when they were homeless and so desperate to put a roof over their heads that they'd do anything. The feds didn't put you in charge of handing out housing subsidies in the city so you could sexually harass poor, vulnerable women."

"Come on, Jenny. You're wrong about this." Brad jumped off the stool and moved toward her. "Yeah, I was involved with those women, but that was long before I met you, and they didn't mean a thing to me. I thought you understood what an emotional mess I was back then. And I didn't promise them anything if they slept with me. They got those certificates all by themselves, and I can prove it."

Brad pressed his hand into the soft flesh of Jenny's arms that were folded tightly over her chest and went on.

"The FBI has all the evidence they need to clear me. That's why I went to see Pedro last night. Everything in his files backs me up 100 percent. Those women got certificates on their own merit. I didn't give them any special favors. I faxed the paper records to the feds last night to back it up. That's why I got home so late."

Jenny pulled her arm back from his grasp and narrowed her eyes at him. "And you think that fixes everything? If the FBI is happy, I should be too? How about what it feels like to be married to a sex addict and have my husband's lack of moral character discussed on the front page of the paper day after day? Do you know how much that hurts?" Her voice cracked for a moment, and then she went on. "Do you?"

"But this isn't about sex for subsidies, and you know that! It's about people coming after me with stories that aren't true because they can hurt you personally and politically. They want to bring you down, Jenny, and I'm trying to stop them. Can't you see that?"

"So you're worried about me and my career now," she shot back. "How refreshing! Venturing out of that self-absorbed world of yours must be pretty scary!"

"I always worry about you," he said, his voice softening. "How can you *not* know that?"

Jenny's eyes sharpened their focus. "Everything I know about you these days I find out in the newspaper or on the internet! And what I read disgusts me. Who knows what I'll learn next!"

"You're pissed because someone used me to get to you and now you look stupid. But you do have enemies, Jenny. Not everyone loves *the* most popular governor in the state."

"People may disagree with me, but I'll stand on my record any day and take them on. It's your stinking life I can't defend."

"What's wrong with my life? I've done important things too!"

"Right, like building shopping malls and fancy overpriced apartment complexes? Let's face it. You do it because you have backers, and with money, you get to mix it up with the big boys. They all want to rub shoulders with you and tell you how brilliant you are. Being married to the governor doesn't hurt. That must be good for business."

"That's not why I married you, and you know it!" Brad's face turned a bright crimson. "I love you," he said pleadingly.

"No," Jenny said coldly. "You love being married to the governor, not to me. It's a power trip for you."

"Like you're not in it for the power," Brad's voice went up. "I see the way you push people around. You like being a bully, but you can't bully me."

She glared at him for a moment, then said, "You're just pissed because I didn't do some kind of 'stand-by-your-man' routine when the press called me. You want some of my credibility to rub off on you. You want me to support you 100 percent even when I don't know who or what you are anymore. And this may come as a shock to you, but not every voter in this state thinks what you do is any reflection on me. I married you. I don't have to act like you."

"Obviously I won't be expecting your help anymore," Brad said with a huff. He could see where this was going. It was just as he thought—all the women he had ever loved eventually betrayed him.

"Damn right about that," she snapped back, and he knew there was no stopping where this was headed. He didn't even care anymore.

"You got yourself into this," Jenny went on, "and you'll have to get out of it. Lucky for you, Everett's been making calls to let people know that I'm supporting you. It may not be on the front page of the paper, but I am. But this has to end. So here's the deal. Clean up this mess, and if nothing else rotten turns up from your past, I won't dump you before the next election. After that, we'll see!"

Without giving him a chance to say anything more, Jenny turned on her heels and stomped out of the kitchen.

"Bitch," he wanted to scream at her. What makes her think she can act so high and mighty with him? "Fuck this shit!" he said under his breath as he hurled himself back to the breakfast bar, where he threw the newspaper and the coffee cup sitting on it to the floor. The cup hit with a clunk and splattered coffee all over the wall.

Jenny was just like Marie. Why hadn't he seen it all along? She showed one side of herself until one day a whole other side showed up, leaving him totally surprised.

These were her true colors, the real Jenny Jablonski! She didn't care about him. She never had. She had made him believe otherwise, but it wasn't true. *Just like Marie,* he thought bitterly. She made him believe he was the father of her baby and then the joke was on him. Except he wasn't laughing, then or now.

Marie.

Why did he always come back to Marie? Why did he go over and over what happened from the first day they met? Because with Marie, like Jenny, it was never over. There had to be something he had missed about Marie, and if he knew what it was, he'd know where it was going with Jenny. God knows, he could use the help. Being married to Jenny wasn't easy.

Was it any easier thinking about Marie?

Maybe only because she was dead and gone, for all he knew—but still, somehow he cared, even though he had never tried to find her all these years.

He slumped back down onto the stool by the breakfast bar and thought about Marie. He let himself go back to a time when there was as much pleasure as pain, in search of something that could make him feel better.

He didn't know what else to do.

❖ ❖ ❖

Monday, April 2, 1979

It was early in April of 1979 that Marie came walking into the SNAP office and changed Brad's life.

SNAP stood for "Stop Nuclear and Atomic Power," an organization Brad worked for during the break he took between his last two semesters of college. He told his parents he needed time away from the grind at college, but in reality, he had broken up with a girl he was engaged to and he was devastated. She was perfect in every way to his twenty-two-year-old heart, but that was before he saw Marie.

Marie was spectacular. That day she wore a light blue cashmere sweater that made her deep blue eyes twinkle and her large, round breasts stand out. They were like beacons signaling his ship lost in a sea of instant lust. Her hair was long and blonde and the navy-blue skirt she wore fit snugly over her hips and hung right above her knee. She looked like a college girl from one of the classier schools, maybe Vassar or Mount Holyoke. And she was classy all by herself.

She came in looking for Brad, smiling and breathlessly introducing herself as Marie Patterson and telling him that she had seen him on TV news the other afternoon. She was upset, too, she said, about the terrible meltdown at Three Mile Island, the nuclear power plant in Pennsylvania, and she was so eager to help that she had run all the way there from the bus stop.

"I can't say that it's that exciting every day around here," Brad said, motioning for her to take a seat across from him at his desk.

He watched her sit down and curl her long, shapely legs around those of the chair. Every move after that seemed like a symphony in motion. How she swung her leather purse off her shoulder and dropped it down next to her chair. How she flipped her long hair back over her shoulder when it cascaded down over her chest, and how the gold cross that she wore on a thin, gold chain around her neck bobbed in the space between her breasts as she reached into her purse for a cigarette.

Brad found himself staring at her chest when he heard her ask, "Do you have a match?"

He blushed and looked up into her face and saw a cigarette dangling between her full red lips. "You don't mind if I smoke, do you?" she inquired.

"Oh, no, not at all. There's an ashtray and I've got some matches here somewhere," he said as he rummaged about inside the top drawer of his desk.

When he finally found a matchbook, he struck a match and held it out in front of him. She leaned forward and placed her hand on his to guide it toward her cigarette. The touch of her hand went through him like an electric current, and when she removed it, the temperature in his body had gone up and his face was flushed.

She took the first drag from her cigarette and sat back in her chair.

"I'm interested in doing whatever I can to help," she said blowing smoke out the side of her mouth and over her shoulder. "I'm really mad about what they're doing to this world with nuclear power."

"It's a serious problem," Brad heard himself saying as his eyes settled again on her chest. "This country and so many others around the world—France, Japan, and the Soviet Union—all want to expand their nuclear energy capabilities."

By then he was imagining how he had pulled that soft, fuzzy sweater up over her head and fondled her large, firm breasts snuggled in her sexy, white lace bra. "Because they think they can reduce this world's dependence on petroleum," he managed to say, "we probably can't stop the facilities that are already up."

Now he had unhooked her bra from behind and pulled her close to him while dropping his hands down past her waist and inside her skirt, making contact with her lace panties. His voice cracked as he continued, the fantasy taking more of his energy now as he struggled to stay focused on what he was saying. "But if we keep the public pressure on what happened at Three Mile Island, we should at least discourage new atomic energy facilities from coming up."

He had to stop there. Steady progress down her body was too much for him to take, so he mercifully ended it by saying quickly, "I'd like to see them all closed down, wouldn't you?"

She took a puff on her cigarette and blew smoke out her mouth.

"You sure know a lot about this stuff, don't you?" she added, letting out a sigh.

"That's my job," he said boastfully, as he regained his composure. "I'm the director here."

"You are?" she asked with surprise, taking another drag on her cigarette. "I'm impressed."

"Actually, I'm only the acting director," he clarified. "I'm filling in until someone permanent is found. I'll be going back to college in the fall."

"Where do you go?" she asked with great interest.

"Capitol College here in the city. I'm majoring in economics with a minor in political science. When I graduate, I'll be going to law school. Where do you go?"

"Oh, I'm not in school right now. I'll be going back to Spellman as soon as my mother gets better. She's sick."

"Nothing serious, I hope." Brad looked at her sympathetically.

"Actually, it's…it's TB—tuberculosis, you know. She's got it pretty bad."

"Gosh, you don't hear of many cases of that anymore. Used to be they put people in sanitoriums for that."

"Well, my mom's at home and I'm helping take care of her. I was going stir crazy being there with her all by myself, so when we saw you on TV, Mom and I thought that I should come down here and volunteer a few days a week so the time would go by faster for me."

"Can your mom be home alone? Isn't TB contagious?"

"Yeah, but I can't get it now. I've been tested. My aunt is filling in for me today, so I can have a break."

"And there's no one else to help out?"

"No, my dad died several years ago in a train wreck."

"Wow! You don't hear of many of those anymore these days either."

"No, I guess not." Marie took another drag on her cigarette and then changed the subject. "So, is there some way I can help around here? I can type a little. High school typing class, you know." She looked quickly around her and when her eyes rested on a stack of envelopes on the table next to Brad's desk, she added, "I can lick envelopes!"

Brad followed her eyes to the table and then back. For a moment there, he would have given anything to be an envelope licked by Marie, but he quickly regained his composure. "Sure. We're working on a mailing for a rally next week. The public's pretty upset about this thing that happened at Three Mile Island last week. We're trying to keep them that way. Don't want them to get complacent after all the initial publicity."

"No, we wouldn't want that, would we?" Marie sounded nervous again. "So just let me know what I can do, and I'll do it. I can stay until three o'clock today."

"That would be terrific." Brad smiled at her this time and held out his hand to shake hers. "Glad to have you on board then."

He held her hand a little longer than he should have, but it was soft and warm and he didn't want to let it go.

She pulled it away gently and then asked, "Is there a ladies' room where I could freshen up a bit?"

Jesus, Brad thought, *if she gets looking any better, I won't get anything done today.*

"Sure." His voice flickered as he tried to control the hormones raging inside him. "Down the hall and turn right."

She put her cigarette out in the ashtray on his desk and smiled at him as she got up from her chair. Brad watched her move slowly and deliberately down the hall. Underneath that cool, calm exterior, he bet she was a real scorcher in bed. And from the way she walked away from him, he knew that she knew what he was thinking about her.

Tuesday, May 1, 1979

It took Brad a few weeks after that to work up the nerve to ask Marie out. Then she put him off for another two weeks, telling him that she had to stay home at night and on the weekends to take care of her mother and he couldn't come to her house for fear that he might get TB. He finally he convinced her to go to a movie with him one night in May after work and then come back to his place for pizza. It was a cheap date, all he could afford, but she didn't seem to mind.

They started necking on the couch after eating the pizza and drinking a few beers. Soon they had all their clothes off and were in his bedroom together.

It was almost twenty years ago now since Brad had first kissed Marie, but he still remembered how soft her lips were and how sweet she smelled. He even remembered how she moaned with pleasure as their kisses became more passionate. For him, it was like making love to all of the girls he had ever wanted in his life in this one person, Marie. Even Jasmine, his old girlfriend, paled in comparison.

During this night of incredible pleasure, all the endless possibilities for his life with Marie floated through his head as he cuddled up next to her. It was almost two o'clock in the morning, and he was exhausted but energized after making love to her for hours.

"Jesus!" he cried out as he suddenly bolted upright on the bed. "I've got to get you home. Your mother will be furious."

"Don't worry," Marie said calmly. "I told her I was staying over at my girlfriend's."

"You mean you didn't tell her you were going out with me?"

"No, it was easier say that I was with Lucinda. She won't worry so much."

"So you think she has something to worry about when you're with me?" Brad teased her, then relaxed and laid back down next to her.

"No," Marie giggled. "But my mother doesn't like me hanging out with boys. She thinks I'm still a virgin."

"Well, you aren't now, that's for sure," Brad said boastfully. "But you *are* one sexy lady—you know that, don't you?" He stroked her naked body as he pulled her closer to him.

"You're not so bad yourself."

"God, I wish this night could last forever."

"I wish that, too, but sometimes good things don't last."

"Don't say that. Say that you'll love me forever. You do love me, right? I've never felt this way before."

"Oh, I do," she giggled. "I love you, Brad Reginald Bufford!"

"Quiet!" he whispered and giggled himself. "You'll wake up my roommates."

"I thought they weren't coming home tonight."

"One of them came home a while ago. But you must've been otherwise occupied," he said, chuckling.

"And you weren't," she pouted. "I'm crushed."

"If you want some more attention, I can fix that."

Marie shrieked and giggled as Brad once again jumped on top of her body and covered her face and neck with kisses.

"God, you're beautiful," he muttered moving down her body and burying his face in her breasts.

Marie moaned and ran her hands through his thick hair. "Are you mine? Are you really mine?" she whispered.

"Yes! Yes! I really am."

"Then you're the cat's pajamas," she squealed.

Brad pulled himself up from her body and looked at her.

"What does that mean?" he asked with a laugh.

"It means that you are all things great and wonderful. You're the best."

"You're just saying that because you liked the pizza tonight," Brad said teasingly.

"No," Marie said, her tone changing. "I said it because it's the truth. You'll always be the best thing that has ever happened to me."

Brad looked at her. He was surprised at how serious she was. "How could you say that? You hardly even know me."

"I know, but it's something I just know. I can't explain it." Then she paused and added, "Don't worry. You don't have to say the same thing about me. I know that you're going to meet a lot more important people in your life than I ever will, but I want you to know that this is my special moment. It won't ever come again." Then she sighed and pulled him down on top of her.

How could she know that? he wondered for a moment and then he lost that thought in the pleasure of her body. *How could she possibly know something as amazing as that?*

❖ ❖ ❖

Thursday, October 15, 2009

It took Ambrose all night, but he finally found Marie's diary.

It was stuck at the bottom of a box he had gone through several times in the course of his search. He had become more and more desperate as the night wore on into the early morning hours of the next day.

He started reading from the beginning again—how Marie had seen Brad on television and how the girls at the club dared her to go meet him and make her fall in love with her. And she did.

Ambrose read the first entry in August 1979:

I'm in love with Brad, and Brad's in love with me. Bradford Reginald Bufford. That's his full name. It's a great name to put a Mrs. in front of—Mrs. Bradford Reginald Bufford—and soon it'll be my name. I never knew that anything this good could happen to me. I am so happy!

Lisette had told Ambrose that her mother died when she was young, maybe ten years old. She also told him that a guy named Ralph was her father, but maybe that was something her mother, in this case, Marie, told her to cover up the truth. But why? Because Brad was the kind of guy who wasn't going to stay with a woman who danced in strip clubs for a living, even if she was the mother of his child. And he could be the father of this child if these diary entries were written about the time Marie got pregnant with Lisette. According to the diary, she was in love with a guy named Brad whose full name was Bradford Reginald Bufford. There was that name again! The one that Ambrose thought he heard at the Community Center last night. He turned the pages quickly to see if he could find anything more about this Brad and a baby.

He found nothing until he came upon a late September 1979 entry, which he read with eagerness and relief. At last he was getting to the good part.

Thursday, September 20, 1979

It's true. I'm pregnant. I went down to the clinic to get tested and got the results this morning. The doctor told me I'm two months gone, and I can't believe it. I'm on the pill, but the doctor said nothing is 100 percent safe.

How can I tell Brad? He'll be furious! Brad is one of those guys who has his life all figured out. He's only with me now because he thinks I fit right into his life. But a baby won't. He's got to finish college and law school and then get a job. He says he plans to get married and have kids somewhere in there, but not now.

I could just not tell him about the baby. I could get rid of it, and he'd never know anything. No muss, no fuss. But if I get rid of the baby and don't tell him, how could I live with him the rest of my life knowing that we made a baby together and I killed it without telling him? Haven't I told him enough lies just to get him to go out with me?

But if I tell him about the baby, he may stay, but for the wrong reason and worry too much about how he's going to support me and the baby. His parents could help out. They have lots of money. Brad told me his dad is a lawyer in a big law firm downtown and his mother sells real estate. But his parents wouldn't like the part about the baby. They waited to get married until his father got out of law school, and Brad said they expect him to do the same.

What a mess! I know one thing. I don't want to have this baby and end up like my mom. After Dad left us, she raised us on welfare and cleaning the houses of rich old ladies. Talk about shame and embarrassment! I left home when I was sixteen and never looked back. At least I earn my own living now, except that with a baby coming, I won't be able to work. Ralph won't let no pregnant bimbo dance in his club. I'll have to quit before I even start to show. I was planning to quit anyway. I don't want Brad to ever know where I worked when I met him.

Oh God! Why did this baby have to come now, just when everything was so perfect between Brad and me? I can't lose Brad. He means everything to me. But I have to tell Brad about the baby. I have to make him see that the only thing to do is to get rid of it. I'll tell him this afternoon and call the clinic tomorrow to schedule an abortion. It's the only way. I don't know what else to do.

Wow! Ambrose thought. *Maybe Marie didn't have the baby after all. Maybe all of this is a false alarm.* He continued reading until he found the next reference to Marie's pregnancy.

Friday, September 21, 1979

I did it. I told Brad about the baby. It was the hardest thing I've ever done, but I told him the truth, and for a minute there, he was really excited about it. There was this kind of glow in his eyes, and then his face turned to sheer terror. Are you sure? he asked me, and I told him what the doctor said. Then he paced back and forth like a wild animal trapped in a cage for a while and pulled at his hair. Finally, he stopped and said, I don't want you to get rid of this baby. So let's get married. Are you sure? I asked him, but by then he was down on his knee proposing to me. Can you believe it? I said yes, but now I wonder. Was it the right thing to do? I'm so happy that Brad wants the baby, but how can he be so sure? I'm not. I've told him so many lies. I only want what's best for my baby. But how can I know what that is? I'll be Mrs. Brad Bufford soon, but will it be all right?

"Bufford!" Ambrose said in a whisper. That was the name when he heard Brad and Pedro talking downstairs. But what were they saying exactly? About Brad giving Pedro's regards to his wife, Jenny.

Ah, yes, Ambrose groaned with revulsion. Jenny Jablonski, our governor! Ambrose hated her then, and he hated her now. Suddenly his scheme for revenge was getting so much more enjoyable! With one bold stroke, he could bring his revenge down on two people he hated the most in this world, not counting his hated ex-mother-in-law, Abigail Durocher.

Now he remembered there was a name in the headlines this morning. What was it again?

Ambrose got up and grabbed today's newspaper from his pocket. He had bought a copy of the overnight edition of Friday's paper last night as he walked to the Community Center.

"Oh my God!" he gasped as he read the headline, "Bufford Nears Indictment," and quickly scanned the front-page article.

Lisette was never going to believe this!

Never!

CHAPTER FIVE

Thursday, October 15, 2009

The Deal is Done

By Friday morning, Brad was in a deep depression. After his knock-down-drag-out fight with Jenny the day before and his long, melancholic remembrance of how he first met Marie, he felt as if he had been in a train wreck.

To make matters worse, if that were possible, he hadn't been out of the mansion since Wednesday night when he had retrieved the housing subsidy records from Pedro's files and then faxed them over to the feds in the hope that it might clear his name and end this nightmare.

But after the article in yesterday's paper, not only was he close to being indicted, if he believed everything he read in the *Enquirer*, but also he was so solidly in the doghouse with Jenny. He had slept on the couch in his office alone last night and woke up this morning resigned to letting his attorney deal with the feds for him and staying clear of Jenny.

So far he had handled the whole matter abysmally. He had taken it too personally, pissed that the allegations of sexual harassment were still haunting him and angry that someone was using him as a political pawn to stall his wife's reelection campaign. He was distracted by who was doing this and why. What was more important for him and Jenny was for him to be exonerated and for people to know he was a good person. He could see that even Jenny wasn't sure of that anymore, and that hurt the most.

So there he sat, feeling like a complete failure, slumped down on the couch in his office and flicking indifferently through the TV channels with the remote control. When his cell phone rang about ten o'clock, he lunged for it.

He put the phone to his ear and heard Everett's voice.

"Hey, are you sitting down?" he asked Brad cheerfully.

"Yes," Brad moaned. "What else have I got to do?"

Everett ignored him and went on. "I've got news! The feds made you an offer."

With that, Brad bolted up straight. "Really? How do you know that? My attorneys haven't even called me yet."

"You don't want to know, but I heard that the feds took a look at the stuff you faxed over to them the other night and agreed that it supports your side of the story."

"Hallelujah!" Brad exclaimed. "So they're willing to settle, just like that?"

"No, not exactly, but if you and your attorney can save them a little face, you can get yourself out of this."

"Why do I have to worry about them looking stupid?" Brad grumbled. "They're the ones who are stupid. What kind of a deal is this anyway?"

"They'll probably want you to accept some kind of agreement."

"Oh, so they know I'm right, but I have to say I did something bad."

"Not exactly, but they do have women who have made complaints against you. The local cops could even bring criminal assault charges against you."

Brad winced. He knew that Everett had spent years as a street cop and knew what he was talking about.

"You know someone convinced those women to make complaints against me," Brad corrected him. "It's all about politics, of course!"

"Look, they need to show these women that their complaints were taken seriously."

"And they have," Brad interjected. "They have investigated them and found nothing to substantiate them."

"No, it's not that easy. You did sleep with them, and while the feds can't prove that you were demanding sexual favors in exchange for their rental certificates, there's certainly the appearance of impropriety, even if the women did qualify for the subsidy on their own merits."

"But I didn't do anything illegal, and I've proven that," Brad insisted. "Why can't they let me off the hook?"

"You know why," Everett hedged. "So let's not go there."

"But it's not fair," Brad whined. He knew it had everything to do with who he was sleeping with presently, and he wanted Everett to acknowledge it at least.

"Don't drag Jenny into this, Brad. Just take the deal. If the feds want you to stipulate that neither you nor any of your businesses will be associated with a rental subsidy program in the future, you should agree. You know they'll want you out of that picture permanently so they can show these women good faith on their part."

"That's extortion!" Brad yelled into the phone. "The only reason I'd even consider agreeing to this is because I'm not in the rental subsidy business anymore."

"Wrong! I just got off the phone with an attorney involved in the Westingham Hills development and you got two problems with staying in the project. First, he's alleging some kind of campaign finance violation against Jenny's campaign because of a contribution that a business made to Jenny last month. Did you know about that? They claim there is a 'quid pro quo' involved. They give money to your wife's campaign and you do them a good deed with a state contract. And second, you'll have to pull out of that project completely anyway since the plans call for some low-income, state-subsidized housing units there along with an expansion of the shopping mall. Besides the deal you may make with the feds, Jenny signs off on those kind of projects as governor. You know that! It's all one big conflict of interest!"

"What!" Brad's voice shook. "I've been working on that mall expansion project for three years. They can't ask me to pull out of it now. I know everything there is to about place. I've memorized the layout and function of everything in that mall. This is unreal!"

"It's the only way to stop the accusations that have plagued you for years."

"But the feds can't legally limit my business, not without convicting me of committing a crime."

"Yeah, but if you go trial and win, what have you won?" Everett paused for a moment while Brad let that sink in. *Nothing*, he thought. By then, Jenny would have lost her reelection because of him, and everything that they had worked so hard for would be gone.

"I'm sorry," Everett said, "but I don't think they're going to give you a free ride on this, buddy. But you need to talk to your lawyers about that. I'm just trying to clear the way here for Jenny's reelection campaign for governor and who knows what else!"

Brad didn't know what to say. The rage inside him was clouding his judgment, and he needed time to think. "Can I have a couple of days to sort this out?"

"No. As I understand it, the offer from the feds expires this afternoon, and even if you take the deal, this won't die down for a while—but it shouldn't get any worse. We are going into campaign mode here, Brad. We've got to be careful."

"Jesus," Brad muttered. "They've got me by the balls, don't they?"

"Sorry. I'd talk to your people, but this may be all they'll give you."

"I understand. But Westingham too! What will I do without that project in my life? I'll have to go out and get a real job!"

"I wouldn't go looking yet. It's best if you keep a low profile. No public appearances with or without Jenny. We don't want to give the press a chance to ask you embarrassing questions."

"Great," Brad said with a sigh. "If I'm alone under house arrest any longer in this dizzy old mansion, you'll have to get me a padded cell."

Everett was quiet for a moment, then he said gently, "I heard that you and Jenny had a row yesterday morning."

Brad winced and then demanded, "Does everyone get to know what goes on between Jenny and me now? When does it stop?"

"It stops when she gets reelected," Everett insisted. "Jenny has to show that she's not a one-term governor. Once she gets to her second term, it will be easy sailing."

"I don't believe that," Brad grumbled. "With her, this job is never going to be easy."

Everett didn't respond, perhaps it was because he didn't believe it either, but then Brad laughed. "I don't think Jenny wants to be seen with me anyway, publicly or privately. And my business has gone down the tubes, so I'm unemployed and unattached. Do you have any envelopes I can lick for the campaign? I do have some marketable skills." Then he asked more seriously, "If I agree to this, will this take the heat off Jenny?"

"I think so. She's happy we got somewhere with the feds. I talked to her a few minutes ago about you keeping a low profile publicly for a while. We need things to quiet down for a while."

"But I wanted to go with her to the event this Saturday. You know, the Tenth Anniversary Gala for the young woman killed on campus ten years ago. I saw pictures of her on the news this morning. She was very beautiful, and they say very talented. That's got to be tough for her family, still missing her after all those years. She was only nineteen when she was killed. She'd be twenty-nine now."

Brad sighed, then continued. "She was so close in age to Jenny's own daughter, Maryssa. This event is going to be hard for her. I should be there with her. Jenny would want that."

Everett went on, anticipating his thoughts. "At first we talked about you going to the event with her to show that things were okay between you two. But with what's happening with the feds deal and Westingham, we both think it's too risky. And you don't want to blow this deal with the feds. Sorry about that."

Brad heaved a deep sigh and tried to focus on what Everett was saying. But all he could think about was how much he wanted things to be different between him and Jenny. It was all his fault. This was the place he had put himself, and he hated it.

"So I'll call my attorneys, tell them to find the leak in their organization that got the news to you before me, and let the feds know we have a deal," Brad said, feeling despondent. "It's a lousy deal, but I'll take it if it makes Jenny happy."

"I know. This isn't fair."

"Life isn't fair now, is it?" he snarled as he hung up the phone and slammed his body against the back of the couch. If only he could end this battle with Jenny, he thought. He'd even let her win the war. He didn't care anymore.

So many things were unfair. For instance, as much as he felt sorry for the family of that girl who was killed, at least they had had a daughter for nineteen years. He didn't. With long blonde hair and a beautiful face, that girl looked so much like the daughter he and Marie could have had. But the baby wasn't his. That's what Marie told him.

Did Marie and the baby ever think of him the way he was thinking of them now? *What became of them?* he wondered. *Were they even alive?*

Suddenly he found himself trying to remember everything Marie had said to him about the baby on that day almost thirty years ago now. As in a dream, he wanted to remember it word for word.

In a flash, he was back with Marie and the baby that wasn't his. The one he had given up on so long ago. Or had he?

◈ ◈ ◈

June to September 1979

Within a week of their first date, Brad and Marie began to see each other or talk almost every day. By June, when he had to go to Miami for an anti-nuke conference and she couldn't come with him, he was devastated that he'd be away from her for two whole weeks. He called her every night, and when his parents invited him to their condo in Palms Springs for the weekend, he asked them to fly Marie there too, but they wouldn't.

Brad tried to explain why to Marie one night on the phone from Miami.

"I know you think that they don't like you, but they will when they meet you. They'll love you as much as I do."

"But why don't they want to meet me?" Marie asked.

"It's not about you. They didn't meet Jasmine until after we got engaged."

"But you're not engaged to her anymore. You're with me. Don't they want to know if you're happy?"

"You don't understand. They have this idea I shouldn't get attached to anyone until I get out of school. They think that if we're apart for a while, I'll forget about you."

"But I miss you so much!" Marie said, sighing. "Can't you just tell them no and come home?"

"It's not that easy. Trust me, I have to play this thing out. If I defy them, they won't pay for my school in the fall. It was hard enough to get them to let me take this year off and work at SNAP. If I stay with them in Palm Springs, they'll see how I feel about you and back off."

Marie sighed once again into the phone.

"What if they keep trying to get me away from you?"

"Oh, they'll try. Hadley and Marian can be persistent, but I'm as stubborn as they are. After all, I *am* their son."

"Can't we invite them over to see us when they get home?"

"I'll try, babe, but I can't promise anything. See you soon. I love you," Brad said and hung up the phone, missing her already. He vowed he'd spend the weekend talking about Marie constantly, no matter how uncomfortable or crazy it made them.

And he did. He talked about how beautiful she was, where she was going to college, how much they had in common since she was interested in the environment, too, and how she was taking care of her sick mother.

His parents made no comment about all this until finally, when they were dining at a fancy, expensive restaurant on his last night in Palm Springs, his mother turned to him and asked, "Who is this girl you keep talking about?"

"Marie, Mother," Brad said with exasperation in his voice. "Her name is Marie Patterson, and I want you and Dad to meet her."

"Oh pish!" his mother sputtered. "You've wanted us to meet every girl you've ever dated since high school. And for what? The next thing we know, you've broken up with her and you're all depressed and despondent. It's getting tiresome, son. Your father and I wish you could be more discriminating. Why can't you date some of the girls from our country club up north?"

"But Marie is different. I'm going to marry her," Brad said definitively.

His mother winced and gave him a disapproving scowl. "You're too young to get married. You've got more important things to think about than that."

"Like what? Going to law school and joining Dad's firm? I told you I don't want to do that. I told you. I'm going to Washington, D.C., to work for the Environmental Protection Agency."

"We'll see about that," his mother snapped and then asked brusquely, "Do you have a picture of this girl? Can I see what she looks like?"

"You can see more than her picture, Mom. You can meet her," Brad retorted, but he pulled out his wallet anyway and took out a picture of him and Marie. It had been taken a few weeks ago in a photo booth at the drugstore, and he proudly handed the picture to his mother.

She stared at it for a moment and then looked up at him.

"*This* is the girl you're so in love with?" she sputtered.

"Yes," Brad said confidently, ignoring the sarcasm in her voice. He couldn't imagine what his mother could object to about Marie. She looked so sweet in that photo, he thought, and so sexy too.

"She's all right," she snorted, "if you like girls with a big head of hair and lots of makeup." Then she flipped the photograph back across the table to him.

"It's the Farrah Fawcett look," Brad said, snatching up the picture and gazing at it fondly. "All the girls wear their hair like that, and there's nothing wrong with her makeup. It's the natural look."

"She looks like a natural-born tart to me," his mother muttered under her breath, as she took a forkful of food from her plate and shoved it quickly into her mouth.

"What did you say?" he asked indignantly, jamming his hands on the table, making everything on it shake. "If you have something to say about Marie, then say it," he went on. "I'm tired of how you are treating her. You don't even know her and you're calling her names. I'm sure she could think of a few names for you, Mother. Or wouldn't that be playing fair?"

"That's enough, son," his father barked, speaking to him as if he were still six years old and he had to show him who was boss. "Your mother is just concerned about you, and so am I. Running around with someone who looks like that bimbo on television is not what we had in mind for you."

"And what is that you have in mind for me?" Brad exploded, his voice trembling and rising as other diners turned toward their table. "You don't own me, and you can't control my life!" Then he got up from his chair and threw his napkin down on the table. "Oh, what's the use? You never listen to anything I say. Never! And you don't care what I want. It's always what you want. I've had it. I'm out of here."

He turned to leave the table, but his father's hand gripped his arm.

"I said, that's enough!" his father said, his voice low as he spoke through his clenched teeth. "Sit down and stop embarrassing your mother. We will talk this out like civilized people. "

Brad eyed his father, and the look on his face infuriated him. He was blaming him for the whole scene in their favorite restaurant, and they would never let him forget it. Soon he'd sit down, and they'd extract something from him for being such a bad boy, but not this time, Brad thought quickly. No, for once, he'd get the upper hand. He had to think fast. There was too much at stake here.

"You want to talk," Brad said talking quickly and with confidence as he sat back down and leaned in toward his parents. "Here's the deal. You come meet Marie, and if you don't like her instantly—and I'm talking immediately here—" He stopped and looked both his parents squarely in the eye for emphasis, and then went on as they nodded, "I'll give the girl up."

His father gave him a stunned look and then took his time taking a bite of meat and chewing it slowly. "You really mean that?" he finally said. "Both your mother *and* I have to like her?"

"Yes, sir," Brad shot back with great confidence. "I'm that sure of Marie. She's very special, and I know you'll see that in her too."

"All right," his father said flatly. "It's a deal."

"Fine," Brad replied. "You come to see us when you get back up north and you'll see what a great person Marie is."

"Great!" his mother said, and then sat up straight. "Now that that's settled, I'm going to have coffee. What about you, dear?" she said, turning to her husband. "Better have decaf or we'll be up all night. How about dessert? I wonder if they have those key lime pie tarts they had here last week. I absolutely loved them. They were the best!"

Brad listened to his mother rattle on and watched his father light up an after-dinner cigar. The argument was over, and he had won. Of course, his parents figured that they got the better part of the bargain, that's why they caved in so easily, but they didn't know how perfect Marie was. But he did, and for once he would get what he wanted because Marie was going to wow them. He told her so when he called her that night from the airport while waiting for his connecting flight home.

"All we have to do is wait for my parents to come see us, and we'll be in the clear. Then no one will ever keep us apart," he gushed into the phone. "I promise."

But summer went by, and when fall arrived, Brad went back for his last year of college. Still there was no visit from his parents. Whenever he talked to them on the phone, they had some excuse not to come, even though they had been back for months. Brad was still confident that everything would work out as planned until one day in mid-September when he came home for lunch between classes and was surprised to find Marie sitting on the couch in his apartment.

"What are you doing here?" he asked in a stunned, concerned voice, sitting down next to her. "You should be with your mom. Is she okay?"

"I have to tell you something," she said in a tiny, squeaky voice.

"What is it? Are you all right?"

"I'm pregnant," she blurted out. "I found out yesterday."

"You're what?" His mind raced. He must have heard her wrong. He was stunned. "I missed my period last month," she went on. "It's my fault that we weren't more careful."

"Are you sure?" Brad asked, his mind still reeling. He felt the shock hit him like a blow to the top of his head and his knees went weak. "Have you seen a doctor?"

"Yes, the doctor said sometimes birth control doesn't work."

Brad pushed his numb body against the back of the couch, and his mind exploded with thoughts about his parents. *Oh God! What would they think of Marie now?* Her being pregnant and they weren't even married would blow that deal he had with them completely. There was no way they'd like her now. It was a lost cause.

"Then suddenly his desperation about his parents was swept away by another sweeter thought. He was going to be father! A warm, fuzzy glow came over him and his eyes grew wide with delight. He leaned over and touched Marie on the abdomen. "Is it a boy or girl?" he asked playfully. "Can they tell yet?"

"I…I don't know," Marie stuttered, looking into his eyes for the first time. "But I think it's a girl."

He kept his hand there for a moment more and realized that soon he'd feel the baby move there. That thought flooded his heart with pure joy. Is that what it's like to be having a baby? *God, it was wonderful!* Is this how his father felt when his mother told him that Brad was growing inside her?

Then Brad's face contorted, and his father's voice roared up inside him. *How could you be so stupid, son? Knocking a girl up! What did I teach you about that?*

Brad jumped up off the couch and paced wildly in front of Marie. "Oh my God! What am I going to tell my parents? They'll go nuts!" He stopped for a beat and then went on with even greater agitation. "And what about your mother? She doesn't want you dating boys, let alone having sex with them and making babies."

"She doesn't have to know," Marie insisted. "I'll go down to the clinic and take care of it."

Brad glared at her. "You're not going to abort this baby."

"I have to. It'll ruin everything. You said so yourself."

"You're not going to do that," he begged her. "There's a human life growing inside you, for God sakes."

"Don't you think I know that?" she yelled back. "I'm not a monster. I'm just being realistic, and so are you. We can't have a baby now."

"But we can't kill it!" Brad's face was red and his voice harsh.

Marie seemed surprised by his reaction, and he narrowed his eyes at her.

"You thought I'd want to get rid of the baby, didn't you? As though it's the only way. Well, I don't," he said adamantly. "We'll just have to think of another way."

"I know what I can't do," Marie said pointedly. "I won't raise this baby by myself."

"No one's saying you'll have to," Brad said but when he looked at her, he could see the pained expression on her face.

"You don't know what it's like not having a father," she went on with a bitterness in her voice he hadn't heard before. "You piss and moan about your father, but he's there for you, no matter what. I never had that."

Then her eyes teared up and she grabbed Brad's hand. "Don't you see?" she went on. "My mother tried to make up for my father not being there, but there was always this big hole in my life that I could never fill up. There still is." Tears flowed down her face and her chin and lips trembled. A sharp, painful sound came up from deep down in her throat.

"Oh God, I won't do that to this baby," she cried out. "I can't! I'd get rid of it or give it up for adoption before I'd do that."

Brad couldn't take it anymore. He sat back down on the couch next to her, took her in his arms and held her as she sobbed into his shirt. Her pain overwhelmed him, and he didn't know what to do. How could he or anyone make up for what she didn't have? She had never talked about her dad before, and so he didn't know how much she missed him.

"There, there," he finally said softly, stroking her hair and comforting her. "Nothing bad is going to happen to this baby. I promise you that." He kissed the top of her head and rocked her until her crying let up a little. Then he reached into his pocket to pull out a handkerchief.

"Here," he said offering it to her. He watched her blow her nose into it and wipe her tears away. After a while, he spoke to her in a calm, even voice. "Look, I was upset because—well, you surprised me, that's all. You've had time to think about it, and now I have too. I want this baby. I really do."

"Are you sure?" she whimpered.

"I love you, Marie." He touched her abdomen again. "And this baby makes what we have together even more special."

Marie looked at him, her eyes brighter now, as though she had hope and trusted him again. He brought her hand to his lips to kiss it and held it as he slid off the couch and onto one knee in front of her.

"Will you marry me?" he asked her.

She gasped. "You don't have to marry me just because—"

"No!" Brad cut in. "I wouldn't ask you unless I wanted to. I want you to be my wife."

Marie took his hand and pulled it up to her face.

"Of course, I'll marry you," she said breathlessly. "I love you so much!"

Brad slid back up on the couch next to her and kissed her passionately. "There, that's settled!" he said happily, as he released her from his embrace. "We'll get married as soon as we can, and when the baby is born, we'll be a family. Won't that be great? Make sure you tell your mom that we'll figure out some way for you to finish school too."

Brad paused for a moment, then he gushed. "I can't wait to call my parents and tell them about our engagement, wedding, and baby all at the same time. That'll make them crazy!"

Marie giggled, and Brad pulled her body closer to him. As she clung to him in that moment, he remembered that nothing else mattered to him but her and the baby.

Isn't this what life is all about? he thought. *Finding and holding on to someone who loves you and who you love with all your heart?*

Having found that in Marie, he really and truly meant it to last forever.

September 1979

"Jesus, we're just having a baby! It's not the end of the world," Brad remembered screaming in exasperation at his father as they sat opposite each other at the dining room table in his parent's home.

It was late September, a couple of days after Marie told Brad about the upcoming birth of their baby, and Hadley was pissed.

"You get someone you hardly know pregnant and now you want to get married before you finish school," he yelled at Brad. "Thank God your mother isn't here right now. This would kill her!"

Brad wished she were; then maybe he could get this over with. Instead, his father would have to tell his mother, who was busy playing real estate agent, and then she'd be upset with him too.

"And I'm still not convinced that this baby is yours!" Hadley continued.

"It's mine, Dad," Brad said firmly. "That discussion is off the table."

"Why—because she told you so? How do you know you can trust her?"

"Because I know Marie. She wouldn't lie to me about something like this."

"But if she's pregnant and needs a father for the baby, it's easy to say it's you. At least let me check her out. Where did you say she went to college? At Spelman? I can get one of the law firm's investigators to start there and...."

"No, Dad!"

"At least, don't say you're the father until you have a blood test after the baby's born."

"The baby is mine. I didn't come to you about this so you would start some ghoulish investigation. What I need is for you to help us until I get out of law school and find a job."

"Your mother and I already have agreed to pay your law school tuition."

"I know, but I'm talking about living expenses too."

"You can't expect that kind of help unless I know all the facts."

"But these are the facts, Dad. I'm in love with Marie. She's a wonderful girl. I'm going to marry her, and we're having a baby."

"I don't agree with those facts."

"You can't disagree with them. This is my life. I need your help."

"My father never helped me. He didn't...."

"I know all about Grandpa and how he didn't care about your problems," Brad broke in. "But this is what I need."

"But what about your career plans?"

"What about them? They're still there if you help."

Hadley took a deep breath and let it out slowly. "Your mother's going to want to meet this girl and have her checked out."

"Marie would love to meet you both. You know that. How many times have I invited you to come see us? Maybe we can come by and see you now?"

His father was silent for a moment. *Could he possibly be coming around?* Brad thought. Then his father went on, "I'll talk to your mother and let you know."

Brad sighed. He reached across the table and put his hand on his father's.

"Thanks, Dad, for talking to Mom. I really appreciate this."

Hadley coughed and sputtered. "Don't count on anything yet. I have to talk to your mother."

Fine, Brad thought. He knew his father picked his battles with his mother carefully, and maybe this was one of them. He'd need his father to persuade her that he and Marie and the baby were a good thing. And when Hadley made up his mind, he could be incredibly persuasive. After all, he was a good lawyer, and that's why Brad needed him on his side. He'd hate to think what would happened if he wasn't.

The next day Brad's mother called him with an offer. It was so like Marian, the consummate real estate broker. Her buyers made offers on houses to the sellers and she made money. That day, she made an offer to her son, and she made him crazy.

"Brad, honey," she purred in a sweet, syrupy voice. "Your father tells me that you want us to meet this girl you've been seeing."

"She's more than someone I've been seeing. I'm in love with her, and I'm going to marry her. She's having my baby."

"Oh yes, I see. Where is she from?"

"I don't know. Somewhere in Newtown, I think."

"You *think*. You should *know*. What part of Newtown?"

"I don't know. I've never been to her house."

"You haven't been to her house? Don't you think that's rather strange?"

"No," Brad said snidely. "She hasn't been invited to my parents' house yet either."

"And you haven't met her mother?"

"No, I haven't, but then you haven't met Marie."

"Your father and I have a perfectly good reason why we haven't," his mother retorted. "But you'd think her mother would want to get to know you right away. You're quite a catch for her daughter, you know."

"Look," Brad said sternly. "I don't know where Marie's mother lives, and frankly, I don't care. I love Marie no matter where she comes from. You will too. After all, she is the mother of your grandchild."

"You don't mean that. Your father told me you weren't sure the baby was yours."

"Oh no," Brad said firmly. "This baby is mine. It's Dad who's not sure of that."

"He must have his reasons."

Brad sighed in exasperation. "Look, do you and Dad want to meet Marie before we get married or not? It's up to you. Either way, we're getting married."

"Don't go doing anything crazy here, son. There's no need to throw your whole life away for some girl."

"I'm not planning to, and I don't have to give up law school if you'll help."

"I don't know if your father and I can. We've promised to pay your tuition, and we'll do that even if I have to work myself to death. But we also have Bethany's medical school expenses, and what you are asking for now is perhaps more than we can handle."

"But only paying my tuition won't get me through. Marie and I need money to live on until she can get a job."

"Is there some kind of work she can do?" his mother asked snootily.

"Of course, there is. She's not stupid. Just because she hasn't finished college yet doesn't mean she won't be able to get something after the baby is born."

"I can see it now," his mother said dramatically. "You'll have to quit school, get stuck in some dead-end job, and she'll sit around all day doing nothing."

"That's not fair!" Brad sputtered, anger rising in his voice. "You don't even know Marie. How could you believe that about her?"

"Because she's got herself pregnant and she says you're the father. Trust me. Girls like her are looking for a free ride."

"Look," Brad said sharply. "I got her pregnant, and I'm the father. Like I told Dad, that discussion is off the table."

"Don't burn all your bridges here," his mother cajoled him. "I think you should wait until the baby is born and get a blood test to see if you are the father."

"NO!" Brad exploded. "I won't do that."

"If you do that," she continued ignoring his outburst, "we'll give you all the money you need. But only if you're the father and you don't get married to this girl...." His mother broke off, flustered. "What's her name again?"

"Marie," Brad responded with a sigh. "Her name is Marie Patterson."

"Yes, all right then, if you don't get married to Marie until we've established paternity. Don't you see? This could all work out. Your father and I need to be sure."

"That your grandchild is really yours?" Brad's voice was full of anger. "Afraid the wrong genes will get into the family pool, is that it?"

"Don't get that way with me, young man. We've made a very reasonable offer to you. You talk it over with Marie and let us know. She'll see how reasonable it is."

"Yes, Mother. Even I can see how reasonable you're being!" Brad said, sarcastically. Maybe that was the way to get through to her, he thought, as he felt rage building inside him. Show her how ridiculous *she* was being! Still he went on, his voice raised. "You'll be sorry for this, Mother! I'm going to marry Marie with or without your approval. Then you'll have to explain to your grandchildren someday why you and Dad aren't in our wedding pictures."

His mother was silent, and for a moment Brad thought he had gotten through to her. But when she spoke again, it was in the same persistent, whining tone.

"Just talk to Marie, son," she said with finality in her voice. "And think about this very hard. This may be one of the most important decisions of your life."

"And driving such a hard bargain could be one of the biggest mistakes of yours," he exploded, unable to contain himself any longer. "You think about that too."

With that, he slammed down the phone and buried his head in his hands.

What had he ever done to deserve this kind of treatment from his parents? He loved them. He cared for them. Why didn't they want him to be happy? Why couldn't they accept what was important to him? Why did they always have to decide what was right for him? He was a grown man. He could decide what he wanted and believed in. He wanted Marie. He believed this baby was his, and all he was asking his parent for was a chance to finish his education and provide for the woman he loved.

What was so wrong with that?

What was it about Hadley and Marian that made them so incapable of understanding something so simple, so basic?

What was wrong with them?

CHAPTER SIX

Thursday, October 15, 2009

Old Problems, New Beginnings

Ambrose spent the morning trying to track down Lisette.

After reading about her arrival yesterday in the newspaper, Ambrose thought it was important for him to get to her before he made his bigger move against Brad and his wife, the notorious Governor Jenny Jablonski.

What he knew of Jenny as governor was not very much. Their paths had never crossed, though he did know her campaign manager, Everett Hall. Before he retired, he was a street cop who patrolled the area around the Community Center. When Ambrose worked there for Pedro, Everett would sometimes catch a kid doing something on the street that he could be arrested for. Instead of taking him down to the station, he'd bring the kid over to the Center and have Pedro give him a talking to instead. Ambrose always thought that Everett had too soft a heart for a cop, but it was probably more that he didn't want to spend the rest of the day processing the kid through the system for carrying around a little weed in his pocket.

Ambrose could get to Brad through Everett because he knew him but also because Everett would want to find out first how the governor's husband had gotten himself into political hot water again this week. After the announcement in yesterday's newspaper, Ambrose knew that Everett wouldn't want Jenny Jablonski answering again in the press for her husband's inappropriate behavior. This time it would be about a daughter he abandoned years ago who had grown up to have her own strip clubs across the country. That would be something voters might be interested in finding out, Ambrose thought.

Yes, Ambrose had the advantage here and there was a deal to be made with Jenny and Brad through Everett to keep the diary and its contents quiet. It was only a matter of money! Ambrose felt justified in wanting to expose a scandal that might screw Jenny the Governor's chances of getting reelected or elected to some higher political office in the future. He bet she would sure like to be the first elected female vice president, wouldn't she? But more than politics, he had a reason to hate Jenny Jablonski. Years ago, then-Judge Jablonski gave full custody of his son, Mark, to his mother-in-law, Abigail Durocher. She had bought the argument that he was incapable of caring for Mark after the car accident that killed Betsy and Jeanine. After losing custody of Mark to Abigail, Ambrose's relationship with his son fell apart, and now—years later—Mark not only continued to refuse to see Ambrose, but he also changed his last name to his grandparent's. Now as Mark Durocher, Ambrose felt, Mark was trying to obliterate his father from his life. It was so unfair!

With lots of reasons to want Jenny to pay for her mistakes, Ambrose also felt no mercy toward Lisette. He'd make her pay him lots of money now and in the future in exchange for the chance to meet her real father and notorious stepmother. But he wasn't planning to lay the deal out to Lisette that simply. He didn't want Lisette to know exactly who Brad was or how the governor wouldn't welcome her entry into the family until the time was right and the most politically embarrassing for Jenny.

However he laid this out to all the parties involved, there was enough good scandal and political intrigue in this to satisfy Ambrose's need for revenge from both Jenny and Lisette now and forever! But today, with a plan in mind about how to get to Jenny and Brad through Everett, his rage and fury was more focused on Lisette and tracking her down.

He reminded himself about how Lisette had, ten year ago, reneged on their deal for him to go into the performance art business as her manager or help him win back his son as a new young person in his father's life. He also remembered how his heart soared when he first learned of Lisette's Atilla the Hunny act after the humiliation of trying to see his son on his birthday.

No wonder Ambrose spent the rest of that day, afternoon, and night drinking himself silly—as only a drunk can know that feeling of oblivion when you have tied one on and nothing else matters. There is no future, no moving forward, and certainly no redemption.

But that was when Lisette came dancing into his life for the first time.

As he remembered how he came to believe she was his ticket out of hell, he could also see she was nothing but a way, ten years later, to get his best revenge against all who had made his life truly miserable.

❖ ❖ ❖

Wednesday, October 20, 1999

The next thing Ambrose remembered the day after Mark threw rocks in his face through the schoolyard fence was waking up face down in a gutter at the end of a dead-end street near the Capitol. Lying on the curb against a stack of garbage bags, he could smell them even before he opened his eyes.

It must have been morning, although he wasn't sure what day it was. Not that it mattered. So what if he lost one or two days?

Trying to see Mark and being treated so badly by him required a few days of blank time to recover, he reasoned. But now he needed to get up and move around to make sure he was still alive.

When he raised his head, the movement set off a pounding in his brain.

"God," he groaned aloud. "I really tied one on."

"So what else is new?" The sarcastic reply came from inside his head. Like most drunks, he was always talking out loud to himself and then answering back.

Who else was he going to talk to?

"It's no skin off your nose what I do," he grunted back.

"You don't remember where you were last, do you?" the voice snapped.

"Sure I do. I got on this bus and then stopped to get some wine at the liquor store on my way back from...from..." His voice trailed off.

"See, I told you!" the voice smarted back.

"Goddamn it," Ambrose growled. He hated when the voice was right.

Where had he been yesterday—or was it the day before? Why couldn't he remember? His mind played tricks on him like that sometimes. The booze blotted out most of what had just happened to him, but it left vague memories like a nasty taste in his mouth. Then it came to him.

"I went to see Mark at his school. That's where I was. See! I do remember," he declared triumphantly.

"So how did it go?" the voice asked, more politely now.

"Like always," he groaned. "Mark hates me like I hated my dad. May he rot in hell!"

Enraged, Ambrose bludgeoned a bag of garbage with his fists until he rolled over on his back exhausted.

"May he rot in hell!" the voice echoed.

"Go away," he growled, waving his hand up in the air as if he could shoo the voice away. "Leave me alone!"

Then his hand dropped down, and to his surprise, he found a bottle lying on the ground next to him. He snatched it up and tipped it to his lips, hoping that a drop, just one drop of wine, was still in there. But the bottle was empty.

"Goddamn it," he roared again, this time slamming the bottle against the curb and shattered it into pieces, one of which caught his thumb and threw him into another rage.

"Shit!" he screamed in pain, sitting up and grabbing his bleeding finger. He tore the dirty bandanna off his head and pressed it on the wound.

Jesus, I needed a drink, he thought.

"Haven't you had enough?" the voice started up again.

"Shut up! I'll drink if I want to. You can't stop me."

"Like you can't stop your hand from bleeding?"

He looked down and saw blood soaking through the bandanna.

Shit! The voice was right. He'd need to get some antiseptic and a good bandage.

Reaching in his pocket with his other hand, he found two dimes. Not enough for a bottle of wine or even a Band-Aid, he thought. He'd have to collect bottles along his usual morning route, beginning with the bar called the Pussycat's Meow, and then get some cash at the package store for them.

Ambrose stumbled to his feet, grabbing one of the garbage bags and dumping out its contents. Dragging the empty bag alongside him, he walked up the dead-end street to where it met La Strada Street in front of the Pussycat.

As he passed the bar's front window, he stopped dead in his tracks. A new publicity poster hung there, and when he saw it, his jaw dropped and his eyes popped wide open for the first time that morning.

He read the top line, "Straight from Appearances in Los Angeles!" and then took in the photograph of the dancer below.

She was young, maybe nineteen or twenty, and had a sultry look on her face. Her wide, sensuous lips were set in a perpetual pout, and her long blonde hair hung down from a helmetlike hat on her head in tangled strands that he thought needed combing. Her breasts were large—probably surgically implanted, he noted— and her derriere was more than ample. She stood in profile, her chest and ass thrust out in opposite directions, and a scanty bikini barely covering those areas of bountiful endowment. Fuzzy, white fur framed those parts of the costume that touched the most intimate parts of her body.

Below the photo were the words: "Coming Soon—Attila the Hunny!"

At the sight of her stage name, he smirked. What was this "Attila the Hunny" shit? There's no "hunny" in Attila the Hun! What was this girl thinking? In the fourth century, the Huns would've raped a woman who looked like her.

"She's something," the voice inside his head said. "Pay attention."

"It's only a poster, for chrissakes," he barked out loud. "What does she know about Attila anyway?"

"You know more about Attila than anyone," the voice agreed. "What are you going to do about her?"

"Nothing," Ambrose muttered…and yet there was something about the girl. He didn't know what.

"She's beautiful!" the voice teased. "She's made you come alive."

"She has not!"

"She's made you angry."

"No, she hasn't."

"At someone other than yourself."

"I'm not angry at anyone."

"Oh, yeah? Then why are you standing out in the middle of a public sidewalk yelling at a voice inside your head?"

"Christ," Ambrose muttered, his eyes darting around to see if anyone was about. He was a drunk, not a schizophrenic. Next he'd be hallucinating, and they'd haul him off to some institution.

"Damn!" he moaned, gaping at the photo again. She was beautiful! A girl like that could make him feel so wonderful. She'd do the tease and make him feel like a million bucks, then take him for all the money he had.

Still, she was beautiful, so beautiful, he mused as he turned to walk away from the window.

"Hey, you!" a voice boomed out from the doorway of the Pussycat.

Ambrose turned to see a guy with broad shoulders and bulging muscles hanging out of the club's front door. The man shook his fist at him.

"If you want to see the girl dance, come back tonight with some money in that mangy paw of yours. Get along or I'll move you along myself."

"Hey, it's a free country, asshole!" he growled back, but by then he was walking away, dragging the garbage bag behind him and listening to the voice inside his head.

"Come back tonight," the voice cooed. "She's been waiting for you. She's come to set you free."

Coming out of that memory, he knew that day set him on this journey ten years ago, but now as he walked toward her hotel, what was in his mind was this day of reckoning.

He knew what he wanted and needed from her.

He was going to get it.

❖ ❖ ❖

Thursday, October 15, 2009

When Lisette got back to her hotel a little before noon on Thursday, she was exhausted after the final haggling with Wiley of her purchase of the Pussycat's Meow Club from him. She was done with the document signing and the real estate transaction. Now Todd and others on the management side of the business would step in and decide what happened next with the name and building of the business she just bought. She wasn't sure that it was a winning prospect for their company, but it felt damn good to sit on the other side of the table and out-haggle the old coot.

Wiley hadn't changed much over the last ten years. He was still a cheat, an ornery son of a bitch, but she had gotten the best of him. She loved it! Made it worth her while coming back here just to see that creep get his due. The business wasn't worth much, and she didn't give him much for it, but she was sure that Todd could make a going concern of it.

Happily, she stepped out of her taxi at the hotel entrance, paid the driver, and was relieved that this would be the one and only trip she'd have to make today outside the hotel.

She had a noon lunch with Sophie and some of the other angel investors for Sophie's nonprofit organization, *Survivor Strong, Thriver Resilient*. But the lunch was right here in the hotel, and then she'd have the next few days to relax until the Tenth Anniversary Gala Saturday night. She had brought a special dress with her that she planned to wear for the festivities. It was the long, black dress that had some significance the last time she was here in town ten years ago.

She had barely stepping out of the cab and was paying the driver when suddenly an old, scruffy-looking guy came running up to her, looking like he was a panhandler about to ask her for some money. She turned to look at him, ready to tell him to get lost, but suddenly she thought she recognized him.

"Ambrose? Is that you, Ambrose?" She was startled at the possibility and stepped back from him just as he advanced on her.

"Lisette!" he said with a wide grin. "You recognized me. So much easier when you know me."

"So much easier for what?" she snarled back at him. "What the hell are you doing here?"

Then she turned quickly and brushed him off. "I'm not buying anything you are selling to me this time. Didn't you get yourself in enough trouble last time we met? Then she looked at him blankly. "Aren't you supposed to be in jail or something? Why are you here?"

Ambrose laughed. "So many questions. I bet you'd like some answers." Then he gestured toward the hotel front door. "Do you have a few minutes for me? Maybe we could go into the coffee shop here and talk. I'd appreciate that."

Lisette looked at him sternly. "I'd appreciate if you never talked to me again. The last time I saw you attacked a good friend of mine and…" She paused to take a breath. "And there was a whole lot of other weird stuff that went on between us. No, I really don't want to talk to you about anything—not now, not ever."

She moved toward the front door of the hotel, and as she did, he grabbed her arm.

"I can tell you all about Ralph and how he isn't your real father," he said quickly, then added, his eyes fixed on her, "I know about Marie and how she met your real father. He's a real important person now. I think you should know about him."

She glared at him and shook his hand off her arm. "Don't you touch me! And I couldn't care less about what you know about Ralph. I know more than you ever will, and that's all you need to know. You don't know shit! Stop trying to con me. It's not going to work!"

"This is no con. I have your mom's diary and…."

"You have *what*?" Lisette stopped dead in her tracks. "How did you get the diary? Where is it now?"

Then she shrieked at him, her face was flushed with outrage and excitement, "Tell me!"

Ambrose stammered, "I...I don't have it with me right now. But I have some pages I can show you."

"Yeah, like I'd believe you. Ambrose, you are such a liar!"

"No, no!" he protested. "I can tell you how Marie got pregnant by this guy...."

"Shit," Lisette interrupted him. "I know how babies happen. And I'm not interested in some story about my mother that you dreamed up to make me think you know something. I'm not paying you for something that you stole from me that's already mine! You think I'm stupid? I was just a kid when you saw me last, but I have my own business now. Don't try and pull something over on me."

Then she stopped for a minute and asked him quickly. "Come to think of it, how do you know Ralph's name? I never told you my father's name was Ralph. I never talk about him to anyone, and never by this name. And certainly not to you!"

"How else would I know Ralph's name unless I had read the diary? Think about that for minute before you start yelling at me again."

"Okay, then show the diary to me. Let me see it now. Do you have it with you?"

Ambrose shook his head. "No, I can't give it to you right now. I have bigger fish to fry first, and I can't show you yet...." Ambrose's voice trailed off.

"Whatever!" Lisette said with a wave of the hand and took off past him toward the front door of the hotel. "You don't have shit, do you? Leave me alone. Come back when you've have something else to bargain with besides just your word. I'm here at the hotel for a few days. You probably already know that, or you wouldn't be waiting to ambush me at the taxi stand. You are disgusting, Ambrose. Get out of my face!"

With that Lisette turned tail and entered the hotel. She stopped inside the door where Ambrose couldn't see her and took a deep breath. *Why does that guy still give me the creeps after all these years? Little does he know that in all of that conversation he didn't tell me much that I don't already know.*

She already knew that Ralph was not her biological father. A few years after she made the business deal to license her stage name and her image on the strip clubs across the country, she had money to hire a private investigator to find Ralph, dead or alive. He was still alive, but barely, and in about the same condition she last had seen him in. The old coot was still alive and kicking. For a sum of money, he agreed to have his blood and DNA tested. She wanted to know once and for all that he was not her father.

He wasn't.

And until today when she met up again with Ambrose, the creep that evidently had stolen her mother's diary, Ralph was the only person she thought should burn in hell forever.

Today, Ambrose joined him.

❖ ❖ ❖

Erick was late.

He had promised Sophie that he'd come early for the lunch with the angel investors, the rich people who had supported Sophie when she started up *Survivor Strong, Thriver Resilient* and had continued to help her do something good in the community. Sophie explained how they particularly liked hearing that she was doing things no one else was doing, and that's why they were all in town for the Tenth Anniversary Gala on Saturday. Erick was invited to talk at the lunch about the men's initiative he was heading up. Sophie told him she needed him to show the investors they were putting their money in an amazing, innovative program.

But this invitation was all very last-minute on Sophie's part, so Erick was preoccupied thinking about how to describe the Initiative as he rushed in the hotel's front door and quickly followed the signs toward the hotel dining room right off the lobby. In his rush, he brushed past and nearly knocked over a young woman standing with her back to him at the restaurant's entrance.

"I'm so sorry," he said quickly, grabbing the woman by the arm to steady her. "This is my fault. I didn't mean to…"

As she turned to look at him, he stopped talking and stared at her.

"Lisette?" he blurted out. "Is that you? I didn't realize that…."

She jumped in to finish his sentence. "…I was standing here minding my own business, just waiting for someone to bump into me like that." Then she laughed. "Sophie did predict we'd be 'running into each other' this weekend."

He laughed too, but added rather shyly, "I thought as much, too. That I'd be seeing you, I mean. And it is great to see you. You look great! Wow! And you are so successful with your Atilla the Hunny clubs and…." He trailed off. "And did I say it was great to see you?"

Lisette laughed. "Yes. I'm pleased to see you, too, and you know so much about my business. And no, I won't be yelling at you like I did when we last met. Or maybe I should say when we broke up. So not to worry about that."

"Okay, yeah," Erick said with a sigh. "That was quite a breakup, but I survived. I'm doing well. I have my own gym now. I'm a personal trainer. Bought the place a few years ago. I like it. I love it some days. You know, some days yes, some days no."

Oh God, he thought. *Stop rambling.* But he was so excited and surprised to see her.

"I'm surprised to see you too," Lisette said, as if she had read his thoughts. "Sophie made it sound like we wouldn't see each other until this weekend. Unless…."

"Yeah, unless," he began suspiciously. "She planned this, right? Don't you see? At the last minute, she asked me to come to the lunch for the angel investors, and she knew you'd be here as an investor. She didn't tell me that, but now I see why I'm here."

"So we could run into each other, just like we did," Lisette teased. "Our friend Sophie is what you might call a matchmaker. Trying to put us back together and see if sparks might fly again." Then Lisette added, "Do you agree?"

"What?" Erick asked with a grin. "That sparks are flying, or Sophie is sneaky?"

"You did try to run me over just now," Lisette replied. "Does that count as something?"

"Maybe, maybe not. It wasn't full-body contact. I'd say it was a skirmish."

"Nice! It was only my second one of the day. I saw that Ambrose guy outside when I was coming back into hotel after my morning meeting. You remember him? The guy that knocked over my friend Radiance and cause all kinds of commotion? Why is he not in jail or something? He always has some scheme going. This time he says he knows who my real father is. Like I didn't know Ralph isn't."

"He isn't? I thought Ralph was and you were really mad at him for what he did to you." He knew that because it had come up during their big breakup blowup, but he really wasn't sure that he wanted to remind her of all that.

"I was mad," Lisette said calmly, "but I'm getting over it. I saw Ralph. I had my business investigator track him down. His blood and DNA doesn't match mine, and he said he had no idea who the real father is. He did tell the investigator that my mother was seeing a guy right before she came to the bar one night and told him she was pregnant. He said a guy was snooping around the bar about the same time asking questions about Marie, but he wasn't sure who he was or if he was my father."

"Ralph didn't have a name to give up?"

"No, Ralph was never good with people's names unless they owed him some money. So I thought it was just a dead end."

"But you think Ambrose has a name for you."

"He might, but he says it's in my mother's diary—which, by the way, he stole from me ten years ago, and I just found that out today. But he won't cough up the actual diary and show it to me. He muttered something about having bigger fish to fry. What does that mean?"

"That his other scheme is to blackmail the real father here and now."

"You think he might be here in this town? What kind of a coincidence is that?"

"I don't know, but I can try to track Ambrose down. I see him sometimes on the streets. He's still pretty much homeless, but he hangs out and does a little legal work for Pedro over at the Community Center sometimes." Then he paused for a minute. "Actually, Pedro might be here today. Let's see if he shows. He's part of our men's initiative, and he also works with Sophie on economic empowerment for the women."

"Okay, but let's not ask too many questions before I get clearer about everything Ambrose is telling us. He's a con man but...."

As they walked and talked on their way to the dining room, Erick noticed how Lisette touched his arm or held his eyes as they talked. He took it as a sign that maybe they could be friends after all. But whatever might happen, he had to admit it sure felt good being in the orbit again of this beautiful and amazing woman. It was like they just picked up where they left it off ten years ago.

Wow!

CHAPTER SEVEN

Thursday, October 15, 2009

Appreciation

At about noon on Thursday, feeling triumphant after making the deal with the feds, Brad made his way down to the kitchen to make himself something to eat for lunch.

As he rummaged through the refrigerator for sandwich possibilities, he found himself mulling over his conversation with Everett earlier that morning. They had talked about the murdered coed, and soon that got him thinking about Marie and the baby again. That baby would have been the same age today as the dead girl.

He shivered.

What if Marie's baby had been his daughter and had died so young too? How would he have handled it? Would the girl have looked like him? Or would she have had Marie's blue eyes, blonde hair, and fair skin? Would she have loved him as much as he would have loved her? And what about Marie? Could she have survived the untimely, tragic death of a child? Would they have survived it together?

Funny, he thought with a smile. All this time he assumed Marie had had a baby girl, but it could have been a boy. It could have been a son that they had together.

His thoughts turned back to lunch as he took some items out of the refrigerator and put them on the breakfast bar. As he turned back to hunt for bread, he heard footsteps. He looked up and saw Jenny standing in the kitchen doorway. At the sight of her, his heart jumped. He wasn't sure if it was because he wasn't expecting company or he was so glad to see his wife again.

"Oh, it's you," he said as nonchalantly as he could, catching her eye.

"Yes," she replied. "I thought you might be down here having some lunch."

"I'm in the exploratory phase right now," he said with a grin. "So far I've got leftover meatloaf and a little hot mustard. Now if I could just find the bread..." He turned back to the refrigerator.

"It's in the bread box," Jenny said, sitting on one of the stools at the breakfast bar.

"Oh!" he said, a startled look on his face. "Why didn't I think of that?"

"That's because the bread is usually in the refrigerator, but I moved it."

Brad looked at her for a moment. "I hate to ask this question. But did you come all the way here just to make sure I knew where the bread was?"

"No," she said simply.

"Because if you came here to argue with me some more, Jenny," he went on, "I'm about wrung out. I don't have the strength to...."

"No, not to fight," she said, interrupting him. "I came to apologize."

He gulped and looked at her, trying to make sure he heard her correctly.

"I was hard on you yesterday," she continued, holding his eyes. "I was angry, and I thought that if I took it out on you for a while I'd feel better."

"And did you?" he asked her curiously.

"No, not really. I think I made things worse. I know you've

been trying to get the FBI thing sorted out, but when the *Enquirer* called the other day, I was pissed that it wasn't going away fast enough. So I treated you like someone on my staff who hadn't done their job right, rather than my husband." She paused for a moment and then added, "Rather than someone I cared about and didn't want to see get hurt."

"I see," said Brad softly, then blurted out earnestly, "Those women didn't mean anything to me, Jenny, if that's what you're worried about. Not then and certainly not now."

"I know," she confessed. "But you are years younger than I am, and I get scared sometimes that someone younger and prettier is going to come along and..." Her eyes filled up and she tried to finish the sentence. But he couldn't stand to let her go there.

"Hey, hey," he said, stepping quickly over to her and putting his arms around her. "I'm not leaving. You're the best thing that's happened to me."

He held her for a moment and then kissed her tenderly. "I love you and I miss you. I'm glad you came home for lunch."

She kissed him back, and they stayed intertwined there for a while.

Brad clung to her, smelling her perfume and thinking how safe and happy he was to be in her arms again. All the bad feelings between them over the last few days were melting away, and he wanted to stay in this moment forever.

Finally, she gently pushed away from him, as if she had something important to say, but still she held him close in his arms. "Everett told me about the deal with the feds. I know it's not a great one for you, but I appreciate that you took it. This is all going to work out, you'll see."

"I sure hope so," he said. "I can't go on like this."

"You don't have to. This FBI thing will blow over in a few weeks and we'll be back on course. No more bumps in the road."

"No, I mean what's going on between us. I hate it when we fight. I'm sorry I made such a mess of things."

"No, no. It's my fault," she insisted.

"I didn't think making up was going to be this easy," he said, laughing. "Now if only lunch were only going as well."

"Do you want me to help?" Jenny asked.

"No, your job is to catch me up on what's been going on the last few days," he said as he moved about the kitchen making the sandwiches. "How are you feeling about going to that memorial for that girl killed on campus ten years ago? Sorry I can't go with you. Everett explained to me about keeping out of public view for a while. Too many reporters with questions to ask!"

"Sad is how I feel," she replied with a sigh. "I remember that tragic murder/suicide on the campus ten years ago. That girl was so young when she was killed. It reminds me of when Maryssa was in school and I worried about her every day she was there. It was too close to me then—and too close to me still today. It makes me realize how we have to make the most of every moment we've got." Then she looked at him. "So let's not argue anymore, okay? I want things to be like they used to be."

"I'm all for that," he said.

"I had to laugh when I read what those women told the FBI about you. If anyone believes that garbage, they don't know you, Brad—not the way I do."

"Thanks," he said softly. "That's the nicest thing you've ever said to me."

"It's the truth," she replied firmly. "And I won't forget it again, I promise."

He looked at her and took in all that he felt for her in his heart. She was an incredible person who trusted him and loved him as much as he loved her. If only he could ask her now—no, beg her—to quit this job and stop all this before everything they had was destroyed. But how could he do that? This job was her life, and she was his.

Then Jenny's cell phone rang.

"Damn," she muttered, reaching down to grab the phone off her belt and reading the message on the screen. Then she looked at him and said, "Sorry, I have to take this. I'll be right back."

But from the sound of Jenny's voice on the phone, he could tell that their lunch plans had changed. Something pressing had happened back at her office in the Capitol, and so, even before she got off the phone, he reached into a drawer, grabbed the plastic wrap, and put Jenny's sandwich in it.

As soon she hung up, she came back to the breakfast bar and said solemnly, "I've got to get back. I'm sorry."

"It's all right," he said, handing her the wrapped sandwich along with an apple and a pear. "We'll have dinner tonight and talk some more. Maybe we'll even get silly."

"I'd love to." She giggled. "We haven't done anything really silly since we went skinny-dipping in the mansion pool in the middle of the night and almost gave the state trooper on duty a heart attack."

Brad laughed and reached over to kiss her lightly on the cheek, but she had other ideas. She pulled him into a tight embrace and nibbled on his ear as he moaned with pleasure.

"*Mmm,*" he sighed, "Let's make up more often. I like this."

"Me, too."

Then she let him go, and he watched her walk out of the kitchen, through the side door of the mansion, and out into her waiting car. *Jenny is amazing,* he thought, as he put his sandwich on a plate and headed back upstairs to watch some afternoon television. Unlike Marie, Jenny could sort out her feelings and be open and honest with him. Unlike Marie, she didn't tell lies and then let them fester until his parents got involved and the whole thing was an ugly mess.

Marie.

Why was he thinking about her again? What was it about him and Marie being together, he wondered, that made his parents so crazy? With not much else to do until Jenny came home, he allowed himself to wonder why his life with Marie and his parents had gone so bad. And as he remembered it all again, he asked himself, *Why did Marian and Hadley do what they did?*

Why?

❖ ❖ ❖

Novemeber, 1979

Hadley called Brad one night in November about a week after his mother had made the offer to him about school, an offer Brad didn't like and hadn't responded to. He decided to wait to see if his parents would make another. But when Hadley called, it was about something else entirely.

Brad picked up the phone near the kitchen table as he and Marie were finishing dinner.

"Are you alone?" Hadley began. "I've got to talk to you about something."

"I'm kind of busy right now," Brad said. He didn't like the sound of his father's voice. "Marie and I are having dinner. Can I call you back later?"

"Is she there?' his father asked in a hoarse whisper.

"You mean Marie, Dad," Brad said with exasperation in his voice. "Yes, she's here."

At the sound of her name, Marie looked up at Brad and giggled as he made a funny face into the phone mocking his father for not remembering her name.

"We need to talk about her," his father continued sounding even more mysterious. "Maybe we should meet somewhere."

"Anything you have to say to me you can say over the phone,"

Brad said firmly, pulling the long cord attached to the phone jack around the corner into the living room and sitting down on the couch. Brad didn't mind that Marie was still within range of hearing him and whatever his father had to say; he wanted it over with as soon as possible.

"All right," his father said, clearing his throat. "I know you're not going to like this but hear me out, okay, son?"

"Are you sure this can't wait?" Brad asked again in a nervous voice.

"No, it can't. I've made some inquiries about Marie and . . ."

"Oh, Dad!" Brad broke in. "I told you not to do that."

"Discrete inquiries, mind you. I think you'll be interested in what I found out."

"Is it about where her mother lives? That's what Mom was all bent out of shape about last week. I can't believe you guys care about that."

"No, it's about where Marie told you she went to school. She said she went Spelman College last year, right?"

"Yeah, so what? Mom knows she didn't graduate yet."

Hadley ignored him and went on. "I thought it was strange that a young, white girl from the Northeast was going to a black college in the South, so I talked to the dean of students."

"You called Spelman, Dad?" Brad asked with a groan.

"Yes, and the Dean of the College said that no one by the name of Marie Patterson has been enrolled there in the past five years."

Brad was silent on his end of the phone. Marie was in the kitchen now stacking dishes in the sink, and he could see her looking back over her shoulder at him. He glanced away quickly before she caught his eye.

"There must be some mistake," he hissed into the phone. "Why are you and Mom doing this to me?"

"Son, we're trying to help. We want you and Marie over for

Thanksgiving, but how can we when we don't know who she is? If she's lying about this, who knows what else she's lying about?"

"Oh, no!" Brad protested. "We're not going there. Jesus, I can't believe this!" He jumped up from the couch and paced the floor wildly. "Look, Dad," he went on, his voice shaking. "I'm going to tell you this one more time, and then I'm going to hang up. I want you to stay out of my business. Marie and this baby are *my* business, not yours. Do you hear me? Stay out! Good-bye."

He slammed the receiver down and fell back down onto the couch. *God! My father is driving me crazy! Why wouldn't he let this go? Why did he have to find out about Marie and Spelman College?*

Brad pressed his trembling hands to his forehead, trying to control the pain and confusion as wild thoughts raced through his head. What if his dad was right? What if Marie had lied to him about college—and the baby too? What if he wasn't the father of this baby? What if she really didn't love him?

No, he thought, pulling himself back. There must be some mistake. The Marie he knew and loved would have an explanation. He was overreacting.

"What's wrong?" Marie asked, walking from the kitchen into the living room. "Did you hang up on your father?"

He scowled at her.

"What did your dad want?" she said as she sat down next to him on the couch.

"He wanted to invite us over for Thanksgiving dinner," Brad began.

"You mean I'll finally get to meet your family?" Marie's voice was exuberant. "That's great!"

"Yeah, except they have this crazy idea that you don't go to Spelman College like you said you did."

"I'm not there this semester," Marie said reassuringly. "I've been taking care of my mother."

"I know that. But my father said no one with your name has been enrolled there for the last five years."

"He checked?" Marie's voice went up.

"Yeah, with the dean's office." Brad desperately searched her eyes. "I don't understand."

"Oh," Marie said and then dropped her eyes down into her lap and twisted her hands around the corners of her cardigan sweater.

"Spelman College?" she said finally, trying to be easy about it. "I...I never told you I went to Spelman. I said Skidmore College. That's where I went."

"Skidmore? Where's Skidmore?" Brad asked, sounding confused.

"You know, it's in...in, you know, Pennsylvania," she stammered.

Brad's voice dropped an octave. "No, it's not. It's in New York. I know because that's where Jasmine was going when I met her."

Marie was silent now, wrapping the sweater tighter and tighter around her fingers. She flinched when Brad spoke again.

"You've never gone to college, have you?" he demanded. "You look like a college girl, but you aren't."

Marie sighed without speaking.

"Answer me!" Brad yelled.

"Oh, all right," Marie spoke indignantly now. "I never got out of high school. I dropped out. I work part-time in a grocery store now."

"Why did you pretend to be in college?"

"Because someone like you wouldn't go out with someone like me unless I said I went to college, and I wanted to go out with you."

"No, you didn't," Brad argued with her. "You put me off for weeks before you'd go out with me because your mother.... Wait a minute!" He paused for a beat. "Is your mother really..."

"No, she's doesn't have TB," Marie broke in before he could finish. "I have a mother, but she doesn't live around here. I live with a few roommates, girls I work with at the store, so I can afford the rent. It's the best I can do."

Brad gasped and felt the breath go out of him as if someone hit him hard across his back with a baseball bat. "I don't understand," he managed to sputter.

"I ran away from home when I was sixteen," she began slowly. "My mother had eight kids including me, and who knows how many more after I left. She wasn't sure who the fathers were. We lived on welfare, and one day when she got tired of taking care of the little ones, she made me quit school and babysit them. I quit school, but I didn't stick around. I took off, just like my dad did."

"You knew him?" Brad was surprised.

"I remember him playing with me when I was little, and my mom gave me a few pictures of him and me together. But he took off one day and never came back, and I thought God was punishing me for being bad. I prayed a lot, but he never came back. I don't even remember his name."

Marie's voice cracked, and she hung her head.

My God, Brad thought, *that's why she was so frightened that he'd leave her baby without a father. Why she didn't want to be stuck raising this baby alone. Why she didn't tell me the truth about her mother.*

She raised her head, and Brad saw tears in her eyes.

"When I met you," she went on, "I made up a mom who was sick and needed my help, and although she was strict, she really loved and cared about me. It was wonderful."

"Not like your real mom, huh?"

"No," she said sadly.

Brad managed a weak smile. "I should be impressed that you went through all of this just to be with me."

"I'd do it again," she gushed. "I didn't mean to hurt you. I'm sorry you found out the way you did."

"It would've been better coming from you," Brad broke in.

"Now my dad has something on me—and more importantly, on you—and he never forgets anything."

"What are we going to do?" Marie asked, sounding scared.

"I don't think we should go there for Thanksgiving," Brad said angrily. "It's better to stay away from my parents for right now. They'll make too much of this."

"I'm sorry," Marie repeated, crying softly. "I've made a mess of everything—the baby, your career, whatever chance we had of being together."

"You didn't ruin anything!" Brad protested. "It's just more complicated now, but we'll figure it out."

Suddenly, looking at her tear-stained face, he knew he had to forgive her. She was his life. What did he care where she went to college—or if she ever did at all? Slowly he gathered her into his arms and kissed her lightly on the top of her head.

"Look, who says that everything I told you about me was true anyway?" he teased. "My real goal in life is to run off and join the circus. I want to be a flamethrower and delight the audience with my daring tricks!"

He was laughing now, and she joined in, giggling.

"And I'll be one of those tightrope walkers and the princess here…" Marie said, patting her tummy. "She'll be a clown and get all the laughs."

Brad roared and then pulled her closer to him. "See, everyone has their secrets." Then his voice got serious. "I love you, Marie," he whispered, kissing her tenderly on the lips. "I forgive you, but no more lies, okay?" he said earnestly.

"This is the real me. I swear it!"

He pulled her down on the couch and made love to her, satisfied that he knew the truth about her. It never dawned on him, though, that the only lie that counted was the one he told himself: that she was someone her parents would admire and want in their family. That they could be the perfect couple—loving, honorable, and true. It was a lie that he clung long after it had any chance to be true. And when all the lies fell into place, Brad could see that the relationship had been doomed from the start.

And he had no one to blame but himself.

❖ ❖ ❖

December, 1979

"Your father and I are finally going to meet Marie," his mother gushed when she called to invite Brad and Marie to spend Christmas Day with the family.

His mother made it sound as if it was a failing on his part as to why this meeting hadn't take place sooner, but Brad let that go by and simply accepted the invitation.

He wasn't sure how or why he and Marie had received it. After the fiasco about where Marie went to college, Brad knew not to call his parents for fear that they'd bottom-line with him and cut him off entirely unless he gave up Marie and the baby. So he took the invitation to Christmas dinner as simply another move in the incredible game of chess he and his parents were playing. He hated that Marie and the baby were pawns in the game, but he decided to let it play out and see what happened. So, as his mother rattled on about her plans for Christmas Day on the phone, he didn't interrupt her.

"Your Uncle Alvin and Aunt Edna are coming over with the kids. But you don't have to buy presents for anyone. Just having you with us is enough."

Brad swallowed that backhanded comment, knowing it was his mother's way of telling him that it was a privilege, not a right, to spend the holidays with them, but he didn't care. When he walked in for Christmas dinner with Marie on his arm, he was proud and happy. Of course, Marie, who was about four months pregnant by then, didn't feel the same way. He could tell she was nervous and felt as though she was on display.

At first, all went well. Before dinner, they sat around the tree in the den and opened gifts. Brad's parents bought Marie a bracelet with a pearl on it, and she told them she loved it. He received new clothes and a stereo system, and, for the moment, it felt like any other Christmas. He took it as a possible sign that Hadley and Marian were finally coming around to seeing his life as he did and everything would turn out fine.

But his good feelings didn't last long. Although Brad had been careful all afternoon not to leave Marie alone with either of his parents, there came a time after dinner when he and Marie were helping his mother clean up the dirty dishes that his father called him into the living room to settle an argument he was having with Uncle Alvin about a college football game on the television.

Marie motioned for Brad to go ahead, saying that when she finished the dishes, she'd join him. He went reluctantly, and when Marie came out to find him a few minutes later, he could see that she was shaken.

"Could you come in here for a minute, please?" she asked in a tight voice, gesturing toward the kitchen.

"Why? What's the matter?" Brad asked as he trailed after her to find his mother standing at the sink, washing up the large platters that couldn't go into the dishwasher.

"Your mother wants to know something very personal about us, and I thought the answer should come from you," Marie said, an edge in her voice.

"What, Mom? What is it that you want to know?" Brad asked her curiously.

His mother turned and gave him a blank look. "Nothing," she snipped. "Marie and I were just talking. Why don't you go back out and talk to your dad and Uncle Alvin? We're almost done here."

"No!" Marie broke in, her voice raised now. "Tell him what you said to me."

His mother gave Marie a tight, grim smile, which Brad recognized as his mother's signal not to push her anymore on whatever it was, but Marie wouldn't let it go.

She turned to Brad and blurted out, "She offered me ten thousand dollars to say the baby isn't yours!"

"What?" Brad blurted out, looking at Marie and then his mother. "Is that true?" he asked. "Did you say that to Marie?"

"Of course, I didn't," she said scornfully. "She misunderstood what I said."

"Then what did you say?" Brad pushed.

"I said that if someone didn't love her son as much as I love you, they could make an offer like that, but I would never do that."

"What!" Marie shouted indignantly. "You can't lie to get out of this."

"Why? Are you the only one who's allowed to do that?" Marian snapped back.

"Bitch!" Marie sputtered, the word flying out of her mouth before she could stop it.

Brad's mother fell back against the sink, her hands crossed over her chest as if she couldn't believe what she had heard.

"Oh my God!" Marie gasped, throwing her hand up over her mouth. "I didn't mean that!" She looked at Brad desperately. "I'm sorry but she's...she's lying. Why would I lie about a thing like that?"

Brad didn't know what to say or who to believe. Suddenly his father's voice came from behind them.

"That's enough," he said firmly, and when Marian made a sound, he cut her off. "Enough, I said, both of you."

Then he turned to Brad. "Why don't you and Marie go see what Bethany and the kids are watching on TV in the den? I'll help your mom finish the dishes."

By this time, Marie was crying, and Brad nodded at his father without speaking as he grabbed Marie by the arm. He commandeered her through the living room until they were in the hallway near the front door.

Behind the closed door to the den, he could hear his young cousins inside hooting and hollering with his sister, Beth's, voice being the loudest. Just like her to be having the time of her life when he was going through a major meltdown.

He opened the door to the hallway closet and found their coats. Marie stood there, whimpering and dabbing at her eyes with the handkerchief he had given her.

"Where's your purse?" he barked at her.

"I left it in the den," she said as she sniffled.

"I'll go get it. You stay here. We're leaving in a minute."

"But you aren't going to say good night to your parents?"

He didn't respond but helped her into her coat and then put on his own. "Don't move," he repeated. "I'll be right back." He walked quickly toward the den and opened the door. Beth was sitting on the couch with the kids all around her, giggling and tickling each other.

She looked up and asked, "Are you leaving? We haven't had a chance to talk."

"Yes, Marie's tired. I need to get her home."

"Is everything okay?" She stood up and moved toward him, studying his face more carefully.

"She's a little shook up."

"About what?"

"I can't tell you about it right now, but can you do me a favor? A few minutes after we leave, go into the kitchen and tell Mom and Dad that Marie and I have left and that I'll call them in the morning."

"Can I say good-bye to Marie?" Beth asked, concern in her voice.

"It's better if we just leave." He touched her arm and squeezed it. "Look, she's waiting for me. I've got to go. I'll talk to you in the morning."

As Brad moved across the room and picked up Marie's purse next to the couch, he could feel Beth's eyes following him. When he got back to the door, he turned around and said forlornly to her, "Merry Christmas."

"Merry Christmas," she repeated, but there was no holiday spirit in either greeting, and Brad closed the door behind him. Back in the hallway again with Marie, he grabbed her arm and said, "Let's go."

"I'm so sorry," she whispered to him as they went out the front door. "I've ruined your Christmas."

"No, it was my mistake. Silly me, I thought I could spend time with my family without someone bringing up the topic my parents can't seem to let go of."

"You mean about the baby?"

Brad was silent as they went down the front steps and headed toward the car parked at the end of the driveway.

"About everything," he muttered as he held the car door open for Marie on the passenger side. "Merry Christmas to my loving, crazy family!" he yelled out at the house as he slammed the car door and walked around to the other side.

As he did, he saw his father coming out of the house, with no hat and his coat unbuttoned.

"Brad, don't leave," his father yelled across the front yard. "Not like this. Your mother is so upset."

"She should be," Brad snarled. "I've got to get Marie home." He pointed to the figure inside of the car.

By then his father was at front of the car. "I'm sorry this didn't work out the way you wanted it to."

"Does that mean it worked out the way you and Mom intended it to?" Brad growled. "You need another opportunity to get at me, and this time, you did it through Marie. Not a good plan, Dad. Big mistake."

Then he reached for the car door. "And what are you doing out here?" Brad added snidely. "Playing good cop to Mom's bad cop? Is this one of your lawyer tricks?"

As he pulled the door open, his voice cracked. "I'm sick of this, and I'm going home."

Hadley sighed and nodded his head in agreement. "You're right, son. It's time for you and Marie to go home. Tell her I said good night." Hadley looked down into the car and waved at her. "You're right about something else too. She loves you a lot."

Brad was stunned by his father's remark. Was it meant to gain back some ground with him, or was it merely a casual observation? Either way, Brad didn't give a fuck.

"Good night, Dad," Brad said as he stepped down into the car. "Merry Christmas," he added sarcastically.

Then he closed the door, put the keys into the ignition, and waited a moment for the car to warm up. He turned to Marie, shivering in the seat next to him, and said, "I have one thing to say to you."

"What's that?" she whimpered.

"Don't you ever do that again. I don't care what my mother says or does to you, if you ever call her a bitch again, I'll...I'll..." he stammered, his voice trailing off. Then he gunned the gas pedal and draped his hands and head over the top of the steering wheel.

His cool leather gloves felt good against his hot, flushed forehead. Then Marie spoke with a panic in her voice that he had never heard before.

"I'm sorry. I told you I was sorry. I'm not used to being around people like your folks. Sometimes things just come out of my mouth. You don't understand. When your mother made that offer about the baby, she made feel like a slut. I've done lots of things in my life, but I'd never taken money for anything like that."

Brad looked up and glared at Marie. "What kind of things?"

She was silent for a moment.

"I'm asking you a question," he insisted. "What kind of things have you done that would make you think that calling my mother a bitch was okay? Because if that's how you treated your mother, you've got few things coming before you'll be my wife and the mother of my children."

"But the baby is already on the way, and I'm the mother whether you or your parents like it or not," Marie shot back. "Don't you see? Your mom and dad aren't going to give you what you want without a fight. They want you away from me. And as hard as they fight to get you away from me, I'll fight even harder to keep you. I love you, Brad, and I want us to raise this baby together. So what's it going to be? Me and the baby—or your parents?"

"Some choice!" Brad snapped back, then went on, "Don't you see? You're feeding right into what my parents wanted from the very start, to drive a wedge between us. If we go on like this, then they've already won."

"Ha!" Marie huffed. "You're living in la la land! You can't be the good little boy who makes mommy and daddy happy and still get what you want if you grovel enough."

"I am *not* groveling," Brad said through clenched teeth.

"You've got to take a stand," Marie went on. Then she took a depth breath and let it out in exasperation. "Oh, what's the use! I'm freezing. Can we go home? I've had enough for one day. My head is splitting."

Brad looked at her without speaking, yanked the car into reverse, and backed down the driveway. She stared out the window and cried softly, but he didn't try to comfort her or assure her that everything would be all right.

That was because he wasn't sure that it would be. He had tried to placate his parents about Marie ever since that awful two weeks he spent with them in Palm Springs last summer. He was sure that they wanted him to be happy and they'd come to love Marie as much as he did. But he could see now how futile it all was. Not only would they never come around, but also Marie would never understand how much being with his family meant to him. She wasn't even willing to treat his mother with respect. It was all so hopeless.

As they drove in silence back to the apartment and went to bed without saying good night, Brad felt that they had both stepped over some line that Christmas Day. He could see now in retrospect that it had been the beginning of the end of his time with Marie. She had called his mother an ugly name, and no matter what he did from that day forward, Marie—the woman he loved and the mother of his child—would never be accepted into his family. That he loved her, adored her, and cherished the baby she was carrying didn't seem to matter. His parents weren't able to let him go, and he wasn't able to stand his ground with them. Marie was right about that. In this war of wills, he and Marie and the baby were indeed the pawns.

Their life together never had a chance.

CHAPTER EIGHT

Friday, October 16, 2009

Calm Before the Storm

By Friday morning, Brad was doing much better. He and Jenny had enjoyed a great evening together. They agreed not to talk about politics, the feds, or even the event coming up on Saturday.

But this morning, Jenny was off and running with some official duties at the office and a few events she needed to attend before the big one tonight that Brad reluctantly wasn't attending.

That only made him think more about what his life could have been without all the politics and the drama. Not that he ever *didn't* have drama in his life.

In fact, the biggest drama in his life revolved around Marie.

Marie again. He realized that for some reason she was so much on his mind these days.

He wondered why as he remembered the drama that had unfolded.

◈ ◈ ◈

January, 1980

In early January, Brad got an unexpected phone call at his apartment one night from Hilda Czarnecki, one the volunteers at SNAP he hadn't seen or heard from in months. At first, he didn't know who she was.

"You remember me, don't you, Mr. Bufford?" she asked with a modicum of hurt in her voice.

How could he forget Hilda? She was more than twice his age, but she insisted on calling him "Mr. Bufford" because he was the boss.

"Of course, I do," he replied warmly. "I'm just surprised to hear your voice. How are you doing?"

"Just fine, Mr. Bufford."

"Look, you can call me Brad now since we're not working together anymore."

"Sure," she said quickly, and then her voice changed to a more hushed, tentative tone. "I have something to tell you. I don't mean to pry, but it's about Marie."

Brad had to think fast about what Hilda knew about him and Marie. She must know that they were living together, and that Marie was having his baby since she was beginning to show. But what else?

Since Marie now had another part-time paying job at SNAP covering some of the administrative duties he used to do until the board hired a full-time director and Hilda volunteered a few days a week, the two of them might interact in some way, but he probed Hilda carefully.

"What is it that you want to tell me?"

Hilda cleared her throat, and he waited patiently as he sat in the empty living room of his apartment. Marie had gone to sleep early, and his roommates weren't around.

"I'm worried about Marie," she began. "She's in trouble, and I don't think she'll tell you about it."

"What kind of trouble?"

"I overheard her talking to this guy today in the office."

"What guy? What's his name?"

"I don't know, but he was tall and husky and had long dark

hair. He wore a black leather jacket and rode a motorcycle. When he came up to my desk and asked for Marie, she spotted him and took him back to her desk, so I couldn't hear what they were talking about. But then their voices got louder, and he was shouting at her. I got scared because we were the only people in the office."

"What were they arguing about?" Brad asked.

"I don't know, but I'm afraid he's going to come back and bother her again."

"Do you remember anything you heard them say?"

"There was a lot of cursing in the conversation, and that upset me."

"You mean like four-letter words?" Brad asked delicately.

"Yes, you know—like in fornication," Hilda replied.

He hadn't heard that word used much in his generation, but he knew what it meant.

"Like they were doing it to each other?" Brad blurted out, and then added, "Are you sure about this?"

"No, I was getting the conversation in snatches," Hilda said. She went on hurriedly. "And when I walked back to see if Marie was okay, she grabbed this guy and they went down the hall to the back door, both of them yelling all the way."

"Was she mad at him too?"

"Oh yes, she was very upset with him, and then he went out the back, slamming the door behind him. Marie went into the ladies' room, and I heard her crying in there. But I didn't go in. As soon as I knew she was okay, I rushed back out front."

"Why?" he asked fitfully. *Who was this jerk that upset Marie like this?* He wanted to beat the crap out of him.

"Because," Hilda replied, "the guy parked his bike out by the curb, and I watched him drive away out the front window. I got his license plate number. Would you like me to give it to you?"

Oh, yes! he thought triumphantly. *Bless you, Hilda!* She might be an old meddling gossip, but thank God, she was there and thinking like a police detective. Quickly he scribbled down the plate number, and Hilda went on.

"I hope you don't mind that I called. I think Marie tries to handle more than she should. I wouldn't want anything to happen to the baby. Next time, I'll call the police."

"Don't worry," Brad said quickly. "There won't be a next time."

"I thought you'd take care of it for me," Hilda said with a sigh of relief. "Thank you for easing my mind. Good night."

"Good night, Hilda. And thank you."

Brad hung up the phone and sat on the couch for a while and tried to stop his mind from jumping to conclusions. Was this guy in the black leather jacket as dangerous as Hilda thought? How come Marie hadn't told him anything about this? Something was fishy here, but he couldn't do anything about it tonight. He turned off the light and went to bed. As he lay next to Marie's sleeping body, he drifted off for a while but had bad dreams. They involved huge gargoyles like the one he had seen on the jacket of a guy at school who belonged to a motorcycle club.

By morning, Brad was a wreck, but he had a plan. He made breakfast and dropped Marie off at work on his way to school. He made a point to tell her that he loved her and for her to be careful. She gave him a funny look as she got out of the car but didn't say anything.

Then Brad headed to school and tried to shake the feeling of foreboding he had. There was a logical explanation for everything Hilda told him, and he didn't think Marie was in any real danger, but he had to be sure, and he knew there was only one way to find out.

When he got to school, he pulled into the student parking lot, raced inside the building, and called his father's office on the pay phone before his class started.

He threw some change in the phone and dialed the number, hoping to catch Hadley before he got into a meeting or had to go to court. His father's secretary rang him through and his father's voice came on the line.

"This is a surprise," Hadley said. "Are you okay?

Brad spoke in a rush of words. "I need your help, but you can't ask any questions about it."

"Can I assume what you want me to do won't get you into trouble?" Then Hadley's voice shifted abruptly. "Are you in trouble, son?"

"No, but I know from working at your law firm during the summer that you have a way of running a license plate."

His father didn't say anything.

Brad went on. "I need you to run a plate for me from a motorcycle. I need to know who owns it and their address."

"The DMV won't give information out to a private individual, only to the police."

"I know I'm asking for something big here, Dad, but it's really important to me."

"And I can't ask why, right?"

"No, not right now."

"Okay. Give me the plate. I'll call in a favor."

Brad read the number into the phone and then added, "Can you call me at home later? But don't leave a message if I'm not there. I don't want my roommates to know."

"Does that include Marie?" Hadley asked deftly.

Brad dodged the question. "Maybe I could call you back at work this afternoon."

"I could have the information by then."

"Good. Thanks, Dad. I really appreciate that."

"Son, you'd let me know if you were in trouble?"

"Yeah, Dad. Don't worry. I'm not. I'm fine."

Brad hung up the phone and heaved a sigh, but the relief didn't last long. His father already had a whiff that this was connected to Marie—and why wouldn't it be? If it was so important to Brad, Marie had to be involved.

There was another way to find out who the guy on the bike was, but he'd have to ask Marie. And surely she'd have an answer for him, but would it be the truth?

This time it wasn't about where she went to school or who her mother was. This was about Marie telling him the truth about the father of her baby, and he shuddered to think that he didn't trust her about that anymore.

How had he and Marie, once the perfect couple in his eyes, come down to this?

❖ ❖ ❖

By late that afternoon, Brad sat in his car in the school parking lot with a piece of paper in his hand containing the information his dad obtained for him.

He stared at the paper with the name and address on it and wondered if it would be better to ask Marie what this was all about first. Maybe this guy was blackmailing her or threatening to hurt her or the baby, and she was afraid to tell him about it.

Maybe she'd tell him about this guy—Ralph Andrew Rozniak—who had come to see her at the office the other day...or maybe she wouldn't. What did he have to do with this baby? Maybe he'd didn't want to know about this Ralph.

Maybe he should crumple up this piece of paper right now and forget about it. Would the truth about Ralph make him feel any better about Marie being the mother of his child?

Now as he looked at the address again, he realized it was downtown, not a residential area. Wouldn't a motorcycle be registered to a person's home—or was this a business address? As he recalled Baker Street, there were nothing but bars on the street, the seedy kind, the kind that the college crowd didn't frequent.

That much made him curious, so he drove out of the parking lot, got on the expressway, and headed downtown. He got off at the Main Street exit and maneuvered his way down to Baker Street. It wasn't long before he got to the 500 block, where he saw mostly storefronts with residences over them. It was possible, he thought, that Ralph lived over a storefront, but as he drew near to the corner of Baker and School Streets, Brad saw a sign that made the blood drain from his face and his head throb.

He was there at 565 Baker Street, the address his dad had given him, and on the first floor, neon lights blared out the name of a bar—Painted Lady—and underneath it the words "Live Shows—Girls, Girls, Girls."

He felt his heart jump a beat and he couldn't get his breath. What did Ralph or the Painted Lady have to do with Marie? Wasn't this the kind of bar women danced in and...

Brad's mind turned to mush. Suddenly, his hesitation and ambivalence about finding out the truth about Marie and Ralph froze his mind almost as much as the bitter cold outside was freezing his body.

His car heater had stopped giving off much heat by now, and he watched the neon "Girls, Girls, Girls" sign blink as the evening sky turned dark. He knew what he had to do, but as he got out of his car, locked it, and crossed the street, he felt his anger and fear. Why was Marie doing this to him? What would he find out about her in a place like this? He almost turned around, but he knew he couldn't. He had to find out the truth.

He walked up to the bar, swung open the outside door, and was immediately hit by a wave of smoke, loud music, and the artificial glow of red and yellow lights. Constructed like a long, narrow cave with a dark wooden bar to his right and booths to the left, this place could've easily been a hangout for students, a place to congregate at night after class, with the regulars from the neighborhood there to have a few beers before they went home to the wife and kids.

But as Brad moved into the room, he immediately felt the difference. Set back from the end of the bar and surrounded by tables and chairs was a runway with small white lights marking its edge. On it were two women, nude but for high heels and G-strings that barely covered them. They were dancing with each other in slow, rhythmic movements, putting on a show for a crowd of guys sitting below them. Each of the girls had a long, glowing light sticklike weapon like the ones made popular in a science fiction movie, and they were playfully dueling while the crowd enjoyed their kinky interaction.

Brad stood for a moment, watching these two pathetic creatures who he thought weren't very attractive or sexy, and he wondered what the connection between Ralph, this bar, and his Marie could be. Why was Ralph bothering Marie, and was it for a reason totally unrelated to this place? He didn't think for a moment that Marie wanted a man like Ralph around her. After all, as Hilda told the story, Ralph and Marie weren't exactly buddy-buddy or anything like that.

Unable to come up with an answer to any of his questions, Brad walked over to the bar and sat down on a stool. The bartender came over to him and asked, "What would you like to drink, son?"

Brad tried to ignore the fact that he had just been called son and assumed that the guy wasn't going to card him but as he looked up at the bartender, suddenly all he could see were the pictures of girls with little or no clothing plastered haphazardly on the large mirrored wall right behind him. Girls in sultry but not necessarily sexy poses showing off everything they had to anyone who walked in the door and sat down to look at them.

Was Marie's picture hanging up there somewhere? If he looked hard enough, he might recognize her beautiful face and full, luscious breasts? *Oh God!* he thought in horror. *What am I thinking? Of course, Marie's picture wasn't there. Not my Marie. No, never!*

"If you're going to sit there, son," the bartender's voice said as he broke in on his thoughts, "you have to order a drink. Those are the house rules."

Mercifully, Brad was forced to peel his eyes off the mirrored wall and look at the bartender.

"A beer, please," he muttered. "Whatever you have on draft."

The bartender nodded and walked away, but Brad's eyes didn't follow him. Instead he kept his eyes glued to the bar top so he wouldn't have to look up at those pictures on the mirror in front of him. He couldn't. He hated them now and stared instead almost trancelike at a bowl of peanuts on the bar. He had to stay focused. He had to ask the question he had come to find the answer to as soon as the bartender got back and then get out of there. This was all a big mistake, after all. Hilda must have written down the license plate number wrong. Ralph Rozniak had nothing to do with his Marie. As soon he found that out for sure, all this would be over.

When the bartender brought him the beer, Brad reached into his pocket and pulled out a five-dollar bill, which was twice the cost of the beer, and laid it on the bar in such a way that the bartender could see the size of its denomination.

The bartender eyed it and reached for it, but when he did, Brad kept his fingers on it and asked, "The bill is all yours if you can tell me if there is a guy named Ralph Rozniak around here."

"Sure," the bartender said. "He's my boss. And who should I say you are?"

"Just someone who wants to see him."

The bartender grinned and grabbed the five, disappearing for a moment through a door behind the bar.

A few moments later, another man—tall and husky with dark hair just as Hilda had described him—came from behind the bar and spoke to Brad in a coarse voice.

"You looking for me? I'm Ralph Rozniak." The man stood with his thick arms stretched across the length of the bar, his hands gripping it tightly. He looked mean enough to deal with anything that might come his way.

For a moment, all Brad could think of was that, no matter what happened next, he did believe that Marie had never set foot in this bar and that if Ralph knew her, it was from some other place, one that was respectable, clean, and noteworthy. He could take his parents and sister there and point to Marie's picture on the glass mirror and say with pride, "My Marie works here."

Holding on to that belief, Brad asked Ralph, "I was wondering if you know a girl named Marie Patterson."

"Marie, sure I know a Marie. Maybe her last name is Patterson," Ralph said cagily. "Who's asking?"

"I'm her brother," Brad lied. "I just got into town, and I'm looking for her."

"Funny," Ralph said suspiciously. "She never mentioned having a brother named—what is your name?"

"Fred," Brad said. "Fred Patterson." He put his wet, sweaty hand out to shake Ralph's across the bar top. "I came to tell her some bad news about our mother."

"Yeah. Her mother, huh? Like what, did she finally die, the old biddy?" Ralph snorted. "I don't mean no disrespect, but your sister didn't like her mother too much. I don't think she'll be all broken up to hear she's dead."

"She wanted Marie to know that she forgave her for running way and ending up in a place like this."

"What's wrong with my place?"

"Nothing," Brad said, taking a gulp of his beer and looking over at the stage.

"Marie used to dance here, you know. She had a better body than those girls up there, and she danced her heart out."

Brad looked at him, stunned. What did he say? Did he say something about Marie dancing here? How was that possible?

"She did what?" was all that Brad finally managed to say, and then he swallowed hard, the bitterness of the beer turning in his stomach.

"She worked here, but she quit," Ralph said quickly. "Said she was going down south to take care of one of your aunts, but I know she didn't. I've seen her around."

"You have?" Brad looked at Ralph and tried to look surprised.

"Yeah," Ralph went on. "And she's getting married. To some rich guy who doesn't know anything about this. Can you imagine that? The bitch married to some jerk-off."

Brad tried hard not to react, but he felt his mind start to blur, and it hurt like hell.

"Where is she now?" Brad asked in that fog, hoping this would soon all be over.

"So she hasn't kept in touch, has she?"

Brad shook his head.

"Doesn't surprise me. Far as I know, she's living with the guy somewhere off Second Street. If you want to see her, stop in tomorrow at the SNAP office on the corner of Second and Washington Streets. SNAP stands for something goofy, but she works there in the morning sometimes, and if she's not there, the nosy old hag at the front desk can tell you when she'll be in."

Brad moved uncomfortably in his stool wanting desperately to leave now, but he had to ask one more question.

"So, what are you to her?" he mumbled, forcing the words out of his mouth.

"Me?" Ralph asked, sounding surprised by the question. "Do you mean did I ever poke her?"

Brad could only nod and then pour the rest of his beer down his throat.

"Nah," Ralph said with a snarl like he had a bad taste in his mouth. "I was just her boss." He looked over at the girls on the runway. "Wouldn't mind getting her back, though. She was good for business." Then he looked at Brad's empty glass and asked, "Do you want another?"

"No," Brad said weakly using all the strength he had left to push himself off the stool. "But thanks for your help."

Feeling queasy and light-headed, he turned and walked out the front door of the bar and into the street. He managed to get out on the sidewalk and over to the side alley before he threw up, retching up the hot, liquid contents of his stomach into the frigid, cold night.

Marie! Marie! he screamed silently. *What the hell are you doing to me, Marie!*

❖ ❖ ❖

When Brad came home much later that evening, he found a note on the dining room table in Marie's handwriting.

It had been hours since he had left the Painted Lady, the bar where Marie had danced—and where his whole life fell apart that afternoon.

He didn't want to think what Marie had written to him in the note. He was pretty drunk. He didn't remember much of what he had done since leaving the Painted Lady except to drive around and stop at a few convenience stores along the way to get some more beer. He told himself he wanted to settle his stomach, but he knew he was drowning his sorrows.

Now, after finally getting home exhausted, dizzy, and ready to puke again, instead of finding Marie there, there was only a note.

He looked at it and turned it over in his hand. Should he open it? Would it be another Pandora's box he was afraid to open, like tracking down Ralph's license plate number? He didn't want to know anything more about Marie tonight. He just wanted to go to bed and wake up the next morning with everything the same as before. No Ralph, no Marie dancing at the Painted Lady. Life would be good again, and yet he knew it was never going to be that way. All of that had vanished into thin air.

Nevertheless, he sat down at the dining room table, opened up the note from Marie and read it:

Dear Brad:

I know this isn't the right way to do this, but I don't know how else to tell you. You expected too much of me, and I don't know that I can ever give you what you want. I've never met a person like you before, and I know that I never will again. I've lied about a lot of things, but not about how much I loved you or how much I wanted to live the rest of my life with you. I can see now that won't happen.

By now, you've heard about Ralph. I'm sorry you found out about him and the baby the way that you did. He's not the man I wanted as the father of my baby, but I've learned that you can't always have what you want. Don't worry. I'll be okay. Ralph is helping out with expenses, and I can stay with him until the baby comes.

I don't want you to think that I did this to you because I'm a bad person. I just wanted what was the best for my baby. So, this is good-bye. I wanted to see you before I left, but I have to leave now. It's best that way. I'll never forget you and all the fun we had. Don't think of me as a bad person, okay? I'm not.

Love, Marie

CHAPTER NINE

Friday, October 16, 2009

A Phone Call Away

Ambrose sat in a booth that afternoon near the pay phone at the back of the hotel coffee shop eagerly awaiting a phone call from Everett Hall at the governor's campaign office.

Ambrose had called him a few minutes ago, but he wasn't there, and Ambrose didn't want to leave a message. So now he called Everett again from pay phone in the coffee shop and left a message on his voice mail to call him there.

Before long the phone rang, and Ambrose jumped up to answer it, almost knocking over his coffee cup as he grabbed the pay phone before anyone else could.

"Hello," Ambrose barked into the phone, his gruff voice tinged with excitement. "Who's this?"

"Who's *this*?" the voice on the other end shot back. "Is that you, Ambrose?"

Ambrose grinned. "Yeah, and this must be Everett? What do you know? How's it going with you, Everett?"

"Cut the crap!" Everett growled. "What's this message you left me? 'Roses are red, violets are blue, the FBI is only the beginning for Brad and Jenny, too.'"

Ambrose cackled. "Don't you like my poetry?"

"You're lucky I didn't report this to the police as a threat on the lives of the governor and her family. You'd have cops all over you right now!"

"That's only if you knew where I was, and you don't know, so be nice. Remember, I'm the one who called you, and you still don't know why."

"What *do* you want?" Everett asked, and Ambrose could hear the impatience in this voice. He was getting to him. He loved it.

"I want to talk to Brad about Marie."

"Marie who?"

"Ah! That's for me to know and you to find out."

"Don't play games with me. It's only because you've worked for Pedro that I'm talking to you at all."

"Tell your boss I have some information about Marie and if he wants to talk, we could arrange something."

"Brad is not my boss. I work for the governor," Everett snapped.

"Same difference," Ambrose said smugly. "What involves Brad involves his wife. I don't have to tell an old political operative like you something like that."

"Is Brad supposed to know this Marie?"

"Yes, and her baby too," Ambrose added.

"A baby! Jesus, are you off your nut? I'm going to hang up now and forget you even called. Good-bye."

"I wouldn't do that," Ambrose said quickly. "I'd check with Brad first. Or is he too busy with the FBI investigators to talk? I read the papers. He'll want to know what I know about Marie and her baby before anyone else does."

"Jesus! You're up to something, aren't you?" Everett heaved a sigh. "Can I get back to you at this number?"

"I'll be here. And if Brad doesn't believe you, tell him I know about Ralph too."

When Everett hung up, Ambrose broke into a big wide grin. That went rather well, and he was pleased with himself. While everyone thought of him as a loser because he lived on the street, at least he hadn't walked away from his child twenty years ago and left her with a scumbag like Ralph. But Brad had, and wouldn't some enterprising reporter at the *Capital City Enquirer* be interested in such a tidbit from the governor's husband's past?

Having read the diary in its entirety and knowing all the secrets in it, he was sure that Bufford wouldn't want any of it out there, not with his wife running soon for reelection.

Ah, Jenny the governor! He loved having a hand in how her life turned out when she had done so much to screw up his. Wasn't it amazing synchronicity? She stood in judgment of him about *his* child, and now he gets to tell her all about how she was the stepmother of a famous stripper! Imagine the political fallout if that information got to the press! What would Jenny do if the world found out who Lisette's real father was?

In the glee of this moment, he thought again about Lisette and what she might offer him financially to find out who her real father was. She had money now. She'd coughed up some to him to find out about Brad. He was sure of that.

It was all so perfect, he thought. What he loved the most was that the situation had so many angles and dangles to it. There were so many people he could manipulate to get what he wanted. He'd start with Jenny. She might be the state's most popular governor in a decade, but nobody's political fortune was boundless. No matter how Everett played this, her stepdaughter's background was sure to hurt Jenny politically as well as the fact that her husband was once again involved in a scandal that had to do with scantily clad women in lurid places. Who knew what might happen next? And that's why Ambrose had the advantage over all of them.

God! this was fun, Ambrose thought, sitting in the back booth, sipping coffee and waiting for Everett to call him back. As soon as a meeting with Brad was arranged for him by Everett, he'd go make copies of the diary and put the original back in a safe place. But for now he just wanted to savor the moment.

He was finally getting his revenge and evening up the score between him and Lisette—and Jenny Jablonski too!

How sweet was that!

❖ ❖ ❖

"Are you sitting down?" Everett said to Brad over the phone, and Brad felt like it was deja vu all over again.

What new tidbit did Everett have for him that he thought might shock him after all that had happened to him already? Unless the feds had decided to indict him anyway but at this point Brad didn't care. All of that was bad enough, but he had other problems. He had been in a funk ever since Wednesday morning when all those memories about Marie and what had happened between them at the end came flooding back to him. It was Friday afternoon now, and although he and Jenny had had a good time together last night, he couldn't shake his malaise about Marie and the baby. He didn't know why. If Marie hadn't had so many things going against her, he wondered, would he have fought harder to find out the truth about the baby? But Marie had flip-flopped so many times about what was real and what wasn't that Brad could see why he had simply given up. But should he have?

"You're not going to believe this," Everett went on, breaking into Brad's thoughts, "but I had a phone call a few minutes ago from this guy who claims to know about some baby that he thinks you are interested in. Do you know what he's talking about?"

Brad couldn't believe what Everett was saying.

"Yes, yes!" Brad said quickly. "What about Marie and the baby?"

"You know a Marie and her baby?" Everett sounded flabbergasted. "And a guy named Ralph too?"

Brad's mind reeled. Who could possibly know about Ralph?

He hadn't seen him in years, and then only once at that bar, that awful bar where Marie had worked.

"Who's telling you all this?"

"This guy, Ambrose. He's homeless, lives mostly on the streets, but he used to be a lawyer. A little too shifty for my taste, but I know him because he's worked for Pedro at the Community Center."

"You're kidding. I saw Pedro the other day. Can he vouch for this guy? What does he want?"

"I don't know. He's saying he knows things you might like to know about Marie before anyone else does."

Oh Jesus! Brad thought. That's all he needs right now—for things to come out about him and Marie.

"Tell him I'll meet with him."

"But who is this Marie and what about this baby?" Everett asked.

Brad ignored his questions. "Do whatever you have to do to get me in a room with this Ambrose as soon as possible."

"All right," Everett said warily. "But I want to be there. He'll be less volatile, and I'm the one he contacted."

"Okay, but just set it up now."

"Does Jenny know about this Marie?" Everett asked carefully.

"Sure," Brad lied. "She and I talked about Marie the other day."

"And about the baby too? You've got to tell Jenny about the baby now before it's too late. I don't want to get caught in the middle between you two. It's not my job to tell Jenny…"

"Just set up the meeting," Brad said, interrupting him. "I'll tell Jenny everything she needs to know."

Everett sighed. "You're playing with fire here. If I were you, I'd tell Jenny."

"But you're not me," Brad snapped. "Just make this happen. This is important to me. Please!"

"Okay but let me call Pedro and find out what he knows about this guy. We don't want him going right to Jenny with this, right?

With guys like Ambrose, you can never tell what they'll do. It could be a disaster."

"No! Don't involve Pedro. I don't want to involve anyone else in this until we know what we're dealing with. Just set up the meeting!" Brad yelled back, and then hung up.

For a moment he just sat there, trying to fully grasp what had just happened. He had been obsessing about Marie and this baby for days, and now suddenly she was coming back into his life.

Was she alive? Would he able to see her again? And what about the baby? It had to be a girl. Marie always said it would be. Where was she now? Was it possible Ambrose had some real proof that he was the father of the child? Could it be, after all these years, he was a father after all?

Feelings of joy and excitement raced through his head. This was nothing short of a miracle. But he had had false hopes before, and he didn't want to get ahead of himself. He'd meet with Ambrose and see what he had to say.

As for Jenny, he decided it was too early to tell her anything. He had just gotten back on a good footing with her, and there was no sense screwing that up right now. He was a man full of anticipation, but he wasn't stupid. He had learned that lesson already. Stick to the facts and let things unfold. He had to be patient.

Miracles can happen, but he'd wait and see.

❖ ❖ ❖

Ambrose couldn't believe how nervous Everett looked as he came around the corner and into the coffee shop where Ambrose was waiting.

He loved it.

He remembered Everett as a finicky man, but he had never seen him this shaken. Of course, it wasn't obvious to the untrained eye, but Ambrose knew about guys like Everett. The consummate spin doctor, Everett could be lost in a swamp being devoured by alligators, and outwardly he'd make it seem like nothing.

But true to form, Everett was moving quickly on all this. He got back to Ambrose minutes after his initial phone call him about Marie's baby and told him that Brad wanted to meet him within the hour. Ambrose knew he was on to something then. He had hit a nerve.

As Everett moved into the coffee shop, Ambrose raised his hand and waved him back to a booth in the rear where Ambrose had set up shop. With the lunchtime rush over, the place was almost deserted. Everett saw him immediately, and Ambrose watched him move through the shop looking as though he didn't want to be seen by anyone he knew meeting with someone like Ambrose. Of course, with the kind of people Everett knew these days, Ambrose figured they weren't likely to be here anyway.

When Everett got to the booth, he stuck out his hand to Ambrose and said in an almost cordial voice, "Long time no see."

Ambrose could tell that Everett had rehearsed that line carefully, so the words and tone of his voice sounded cool and unaffected. But underneath he was scared. He must be wondering how this guy was going to rock his world today.

Little did he know, Ambrose mused with a sly inner grin. Then he grabbed Everett's hand and played along.

"You look the same," Ambrose said. "Neat as a pin."

"And you, my friend, look like you've been going through hard times."

"No," Ambrose said boldly, "things are actually looking up for me."

He gave Everett a mysterious look, and he could feel the guy bristle inside his expensive three-piece suit.

Ambrose went on. "Have a seat. Take a load off."

Everett looked down at the seat across from Ambrose and

frowned. He pulled a handkerchief out of his pocket and cleaned off the vinyl covering of the seat before he sat down.

"Sorry," Ambrose said quickly, suddenly feeling as if he had to apologize. "It's not the swankiest place in town, but I don't think anyone will disturb us here."

"Are you sure?" Everett asked grimly, as he sat down and pushed a pile of sugar that had been left by a previous customer to the middle of the table in front of them.

"Chill out, man! The cops swept the place for bugs right before you got here."

Everett looked at Ambrose for a moment as if he wasn't sure he was kidding. Then he mumbled, "Not funny. It's my job to worry about these kinds of things."

"Don't worry. I'm not here to shake anyone down."

Everett looked at him suspiciously.

"Aw, come on, lighten up!" Ambrose said. Then he went on. "How about a cup of coffee or a chocolate-covered doughnut? They are real tasty here. Take my word for it."

"Like I should take your word for anything," Everett snapped back. "This better be on the up-and-up, or I'll…"

"You'll do what? Report me to the bar association? I'm not even a licensed attorney anymore. Oh, you've got me shaking in my boots," Ambrose said sarcastically.

Just then, the front door of the coffee shop opened, and Ambrose looked up to see a man walk in. He was wearing a baggy sweatshirt, an old fishing hat pulled down over his face, and a pair of sunglasses even though the day was overcast and dreary.

Everett looked up, too, then turned around and waved the man over to their booth. "That's him," Everett said to Ambrose with a nervous sigh. "We can get this show on the road now."

"Sure, sure," Ambrose replied, but he was mesmerized by this guy who was shuffling toward them, looking like the most unlikely person to be married to a sitting governor.

He was in disguise, of course, but he looked so down and out that if Ambrose didn't know better, he'd have thought this guy was some wino on the street. And he was even more paranoid than Everett, looking around the place like someone could be watching.

When he got to the table, Brad thrust his hand out and introduced himself. Ambrose recognized his voice immediately. It was the one he had heard the other night when he was hiding in the closet at the Community Center waiting for Pedro and his friend to clear out, so he could go upstairs and get his stuff. This was the Brad who was in trouble, Ambrose decided. The pieces were falling into place. He remembered the tension and anxiety in Brad's voice that night, and it was still there. What Ambrose had to share was going to complicate things even more. This guy was going through hell, Ambrose thought, and he loved it. It didn't get much better than this.

He gestured for Brad to join them. Brad nodded and sat down next to Everett in the booth across from Ambrose.

"I have something of great interest to you," Ambrose began, "but I'm unwilling to give it to you without some assurances."

"You want assurances from us?" Everett said with a huff. "It should be the other way around. You should be assuring us you won't be spreading information around in connection with Mr. Bufford that isn't true."

"Oh, it's true, all right. I can prove it. That's not the problem."

"Then what is the problem?" Brad broke in. In addition to being tense and paranoid, he was impatient too, Ambrose thought. He liked that.

"I want to know that you won't do anything to hurt Marie's baby."

"Then there *is* a baby!" Brad said excitedly, his dour face suddenly full of emotion. "Where is she? What's her name?"

"Slow down," Ambrose said. "Don't you even want to know how I know what I know?"

"Yes," said Everett quickly.

"No," Brad blurted out, then he asked eagerly, "When I can meet her?"

Ambrose laughed and looked at Everett. "Then for your benefit, I'll tell you all about Mr. Bufford's daughter."

"His daughter?" Everett exploded. "Jesus Christ, Brad! Is that possible?"

Brad looked at him, his eyes steely as though he wasn't going to lie, Ambrose thought, but with a determination that he didn't have to explain himself to anyone, including Everett.

"This is crazy! Pure political suicide!" Everett's voice was raised now, and he kept on going. "Why didn't you tell me this before we got here? Is this another piece of dirty laundry that I'm going to have to clean up for you?"

Brad ignored Everett and looked earnestly at Ambrose. "Do you know for sure she's my daughter? What proof do you have?"

"It's all in here," Ambrose said, pointing out a wad of papers in the pocket of his jacket. He pulled one out and put it on the table in front of them.

"What's this?" Everett asked brusquely, picking up the page by the edges like it was yesterday's garbage.

"One of the pages of Marie's diary," Ambrose said, tapping the other pages still in his pocket and adding, "According to this, Marie's baby was born in 1980, but you'll be most interested in the nine months prior to the birth."

"Marie didn't keep a diary," Brad said suddenly.

"See," Everett jumped in. "I knew this wasn't right."

"That's where you were mistaken," Ambrose said. "She kept it meticulously from the day she met you to the day she left you the note telling you that the baby wasn't yours."

"Aha!" Everett broke in. "That's proof that Brad isn't the father of this baby. Even she says he isn't."

"What does she say about the note?" Brad asked eagerly, ignoring Everett. "Does she explain why she wrote it?"

"That's the interesting part, the part that I'm willing to give to the highest bidder."

"What do you mean by that?" Everett queried. "You said you weren't out to blackmail anyone."

"Did I say that?" Ambrose replied with a grin. "Let's say that I'm testing the political waters here."

"What do you want?" Brad shot back, his manner more suspicious now.

"I'll give you the original of the diary and bring Marie's daughter to you, but I want a finders' fee. That's it—take it or leave it." Then he turned to Everett. "See, that's not extortion, just payment for services rendered."

Everett snickered. "And that's it?"

"I told you, I want assurances too," Ambrose said testily to Brad. "I want to be sure that if I find this girl, you won't abandon her again and be a jerk. I know the whole story. How a now politically prominent man early in his life got a young girl pregnant and tossed her aside when the situation got a little dicey." Then Ambrose turned to Everett. "Did I mention the part about what Marie did for a living at a bar called the Painted Lady? The place could still be around, and they'd have employment records somewhere for a Marie Patterson, I'm sure."

At that, Brad leaped up from his seat on the other side of the booth and grabbed Ambrose by collar with both of his hands. "You tell that story to anyone, and I'll kill you. Do you understand me?"

"Easy, easy!" Ambrose said, as he grabbed Brad's hands. Bigger and stronger than Brad, Ambrose easily broke his hold and sent him flying back into his seat, crashing against Everett as he did.

"Hey!" Everett shouted. "Let's not get crazy here. Settle down, the both of you."

Brad looked at Ambrose, his eyes wild, but he let himself be calmed by the sound of Everett's voice.

Now Everett went on with Ambrose. "All right. We get the idea. You've got some damaging information about Mr. Bufford's past, but you're willing to find this girl for him if you are assured she'll be treated properly."

"Yeah," Ambrose said. "She hasn't had a great life, thanks to her father. I don't want to see her get hurt anymore."

Brad eyed Ambrose suspiciously.

"Why do you care about this girl? You must know her or Marie or you wouldn't have the diary. I can't believe that if Marie kept a diary, she'd let anyone see it unless…." He paused for a moment. "Unless…," he repeated. Suddenly Brad's voice got softer, and he said sadly, "Oh, I get it. Marie's dead. That's why her daughter has the diary. But then how did you get it?"

Ambrose ignored Brad's last question and looked at him with disgust. He hated how he was wallowing in self-pity as though he had been the one wronged by Marie and Lisette, and he couldn't help himself.

"You stupid jerk," he screamed at him. "You threw it all away. You fucked her and left her, and what do you have to show for it? A daughter you have never seen or even tried to find. Maybe you should go tell Mommy and Daddy and see if they'll help you out here. Just like they helped you dump Marie for no good reason."

Ambrose continued, his anger building. "If I had this chance with my son, I'd do anything to see him again. Someday I'll find him, even though he changed his name so he wouldn't have the same one as mine. Mark Durocher. That's his name now. But at least I know my son's name. You don't even know your daughter's name, do you? What a poor excuse for a father you are. You're disgusting!"

Provoked, Brad spit out the words at Ambrose, "You don't know shit about anything." But before Brad could grab Ambrose again by the collar, Everett put up his arm and stopped him.

"Are you crazy?" he hissed at Brad. "Starting a brawl in public. That's going to go over really well here." Then Everett turned to Ambrose. "Enough of your histrionics too. The two of you need to sit here for a moment and cool down."

The two men sat in silence, their breathing becoming more even. Everett took his handkerchief out and gave it to Brad.

"I want the diary," Brad finally muttered, using the handkerchief to wipe the sweat off his brow. "Then I want you to find my daughter, and that's it. After that, you tell no one about any of this."

"That's seems like a reasonable offer," Everett said cheerily to Ambrose. "What do you say to that?"

"Fine," Ambrose said gruffly. "And with same assurances as before."

Brad nodded, and Everett said, "Fine, we have a deal."

They sat in silence again for a moment, and then Brad asked Ambrose in a quieter, more subdued voice, "What's the girl's name?"

"Lisa."

"That's it?" Everett jumped in. "You're not going to give us her full name?"

"No, of course not. Otherwise you could just go find her on your own."

Then Brad asked, "Do you know her?"

"Yes, and I can find her without much trouble in a day or two. She doesn't live around here, but she's in town. Not for long, though, so we have to hurry it up."

"How much is this going to cost me?"

"I want fifty thousand dollars total. Half up front, the rest when I find her. That's the deal. Take it or leave it."

"Jesus!" Everett exclaimed. "Now *that* is extortion!"

"I'll take it," Brad said, as he grabbed for his wallet, took five hundred dollar bills out, and laid them on the table. "Here's five hundred dollars cash, right here, right now. You tell me where to wire the rest of the upfront money."

"Brad," Everett interrupted, looking flustered. "Are you sure you want to do this? That's a lot of money to pay him!"

"This is my daughter, for Christ sakes, Everett!" Then he turned to Ambrose. "I got a burner phone for you to use." He reached for his cell phone clipped to the waistband of his sweatpants and handed it over. "Take this," he said. "Call me day or night when you find her. I'm on the speed dial."

Ambrose took the phone from Brad and crammed it in his pocket. From the other pocket, he took out the other papers and pushed the rest of the pages of the diary toward him. Brad grabbed them and stood up.

"One more thing," he said in a firm voice, "don't assume because I left her mother that I don't love my daughter and won't take care of her. I am her father. That's all you need to know. I'll do the rest."

Then he looked at Everett. "Are you coming?"

Everett looked at Brad then back at Ambrose. Without saying a word, Everett nodded and stood up to walk away with Brad.

"Hey!" Ambrose yelled after them. "Don't I even get a 'thank you'? Thanks for finding my daughter. Or even a 'Nice doing business with you'?"

When neither Everett nor Brad turned around, Ambrose added, "Up yours!" and pocketed the money Brad had left on the table.

So what if Everett barely believed him and Brad hated his guts? He was on the clock now, looking for Lisa, who Brad doesn't know had changed her name to Lisette and was staying in this very hotel. Not information he was about to share with Brad at this point. Now he had to focus on getting Lisette back on his radar screen.

Still, he wasn't worried. By this time tomorrow when he got the first $25,000 wired to his bank by Brad, he'd still have a few tricks up his sleeve. Now that he had met Brad face-to-face and saw what a whiner he was, he'd have no trouble playing this thing out to the very end—the bitter end. He would have his revenge. He was sure of that now.

And he wasn't worried about Lisette being hurt by this clown. He was just playing with Brad about that. Trying to make him feel more like a heel than he already was. Once Brad found out the whole truth about Lisette, what she did for a living, he'd be out of her life anyway. Just as he had left Marie after he found out about her life as a dancer. Just as Ambrose suspected from reading the diary, Brad was a spineless idiot who didn't know how to stand up for the people he was supposed to care about. At least Ambrose cared about his son, Mark, and wanted him in his life.

For what Brad was as a father, Ambrose would have no trouble taking him down.

None whatsoever.

◈ ◈ ◈

Luckily, Brad was still wearing his sunglasses as he and Everett left the coffee shop and headed back downtown. He couldn't chance being recognized or spotted in public. Especially now with his daughter in the picture. It was fortunate that Everett was there to keep him out of trouble. Why did he let himself get triggered by such an asshole?

What Ambrose thought of him didn't mean squat to him. It was more about his daughter now and finding her. But it wouldn't have been so easy for Ambrose to get to him if he hadn't been brooding over the last few days about Marie and the baby. Or if he hadn't blamed himself for not standing up to his parents, for letting them convince him he wasn't the father of the child. Hadley and Marion were both dead now, so there was nothing he could say to them, but he could forgive himself. And he hoped that his daughter, his Lisa, would forgive him too.

And Marie. Did she forgive him before she died? What made her tell him he wasn't the father when he was? Why did she do that to her daughter? Why?

The diary.

He had the pages now. Maybe something in them would prove to him that all of this was real. Maybe the diary would tell him what he needed to know before he met Lisa so they could start fresh and new.

He knew what he had to do. He had to sneak back into the governor's mansion the same way that he left, hidden in the back seat of a state police cruiser so the press corps camped out at the end of the driveway wouldn't see him, and read the diary. So he tucked the copy of the pages of the diary into the waistband of his sweatpants, covered it with his baggy sweatshirt, and headed back to the car with Everett.

When he got to the mansion, he raced upstairs to his study and locked the door. He sat down in his armchair and opened the diary to the first page.

It shocked him to see Marie's tight, precise handwriting again after all these years. He rubbed his hand over the page and felt tears well up in his eyes.

Oh God, he thought. *She's dead, and I'll never see her again.* He had pictures of the two of them somewhere, the ones they had taken at a booth at the fair the first summer they were together; they were so happy then. He still remembered how she glowed.

Now those pictures and the copy of this diary were all he had left, except for Lisa. In a rage, he had destroyed the note Marie had written to him at the end. He wished he had it now because it would have verified her handwriting for sure, but he knew this was Marie's all right.

He began reading the diary pages. First, he read about how Marie had purposefully changed her appearance and came to see him at the SNAP office on a bet. He cried when he read how much she enjoyed making love to him and how it pained her to have to tell him about where she went to college. But he was shocked to see the entries about Ralph after she had told Brad she was pregnant. One of them in particular he found himself reading in horror.

Thursday, September 27, 1979

I haven't told you about Ralph yet, have I? Remember how I said that nothing could touch me now? Well, today I realized I was wrong. Ralph, the owner of the bar where I dance, saw me on TV at an anti-nuke rally. I was only on TV for a second waving around a sign, but Ralph recognized me and figured out that I didn't want anyone at SNAP to know where I worked. So he told me that night that if I'd go out with him, he'd keep quiet.

I tried to laugh him off, but he's such a creep I'm not sure I can. So I've been thinking. I could go out with Ralph, even fuck him, if it's not too gross. Then, if he wants to see me again, I'll tell him I'm pregnant and he's the father. Boy, will he be out of my life forever! Trust me, I know guys like Ralph. They never take responsibility for what they do. Not like Brad.

But I love Brad! Why would I even think of fucking someone like Ralph?

Not that things are easy with Brad these days. His dad wasn't happy when he told him about me and the baby. Hadley even asked Brad if he was sure he was the father. Imagine that. "Of course, I'm the father," Brad told me he said. Then he told me not to worry. He said they're just upset, but they'll come around.

And then, worst of all, I've got to find a new place to live. Can't stay in the apartment I rent with girls from work anymore. I'm quitting there next week. I told everyone at work I was going down south to take care of my aunt. I asked Brad if I could move in with him, but I had to make up a different story. That I can't live with my "mother" anymore because the doctor told me that her TB could hurt the baby. He bought it. Poor Brad. He's such a sucker. I wish I didn't have to keep lying to him.

But Brad lives in a small place with two other guys. Who knows what will happen when the baby comes?

I have to stay positive. I love Brad and he loves me, and we're having this baby. It will all work out. I'll have to think of a way to deal with Ralph. I can do this. I know I can.

Thursday, October 4, 1979

I can't believe this happened to me. I thought I had everything under control, and then tonight everything went terribly wrong. I'm crying as I write this, and I feel so alone. But I can't tell Brad. I can never tell Brad. This would kill him. It's killing me.

Oh God, what am I going to do? Ralph raped me, and it was all my fault. It was at my farewell party from the bar, and everyone was drinking a lot. Ralph was plastered when he got me alone, and he told me that tonight was the night he was getting what he wanted from me or else. I wasn't going to do it with him, but I had a plan about how to trick him into leaving me alone. So I went out with Ralph to his truck, thinking he was so drunk that he'd pass out before we did anything, and then later I'd tell him that we did, and he wouldn't remember. It would've worked, but Ralph wasn't as drunk as I thought. He got me into his truck and forced me to do it with him. It was so awful. I cried and cried the whole time and prayed that he wouldn't hurt the baby. He put his hand over my mouth so no one could hear me scream, but I kept yelling, "No! No!" over and over again as he did it, but he didn't stop.

At least, it's over with now, and Brad won't find out that I was a dancer from Ralph because I don't work there anymore. It was worth it, right? I feel so dirty and disgusting that I have to go take another shower. I've already taken two since I got home, but I can't get the smell of Ralph off my body. Please, God! Please don't let Brad find out. I don't want to lie to him again, but how can I tell him this? Oh God, how could I tell so many lies and still have won the prize?

By the end of reading these entries, tears were running down Brad's face, but he was furious too. *Why didn't Marie tell me about Ralph?* he fumed. *What made her think that just because Ralph raped her, he was the father of her baby?* Isn't that what she wrote to him in the note she left? But how could that be? Ralph had raped her in October and Marie had told him she was pregnant in mid-September.

So she knew that Ralph wasn't the father, and yet she wrote that in the note. Maybe she assumed that Ralph had told him something the night that Brad went to see Ralph at his bar. But how could she have known about that? Things were happening fast at the end, Brad remembered, but not that fast!

Something was wrong here. There had to be an explanation for why she had written him that note telling him that Ralph was the father of her baby.

Brad paged quickly through the rest of the diary and found what he was looking for in the very last entry.

January 10, 1980

I've done a bad thing, but I had no choice. I got backed up against the wall, and I did the only thing I could do. I did it for my baby, and while I'm not proud of it, it's for the best.

Brad's parents won't give up. I can't understand why they hate me so much and are so dead set against me marrying Brad or having his baby, but they are.

Of course, the baby is Brad's, although I told him differently in the note I left for him this afternoon at his apartment. As I write this now in my diary tonight, Brad already has read the note and probably hates me.

I hope someday he'll forgive me for what I've done. I wanted to believe that his parents would come around, just like Brad believed they would, but he lives in such a la-la land. They have this crazy idea that I'm going to ruin their son's life and that the baby isn't his. I tried to tell Hadley otherwise when he came to see me today at work, but Hadley knew too much. He had found out about Ralph and threatened to tell Brad. I can't have Brad knowing about Ralph or how he raped me or that I danced at his bar. That's my bottom line. I'll do anything to make sure that Brad never finds out any of that. So I took the deal Hadley offered me. He told me that this was all I could expect. Brad had no money of his own, and if I don't take this now, I'd get nothing. Besides I can't believe that if Brad knew everything, he'd stay with me anyway.

So, it wasn't a bad deal. Hadley said that I was never to see Brad again, only write him the note and tell him whatever I want except the truth and leave it at the apartment. Hadley took me there to get my things. I guess he wanted to make sure that I kept my part of the bargain before he'd give me the check.

I got $10,000 for me and the baby. I had to sign a paper that Ralph was the father of the baby, even though that's not possible. Hadley gave Ralph some money, too, when he agreed to sign the paper and put his name on the baby's birth certificate as the father. So with the money he got, at least for a while Ralph will leave me alone. I don't need anything from him. I'm going to buy a nice trailer for me and the baby when she comes. It'll be a girl. I just know it, and I'm going to call her Lisa. Isn't that a nice name? It was the one Brad liked too. I hope that Brad will see *that this is our only way out of this. If his parents had wanted what I wanted—which was for him, my one and only love, to be with the father of my baby—this could have been different. Brad and I could have been together, until death do we part! But I know you can't always get what you want. I aimed too high. The girls were right. The hard part was getting Brad to marry me and taking me home to his folks. He tried. He did all the right things, but some things weren't meant to be. Brad and I are one of those things. But I do love him, and he'll stay in my heart forever. If he ever reads these word, which I know he won't, I hope he know this. I love you, Brad, and I always will.*

"Oh God," he wailed as he put his head down and wept until his shoulders shook and face was covered with tears. What had he done to Marie? And that baby, that poor baby! How could he have let his only child be raised by someone like Ralph?

What would his Lisa think of him? How had she survived all this?

Not that his life was great after Marie. All the other girls paled after her. That's why he never married, not until Jenny came along.

His parents weren't happy about his misalliance with Marie. They wanted their son married and producing grandchildren, but Hadley and Marian never realized the damage they had done by working so damn hard to keep him away from Marie.

How could they have treated him and Marie like that? And the baby, their own grandchild? How could they buy off her happiness for $10,000?

He couldn't tell Jenny any of this. It was so pathetic, and he was embarrassed to admit that this was how his family was. He was so overwhelmed by it all.

He had to tell Jenny, though. But maybe he should wait to tell Jenny until he was really sure that Lisa was his daughter. Wait—what was he thinking? Lisa *was* his daughter. The diary confirmed it, and he wasn't going to screw this up again. He'd find her and bring her into the family. Jenny would welcome her the the same way that Brad had brought Jenny's daughter, Maryssa, into his.

He couldn't wait for Lisa to call him "Dad." He had been waiting for that moment all his life. He was a father, and he couldn't wait to see his child. He was sure she was the most amazing young woman on this earth. She would be everything he ever wanted in a daughter. He would put no conditions on his love for Lisa. Not like he did with Marie. He wouldn't make that mistake again.

After all, these years, he could finally say it. He had a daughter, her name was Lisa, and she was the best, whoever and whatever she was.

CHAPTER TEN

Saturday, October 17, 2009

The Day of

Ambrose woke up Saturday, feeling jubilant by the way he had handled Brad and Everett the day before. The deal he had made with them was sweet, and he had an ace in the hole. When the news got out that the governor's stepdaughter had done a few twirls around the old pole at the Pussycat, wouldn't life get very interesting for Governor Jenny Jablonski and her husband, Brad, his pal?

God, he was good! He still had it in him after all these years. Just as everyone used to say about him when he was still trying court cases years ago in his glory days as a trial attorney. If there was a hopeless one, the other attorneys in the law firm would give to it Ambrose, and he'd make lemonade out of lemons.

Now I'm doing the same thing in this situation, he thought as he headed down La Strada Street past the Community Center toward Lisette's hotel. He was turning his life around, even if it was at the expense of Bufford and his wife. If only all his lawyer buddies and the snobs at the bar association could see him now! They'd be dazzled by how he had closed the deal with Bufford without Brad ever catching a whiff of the real truth. But that truth would have to wait until he talked to Lisette again.

As he neared her hotel a little after noon, he reviewed what he had done to find her since he left Brad and Everett yesterday afternoon. First, he had called the hotel and left several voice mail messages on her hotel phone. Unfortunately, she hadn't offered to give him her cell phone number when he saw her two days ago, and now the hotel wouldn't give out her room number, so he couldn't leave a note under her door. But he figured he'd go to her hotel, ask for her at the front desk, and have them connect him to her room. He wanted to invite her out to lunch and talk. He'd even pay for the meal. After all, he had that five hundred bucks he got yesterday from Brad burning a hole in his pocket, and he was on the Bufford's time clock now.

When he got to the hotel and went up to the front desk, he was told by the clerk that Lisette was not available.

"Does that mean she isn't here," Ambrose quizzed the man, "or she is here but won't take my call?"

The desk clerk looked at him blankly and repeated, "The guest is not available. Would you like to leave a message?"

"No," Ambrose spurted, "I don't want to leave another message. I've been leaving her voice mail messages for days. I want to see her!" Then he stopped and calmed himself. It was not worth fighting with the stupid man and causing a scene. He had to re-group, so he quickly added to the clerk, "I'll come back later."

Damn it! he swore to himself. *Time was short here!* She was making it difficult to get in touch with her again. Didn't she always? But he wasn't going to let her get to him. So much more of his plan was already in place, including his deal with Bufford, and soon he'd show Bufford that he had some results for him. So much to juggle!

Ambrose decided to sit in one of the chairs in the lobby and consider his options for a moment. He knew Lisette was at this hotel. The front desk clerk had said as much, and Ambrose had seen her outside the hotel as she arrived the other morning. And he had left her voice mail messages since yesterday saying that he wanted to meet with her as soon as possible.

Furthermore, he had worked out all the other parts of this plan. He had read about the event last Wednesday in the newspaper and how Lisette would be in town for it. On Thursday he confronted her outside the hotel in the morning, and then on Friday he met with Everett and Brad at the hotel coffee shop in the afternoon. Tonight, his plan would culminate here in the hotel at the event with Lisette and Jenny attending.

He didn't expect Bufford to show tonight. The publicity he had this week about the federal indictment would have Jenny and Everett too nervous about having the happy couple appear together in public. But Ambrose also planned on Brad being too chicken to tell Jenny about Marie and the baby until he had to. If he did tell her now or anyone else, someone might be able to pull up a few websites on the internet and find that the governor's stepdaughter was Attila the Hunny, the queen of the internet male sex websites. Pictures of her were all over the web. Some were authorized and fell in line with the images that her chain of strip clubs used for marketing purposes. But many of the more revealing and obviously pirated photos of Lisette in many poses and in various states of undress were unmonitored and uncensored by anyone. That's how the worldwide web operated!

Besides the public relations nightmare, Ambrose suspected the revelation that Lisette was Brad's daughter and now Jenny's stepdaughter would tear at the fabric of the personal relationship between the governor and her husband. Just as this week's allegations that Brad has sexually harassed women in the past must have caused havoc in their relationship, Jenny would once again learn in a most surprising way about more of Brad's past love trysts—and this one had produced a love child! *Oh my!* Ambrose thought sarcastically. *How wonderful!*

These delicious thoughts made Ambrose grin as he sat contemplating the final piece of his plans for Jenny, Brad, and Lisette to play out so his revenge against Lisette and Jenny would be complete. But he had to get these copies of the diary pages he had in his pocket to Lisette, so she could verify that it was her mother's handwriting and make his deal with her. Of course, he had crossed out the full name of her real father, Brad Bufford, so she wouldn't be able to place him or find him before Ambrose was ready for the big reveal. All in all, things were coming together—if only Lisette would show up.

At that moment, Ambrose noticed a big lug of a guy standing at the front desk talking to the front desk clerk. Any other time, he might have ignored this guy with the big broad shoulders and huge forearms, but Ambrose recognized him immediately.

He was the guy who had been in this very hotel ten years ago. He knew Lisette and had led Ambrose to her at the apartment of that shaman woman. Things didn't go great for Ambrose that night, but this was the kid! What was his name? Ambrose thought for a minute. It was Erick, he remembered suddenly. Maybe Erick and Lisette still had a little thing going. Maybe he was going up to her room to see her right now. Just as ten years before, all Ambrose had to do was follow Erick to find Lisette.

Ambrose watched Erick, carrying some grocery bags, leave the front desk and walk toward the lobby elevator that led to the hotel rooms upstairs. If Ambrose kept a distance behind him, Erick wouldn't even know he was there until it was too late. Luckily, as he got up from his chair in the lobby and walked toward the elevator, Ambrose got lost in a group of hotel guests also going up in the elevator to their rooms.

At the elevator, Ambrose let Erick get in first and held back, then stepped in himself right before the door closed. Once the elevator started to ascend, Ambrose watched for what floor Erick would get out on.

On the fourth floor, the elevator stopped, the doors opened, and Erick politely pushed his way out of the elevator. Ambrose waited until Erick was moving down the hall before jumping out of the elevator seconds before the doors closed.

Worried that he'd lose sight of Erick, Ambrose quickly moved down the hall and saw Erick use a pass key to enter a door on the right at the very end of the hall. Either Erick was spending a very expensive night alone in a hotel in his own town or he was shacked up with Lisette there, perhaps for the last few days, and he had just gone out for groceries to make Lisette some breakfast.

How sweet of him! Ambrose thought cynically. His plan was moving again!

He'd only have to wait a few minutes for Erick to get in the room and start breakfast, then Ambrose could pounce.

How perfect!

◈ ◈ ◈

When Erick woke up next to Lisette that morning, he wondered why he was so damn lucky to be there.

It was hard to believe that after bumping into each other at the lunch with the angel investors, he and Lisette had spent the afternoon talking, then gone out for dinner and talked some more. She told him a lot more about her life. Even when they lived together for that short period of time ten years ago, she had never really let him know what a disaster her childhood was. Now he knew why.

Yesterday he had taken her to see his gym, which she really liked. She told him she was impressed with what he had done with the place. Then after spending a few hours at work, he met Lisette at her hotel for dinner and they ended up in her room for the night.

He rolled closer to her, now sleeping soundly, and wrapped his arms around her in a soft, gentle hug. God, she was as beautiful and sexy as ever! It was an impromptu lovemaking session last night, but it was spectacular as far as Erick was concerned—so full of passion, but also so gentle and easy. As with their conversation the day before, they simply picked up where they left off with the lovemaking, and it was good.

To top off last evening's pleasure this morning, he wanted to cook her a nice breakfast in the small kitchenette of her hotel suite, but he needed groceries. So he got out of bed, gathered up his clothes, quietly left the bedroom, and walked out into the outer suite of the hotel room. There he got dressed and left her a quick note in case she woke up while he was gone. In it, he told her he'd be back soon and that he had taken one of her hotel room keys so he could get back into the room. He wrote that he'd stop at the front desk on his way back to see if there were any messages for her from that Ambrose creep. She had told Erick last night that maybe she should have given Ambrose her cell phone number the other day since the voice mail wasn't working on the hotel room phone. She also confessed that it was still her habit from her days of traveling from one seedy strip joint to another across the country to tell the front desk clerk that she was unavailable if anyone called and to take messages for her even if it she was in her room.

Back in the room now with eggs and bacon, Erick happily started on breakfast. He was sure Lisette would wake up soon to the smells of a good hearty meal. But before he even got the food unpacked, he heard a rustling noise at the hotel room door and saw something being shoved under it. He quickly walked to the door, grabbed the paper stuck under it and flung the door open. To his surprise he saw an old guy on his knees with a sheaf of papers in his hand.

"Jesus, what the hell are you doing?" Erick yelled at him. "I'm going to call hotel security if you aren't out of here in two seconds."

The guy jumped up and started yelling at Erick. "Hold your horses! I'm trying to leave Lisette a note and some pages."

Suddenly Erick realized that this guy was Ambrose. But how did he know this was Lisette's room?

"What are you doing here? You're looking for Lisette, aren't you? How did you get her room number? I'm sure the hotel didn't give it to you."

"I'm good at getting information people don't want me to know," Ambrose replied slyly.

"I bet you are. Lisette told me you accosted her yesterday morning in front of the hotel. You have some deal to make with her?" Then Erick held up the disheveled page that Ambrose had crammed under the door. "Is this one of the pages of the diary you say you have? Are you here to make deal or do you still have 'other brands in the fire'?"

Ambrose smirked at him. "As a matter of fact, lover boy, I do have a deal for her. I've been trying to make contact with her since yesterday afternoon. You can tell her I've found her real father, and he's on board. But I have to see her, and she has to agree to our deal before we can go any further."

Suddenly Lisette's sleepy voice came from the bedroom as the door between it and the outer room swung open. "What kind of a deal? What madness are you proposing now, Ambrose?"

"Ah, Lisette!" Ambrose cried out, his voice suddenly cheery and overwhelmingly sweet. "Good to see you again. Rise and shine! Greet the new day!"

Lisette came sweeping into the room with her long robe flowing behind her and her hair cascading down around her face. "Jesus, Ambrose. What the hell are you doing?" Then she moved close to Erick and said, "He can come into the room as long as you are here with me."

"Sure," Eric responded, then turned to Ambrose. "Get your ass in here and say what you have to say. Be quick!"

Ambrose scurried into the room, and Erick closed the door.

Holding some papers up in his hand for Lisette to see, Ambrose said to her. "I have some pages of the diary for you to see. I crossed out some of the words. I don't want you to learn too much before we make our deal."

Lisette looked at him suspiciously. "And that deal is?"

"Money, first of all. A good sum. But something else. Something you promised me years ago and never came through with it."

"Are you talking about that ridiculous idea you had about making Attila the Hunny into a performance art act? You knew ten years ago it was a stupid idea. Today, ten years later, its time has come and gone. A bad business proposition then and now. So no deal."

"No, that's not the deal I want with you now. It's something new I dreamed up."

She grimaced but let him go on.

"I know you have licensed your name, Attila the Hunny, and your image to the chain of strip clubs around the country. I'm sure it's very lucrative for you, so now you have the money to start a new business."

"What kind of new business?" Erick chimed in.

"You know that pole dancing—the kind that's done in a stripper routine—is being used now by women and men as exercise. It takes a lot of strength and stamina, I know, but people can learn it. So there are pole dancing clubs sprouting up around the country—and all over the world. I looked it up on the internet. It's catching on. There are even competitions and talk of pole dancing becoming an Olympic sport!"

"So what does pole dancing have to do with me?" Lisette asked.

"You could open up pole dancing exercise clubs, and I'd be on the ground floor as an investor. Of course, it would be with money that you put up for me. I would get the initial investment you put in free and clear and any returns on that investment over the years. If we agree, this time you'd sign a paper to that effect, and I'll give you back the original copy of the diary, no questions asked."

"How much of an 'investment' are you asking for?" Erick interjected.

"I'd say $50,000 to start."

"To start?" Lisette screeched. "What kind of deal is that? Sounds like the amount keeps growing however you want it to."

"No, we'll have clear terms. I have worked it all out. I want to be sure I don't lose out if the business falls flat. Plus, it would give you some incentive to make it work. But we make the deal in writing now, tonight, no going back like before."

He reached into another pocket and pulled out a single piece of paper. "I've written it all down. You can review the terms before you sign it, but it must be signed by eight o'clock tonight or the deal is off." He gave her a sly grin, then added, "I have located your real father. He is living in this area. He is very anxious to meet you. Wants to do it real soon."

"You found him! That was fast," Lisette said excitedly, gripping Erick's hand. Then she turned to Ambrose. "First, I need to review the copies of the diary pages you have for me and make sure that you really have my mom's diary."

"Sure," Ambrose replied, waving the disheveled pack of papers in his hand at her. "I have inked out the full names of people on the copies of the diary pages. You have until tonight to let me know if you are in or not. If not, I'll release the relevant pages to the press."

"The press?" Erick asked. "Why? What difference does it make to Lisette if the name of her real father is released to the press?"

"It doesn't," Ambrose replied with another sly smile. "But your real dad is a big important person now. You wouldn't want his name and yours—and what you do for a living—smeared all over the newspapers and the internet. Not a good way to start a father-daughter relationship!"

"So that means you are negotiating with him too," Lisette snarled at Ambrose. "Why am I not surprised? How much are you asking him to pay you?"

"Nothing you have to worry about," Ambrose replied. Then he flung the pages in his hands in Lisette's direction and turned to walk toward the door. "My cell phone number is on the top page. Don't forget to sign the sheet for our deal by tonight at 8:00 p.m. or the whole deal is off. Then I get to keep the original copy of the diary, and you never get to meet your father. Do you understand?"

"Seems very rushed to me," Erick commented.

"Sorry! It's this deal or no deal. Let's keep in better contact," Ambrose replied. "I'll be waiting."

With that, Ambrose was out the door. Erick helped Lisette pick up the pages on the floor in front of her. As they put the pages on the desk in the outer room, he looked at her and smiled.

"It's a crazy deal, you know that, don't you?"

"Yeah, but he's got a point. If I want to know who my real father is, Ambrose is the only way to find out. Without his full name and some idea who he is, no private investigator would even take the case. Or if they did, it would be a very expensive wild goose chase that would probably go nowhere fast."

"You do want to find out who he is, right?"

She gave him a beguiling look and then a nod.

"Okay! Let's get a look at those papers! No time to lose."

She looked up at Erick and smiled one of her big, beautiful smiles. His heart melted. Lisette was back in his life, and he was happy!

❖ ❖ ❖

Lisette was overjoyed as she read the pages of Marie's diary. She couldn't believe she was reading her Mom's words. It was like she was talking to her after all these years!

With Erick on call if she needed help with any words she couldn't read, she loved that she was learning how Marie used the disco song *Bad Girls* in her act too. How was it that her mother never told her that? True, she was only ten years old when her mother died, but before that, Marie never talked to her about what she did when she danced. She wouldn't allow her to go to Ralph's bar back then either. Later of course, that's practically where Lisette lived up until the event that changed her life on her sixteenth birthday. But she had a feeling long before reading the diary that Ralph—the world's greatest liar—wasn't her real father.

Overwhelmed by what she was reading of the man called Brad (that was all of his name that Ambrose allowed her to see), she couldn't help but think what it would have been like if Brad had been in her life earlier. From the diary, Lisette could tell that Brad's family had money and a stable life. Those were the things that Marie saw in him and wanted herself and her child—a better life for her and her daughter. But who was Brad? Ambrose said he was well known, at least in this town. So who could he be? And, more importantly, did Ambrose really know where he was?

She hated that Ambrose was in control right now. Why hadn't she been more careful about the diary and its whereabouts? Why hadn't she read the diary years ago? She could have found out earlier who her father really was and had a life so different than the one she had. But most of all, she wanted to know why her mother had never told her, even when she was dying, that Ralph wasn't her real father and that Brad existed? Why didn't her mother tell her and let her decide for herself who she wanted to be with after she was gone? Lisette let her mind wander for a bit, making a mental list of all the things she wouldn't have had to deal with if only she had been able at age ten to go live with Brad instead of Ralph.

Suddenly, she heard Erick's voice from the other side of the room, bringing her out of her thoughts and back to the present.

"How are you doing?" he asked sweetly.

He was sitting quietly in a chair, patiently waiting for her to finish reading the diary pages. "I've gotten in touch with Todd to ask about the paper Ambrose wants you to sign."

Lisette looked at him blankly for a moment. She had forgotten that she had asked him to call Todd, her business manager, and let him know they were faxing him the agreement Ambrose wanted her to sign. She needed Todd to review it for her.

"Yeah, I'm okay," Lisette said, brushing sudden tears away from her eyes. "I was just reading about my real dad. I'm thinking how my life would have been do different if I had known him years ago. His name is Brad. That's all I know, and he sounds wonderful, at least the way my mother describes him."

She stopped and wiped away more tears. "He didn't know my mother was a dancer and he never found out about Ralph. My mother told him a lot about things that weren't true, and then she lied to him about the things that were most important—that she loved him and that I was his daughter."

"I'm so sorry," Erick said, crossing the room now to sit next to her. "I don't have much family. You know from our conversation the other night that my grandparents, raised me after my mother and father were killed in a car accident when I was a little kid. I don't remember much about my father, but I know that I would do anything to see him again if I could. So that's what I think you should focus on now. Seeing your father, getting to know him. Having a real dad."

"But what if I come into my father's life right now and cause him so much trouble and make his life so complicated? Ambrose makes this deal sound so simple. But with creeps like Ambrose, who knows what else you get? I have a feeling there is so much more here than we're seeing. There is danger, not only for me but also for my real father too. What if he has other kids, a wife, a whole family? In the diary, Mom talks about how his parents weren't too nice to her, and Brad has a sister, Beth, my aunt. What about her? How will she take all this?"

Lisette stopped for a moment, filled with emotion, and then continued, "Will my showing up in their lives make them all miserable? What if I get only more pain and misery from all this? What good is it?"

She continued with tears coming down her cheeks. "Maybe I should just walk away and let it be. I don't need the diary. I don't need to know who my father really is. As long as I know who I am, and I have people around me who care about me—like you—I'll be okay."

She squeezed Erick's hand, and he leaned over to kiss her.

"I'll always be in your life," he said softly. "For as long as you want me, I'm with you." He kissed her again, and Lisette sighed.

"But," he continued with a softness in his voice, "you have to realize that this guy Brad may want you in his life, no matter what embarrassment or misery you may cause him or others. Maybe he regrets as much as you do that he never knew you existed. And Lisette, you deserve to have unconditional love. Isn't that what we all want from our parents? Love that we can rely on no matter who we are or what we do. It's love like that we all need."

Lisette sighed again. "I love that. What you said about unconditional love—love that is reliable. I haven't had a lot of that in my life since my mother died. I've gotten more of that from you and Sophie and Radiance for sure. Even Lacey talked to me about that kind of love when she crossed over and got to see her mother again."

"So what do you think?" Erick asked her. "What do you want to do here?"

"I want to do this," she said quietly at first. Then her voice got louder. "I definitely want to do this. I want to feel love again,

Erick, not only from you and people like Sophie, but also from someone who loves me as a father loves a daughter. I want to be a Daddy's girl!" she giggled.

Erick swept her up into her arms. "Wonderful!" he said. "But there is one thing that I would ask—that you are still my girl, too."

And before he kissed her, Lisette said, "Always! Don't you know I love you to the moon and back?"

◈ ◈ ◈

Ambrose was thrilled when he got the cellphone call from Lisette about an hour after he had left her hotel room. That she responded so quickly made Ambrose believe that he had really roped her in good. She wasn't going to talk to a lot of people or wait for legal advice. She had read the diary, fell in love with this Brad guy, and was going for it.

She needed a little more time to fax the written agreement to her business manager to make sure it didn't mess up her current business agreement with him. Otherwise, she was ready to sign. "He's just going to make sure that everything is in order," she told him over the phone. "I really want to do this, and I want to meet my dad. You say he lives around here, right? Would it be possible to meet him tomorrow, Sunday?"

Wow, Ambrose thought. *She is hot to trot.*

"Of course," he replied smoothly. "Let's get the paperwork done first and I'll let him know that you are awaiting his call."

Lisette got quiet for a moment, then she asked him, "Ambrose, you are not going to screw me up on this, are you? Please don't do that! This is really important to me."

"Of course not," he reassured her. But he didn't let her know that who he was more likely to screw in all this was not her, but Brad and his favorite girl governor, Jenny Jablonski.

CHAPTER ELEVEN

Saturday, October 17, 2009

What Jenny Doesn't Know

Later that afternoon while waiting for Lisette's answer about their deal, Ambrose sat in the hotel coffee shop enjoying a mocha latte, thinking about all the things that he was going to put in motion in the next few hours that no one else knew about. He had worked hard, spent some money, but the thought of the rewards he'd reap for all of it warmed his heart. Of course, the hot, expensive cup of coffee that he was pouring down his throat was raising his temperature, too! It was one of the ways he was burning though the $500 in cash that Brad had given him yesterday, but all his planning and plotting would pay off immeasurably for him.

True, he was still awaiting the wire transfer from Brad for the first half of the $50,000 they had agreed on yesterday. His bank had warned him that such a transfer can take more than twenty-four hours. Still Ambrose wasn't sure he'd ever see the money, not if he could pull off what he planned for Brad and Jenny tonight.

Money wouldn't be the measure of his revenge from those two. Besides, he knew that a guy like Brad was going to bluff his way through the deal and try to weasel his way out of paying him the money. His deal with Lisette was where the money would come, not just the initial investment she'd make for him of $50,000 but the ongoing dividends that the business would pay him for years to come. Pole dancing exercise clubs were the wave of the future, he was sure of it.

That's why he sat nervously waiting in the coffee shop for Lisette to come through with her end of the deal. She'd sign the papers, tomorrow he'd give her the original copy of the diary and it was done. With her new pole dancing venture, he'd soon have a piece of that cash coming in and he'd be rich. He liked deals like that— simple and lucrative.

Then a cell phone rang.

The guy at the table next to him gave Ambrose an irritated look as the phone rang again. Suddenly Ambrose realized it was coming from the pocket of his jeans.

"Oh, yeah, sorry," Ambrose said, grabbing for the phone. "I forgot I had it."

Ambrose punched a button to answer the call but all he got was static. He hurried to a table by a window for better reception.

"Hello? Who is this?" he asked as he spoke again into the phone.

"What do you mean, who is this?" the voice on the other end yelled back.

"Oh!" Ambrose said realizing who it was. "It's your phone, so it's you. Sorry."

"Yeah, it's me, Brad. Remember?"

"Sure, sure, I remember."

"So, how's it going?"

"It's going," Ambrose said trying to sound nonchalant. "It's going good here. How about you?"

"Don't ask about me, you idiot. Who cares how I am? Have you found her yet?"

Damn, Ambrose thought. *What did Bufford expect, instant results?*

"I'm close," Ambrose said carefully, trying to keep the irritation out of his voice. "But it's not in the bag yet. I'm working out a few snags." That wasn't a lie, he thought. He was close to Lisette if he didn't count how many floors up in the hotel she was from where he was in the coffee shop.

"So how close is close?" Brad cut in.

"Jesus, Bufford. You've got to cool your jets. You've had this daughter for twenty-nine years and you couldn't care less about her, but now suddenly you have to see her."

"I know," Bufford said apologetically. "But until yesterday I thought she belonged to that bastard Ralph. Listen, if you find her in the next twenty-four hours, I'll give you an extra five-hundred-dollar bonus."

"Really? On top of the 500 bucks and the $50,000? No shit!"

Ambrose wasn't impressed, but he'd take the cash. He had bigger fish to fry and he didn't even mention the $25,000 Brad was supposed to wire him upfront. Ambrose doubted he would.

"Yes, I told you it was important for me to find my daughter," Brad replied.

Ambrose grinned from ear to ear, feeling like a dog that had been thrown a bone by a guy who in a few hours wouldn't realize what hit him.

So Ambrose played along with him. "In that case, I'll really get on it. Yes, sir. I will."

"Great!" Bufford replied. "Call me anytime day or night if you have news."

"You've got it!" Ambrose said enthusiastically. Out of the corner of his eye, he saw Erick enter the coffee shop. "Look, something's come up," Ambrose said into the phone. "I've got to go."

"Is she there?" Brad yelled. "Is that what's happening? Oh my God! Did you find her?" Brad's voice went up a few more octaves with each question.

"Sure, sure I found her, but I'm not sure…" His voice trailed off as he waved Erick over to his table.

Ambrose couldn't tell from the sour look on Erick's face if something was wrong or not. Damn! Was Lisette going to renege on this deal? He needed her to sign the papers tonight and for Brad to believe that this was all going to happen for him and Jenny tomorrow. It was a lot to juggle, but Ambrose had his priorities. If his deal fell through with Lisette tonight, his scheme wouldn't work. Still he had to play along with Brad and get him off the phone.

Brad was shouting at Ambrose now. "Not sure about what? What's the problem? What is it about her?"

Ambrose hedged. "She's like her mother, you know."

"Like Marie? How is she like Marie?" Brad was frantic. "Where are you? I'm coming there right now."

"No, don't come here," Ambrose had said too much already. He was worried about Lisette, though. Was she a liar like her mother? In the diary, Marie had told Brad all those lies. Had Lisette sent Erick here to tell him something different than what she had told him upstairs in the room? Had she lied to him too?

"Brad, I've got to go," Ambrose's voice exploded into the phone, but he added before he hung up, "I'll let you know as soon as I've got something."

Shit! He couldn't have Bufford racing down to the hotel this afternoon or tonight. He was counting on him being off the social circuit with the governor after all the public scandals and front-page stories. And he was counting on the fact that Brad wouldn't tell Jenny, his wife, anything about Lisette either. Men are such cowards. He needed Jenny to be unaware of Lisette and all that had gone on between him and Brad for the last few days. The less she knew, the more she'd be embarrassment, humiliated, and destroyed by what Ambrose had in store for her tonight.

As Erick approached the table, Ambrose motioned for him to sit down. Maybe he was going give him the signed paper from

Lisette. But why would Lisette trust a guy like Erick—someone she barely knew—to represent her in such an important matter? Still, he didn't care who brought him the signed paper. He just wanted to seal the deal.

Yes! Ambrose thought, and beamed at the paper Erick laid down on the table with Lisette's signature.

Oh my God, yes!

◈ ◈ ◈

Brad was burning with excitement and frantic with anxiety as his call to Ambrose ended.

Thank God he had taken Everett's advice and given Ambrose a "burner" phone, not only so no one could trace the account back to Brad or the governor, but also so he could trace where a phone call was coming from with the GPS feature on it. With that tracing device, Brad would know where Ambrose was when he took the call. With guys like him, Brad knew he'd have to verify everything and use a few tricks of his own.

The GPS from the call told Brad that Ambrose was in the same hotel coffee shop where he and Everett had met Ambrose yesterday. That fact made Brad think that either Ambrose really liked that place or the particular hotel where that shop was located had some significance in all this. Ambrose did say that Lisa was in town for only a few days. Maybe she was staying at that hotel. With Ambrose stationed there, he could easily have access to her and deal with Brad as well. Maybe Lisa was in town for an event or a program. That could be it. Ambrose didn't say she'd come into town specifically to meet him about the diary.

That made Brad wonder. What was going on at that hotel this week or this weekend? He got on his laptop and found the hotel's website on the internet. He clicked on the "Events" tab at the top of the page and scrolled down to see if any conferences or meetings were being held for businesspeople. But then, he thought, maybe

Lisa wasn't in that crowd. At only twenty-nine years of age, she might not yet be a business owner—or married to one.

Then he saw the listing that read: "*Survivor Strong, Thriver Resilient Tenth Anniversary Gala starting at 8:00 p.m. tonight.*" That was the event Jenny was attending to honor the college student killed ten years ago on the college campus. The listing went on to describe the event as "celebrating the many accomplishments made since Lacey's death by the nonprofit organization formed to combat violence against women." It looked to Brad as though people were coming from all over the country, including a group of wealthy angel investors who had put their money into the start-up of this program. Brad clicked on the link to organization's website and found the list of the investors there. No Lisa was listed, but once again, Brad reminded himself a twenty-nine-year-old woman was unlikely to donate a sizeable amount of money to charity.

Still, he was intrigued by the possibility that this could be the event his Lisa was in town for. Although he had been included on the invite to the governor for the event, Jenny and Everett had crossed it off the list for him. It was too public, too many press people would be there, and the topic was too close to the focus of his own near-indictment this past week on sexual harassment charges. But none of that made a difference to Brad now. He had to be there. This was important to him. His daughter might be there. He had to see her!

He grabbed his cell phone and auto-dialed Jenny's number. He knew that she had a busy Saturday planned, probably appearing at several events during the day before going to this event at the hotel in the evening. When she had one event after another on her schedule, it was difficult to get a personal call in to her. But he had to talk to her now and finally tell her about Lisa. Sure, she'd be shocked and surprised by the news, but he also wanted to gush to her about being a father and congratulate her on becoming a stepmother. For years, he had been a stepfather to Maryssa, who was about the same age as Lisa. Now it was his turn to be a daddy.

Placing the call, Brad expected to hear Jenny's voice on the other end, so he was shocked to hear Everett's voice instead.

"What the hell, Everett? I'm calling Jenny's cell!"

"She must have forwarded her personal calls to me," Everett replied apologetically. "She does that sometimes."

"What? When she's trying to avoid me?" Brad replied angrily, but his voice changed suddenly. "You were my next call anyway." Then he went on exuberantly, "I found her, Everett. I found Lisa. Or at least Ambrose has found her. I'm going to meet her probably tomorrow. On Sunday. Isn't that amazing?"

"I'm very happy for you," Everett said earnestly. "It must feel wonderful."

"But there is something our old pal, Ambrose, said about her that is very curious."

"What's that? That she killed two priests and a nun last week?"

"You're close."

Everett gasped. "I was kidding."

Brad took a breath. This was hard enough to tell Everett. How was he ever going to tell Jenny? He took another breath and then continued, "She may be a stripper, like her mother. Ambrose said something like that on the phone just now. About her being like her mother."

Everett signed. "That could mean anything. But I'm concerned that you haven't told Jenny anything about this yet, have you?"

"No, not that I have a daughter. I'm hoping she'll take it as it comes."

But even as he said it, the enormity of what he wanted Jenny to accept was sinking in. Could Jenny, who had become so unglued with the FBI investigation into his past, embrace Lisa as her step-daughter? Was he out of his mind to think she'd be anything but fu-rious at him? Or that Jenny would accept her? His parents never did.

"I told you. You should've let Jenny know about this Marie and the baby days ago." Everett broke in and then he stopped. "Never mind. Even if you had told her ahead of time, this would still come as a shock. I don't envy you, man. Can I do anything?"

"You mean like tell her for me?" Brad said, half teasingly. For a second, he let himself feel the relief he'd have if someone else could deliver the news to Jenny. But Everett fell silent on the other end of the phone, and Brad came back to reality.

"Don't worry," Brad reassured him. "I'll tell her. But could you try and get me an audience with the Queen as soon as possible? I need to talk to her about tonight. I think Lisa is staying at the hotel and will be at the event. If I can go, Jenny and I can meet her there together, and Ambrose will be out of the picture. Don't you see? We'll have figured it out ourselves, and I won't need to pay him or be beholden to him in any way. So what if Lisa is a stripper? I don't like that, but she is my daughter."

"Jenny will hate it," Everett interrupted.

Brad moaned. "I know, I know. Already this being a father is tougher than I thought."

"Maybe we can get her into one of those job training programs Jenny has been touting. Get her a reputable job. Show the press that these programs do work."

Brad chuckled. "You're good, Everett—that's a really good maneuver. A little far-fetched, but did anyone ever tell you that you'd make a great campaign manager?"

"It has been rumored that I am the governor's campaign manager," he said sarcastically. "But on days like this, I'm not sure that I want the job."

"We'll get through this," Brad assured him. "Keep me posted about Jenny."

Everett signed off and Brad hung up his phone. He was prepared to wait as long as it took for Jenny to return his call. He'd ask her about tonight, but he knew that no matter what Jenny said, he was going to show up and be there for Lisa. He had learned that lesson the hard way with Marie, and he wasn't about to make that same mistake again.

This time he'd be his own man and make his own decisions about how he wanted to live his life.

This time he was going to do it right.

❖ ❖ ❖

Sophie was nervous. She stood at the side of the stage and watched as the hotel workers and her volunteers worked to arrange the Tenth Anniversary Gala. There was about an hour left before the gala started and only half an hour until the VIP reception began in a small area behind the stage.

On the stage, bleachers were being assembled for the women's choir that would sing a few inspirational songs. In addition, there were bouquets of flowers being placed around the podium in the middle of the stage. There she and the other presenters would speak, including Governor Jenny Jablonski. She was one of the few politicians who had supported Sophie's work from the beginning, and Sophie wanted to honor her tonight.

It wasn't easy for the governor to do so in the beginning when she was the lieutenant governor and the governor she served under was accused of abusing his first wife. But Jenny always showed up at Sophie's events, helped her find state funds, and ever since she became governor, she had supported many of the issues Sophie was working on, even when she was criticized for doing too much for women. Sophie liked the stance the governor took when she was asked by the press about being a woman governor. She'd say, "I'm not a woman governor; I'm a woman who happens to be a governor." Sophie was happy to have her by her side for this occasion.

Sophie was also pleased that the governor's husband was not attending tonight. There had been too much in the press lately about his sexual harassment of women in a previous job, and his presence could be an embarrassment given the topic of tonight's event.

But mostly Sophie was nervous. This was her night, as much as it was Lacey's. It was the tenth anniversary to mark the death of her best friend, a woman she met on her first day of college, with whom she felt such an immediate bond that she couldn't imagine them not spending the rest of their lives somehow together. And yet, the unimaginable had happened. Dead at nineteen years of age, Lacey had been struck down with a volley of bullets by a crazy man who thought if he couldn't have her, no one else could. Yes, now she was bound to Lacey for the rest of her life, but in another way. Lacey's death has given Sophie her life work, her passion, her reason for being. Sometimes she felt bad that something so good came out of such a horrible action. If she had her choice, Sophie would give up finding her life's passion just to have Lacey again by her side, alive, laughing and joking as she was always able to do no matter what the situation.

Yet in spite of her sadness and ambivalence, at times Sophie did want to celebrate the good things that had come since Lacey's death. With all the speakers and dignitaries talking about Lacey and the legacy she left behind, Sophie knew that Lacey was not forgotten, and that was so important. From the moment she heard that Lacey was gone forever, Sophie had made a vow to do everything that she and Lacey had planned to do together after graduation to change the world.

She knew that many people in her life had expected her to do something very different, and she fought those expectations every day. To please her parents, she did enroll in law school after college and finished after three years, even taking and passing the bar exam. Her father wanted her to work in his law firm, but she turned him down. It just wasn't in her heart. Lacey was still there, poking at her to do what they had planned to do together—using the law to help poor people. Instead she went to work at Legal Aid, a good experience, but again not enough for her. She lasted two years and then she was done. She left there with no other job prospects, and her parents were very upset.

"What are you doing to do?" her mother had wailed.

Her father was even more direct. "I spent all that money sending you to law school, and you're just throwing it away."

"I'm not, Daddy," she insisted, trying to explain it to him. "I'm just trying to find a different way to use the knowledge I gained. It will be okay, really, Daddy, it will."

But he wasn't happy. "Don't think you can be one of those boomerang kids," he added. "You can't come back to live with your parents and have us support you long after your childhood is over!"

But she didn't plan on doing anything of the kind. She struck out on her own and slowly built an organization, focusing first on making changes at colleges so students like Lacey wouldn't be so vulnerable and alone in dealing with relationship violence, sexual assault, or sexual harassment. She then focused on helping to ensure that women would have equal pay with men and the opportunity to pursue any career or interest, including law, science, medicine, or any other field not traditionally open to women. She called this economically empowering women, and the idea caught on.

At Lacey's school, in her part-time job Sophie worked hard to make that campus safer. Initially only a few hours a week, she was now working there on a part-time basis coordinating the effort to get federal and state funding for a Campus Coordinated Community Team (CCT) to reduce domestic violence, dating violence, sexual assault, and stalking on the campus. She got support from government officials, such as the current Governor Jenny Jablonski, to build this multidisciplinary team that included police, local victim services, and other mental health and substance abuse program providers for both adults and children. She worked closely with the team to address issues and make the school safer for all, students and staff alike. Many of those community programs, such as the town's YWCA, now had open office hours on campus to help students. She also implemented a bystander program to teach students how to intervene if they witnessed violence on the campus—including sexual assault, stalking, and relationship violence. This program, the one Sophie believed could have saved Lacey's life ten years ago, attempts to override the common bystander effect, which is the tendency for people in crowds to do nothing when they see something wrong. Or they assume someone else will help.

But Sophie's real passion was her *Survivor Strong, Thriver Resilient* program that brought women who have experienced abuse together to take the journey from victim to survivor to thriver. Sophie knew that no one, including Lacey, saw how much danger she was in when she left her relationship with Ari. While she had never been physically assaulted or threatened by him, it was only at the moment of her death that she realized she was in a dangerous situation. Because Lacey didn't survive that night, Sophie wanted to help other women to thrive after abuse as Lacey could not!

Sophie started with the idea of providing a workshop with exercises and activities to bring more positive energy into the lives of women who had been abused and help them manifest their dreams and desires now that they were safe. When this material resonated so strongly with the women and helped them move on to new and better lives so successfully, Sophie developed the material even further and now was close to publishing a *Thriver Workbook* and spreading her work even farther out into the world.

All this and more—for instance, the men's initiative, A Call to Men—was happening now, and Sophie knew that tonight was their night to celebrate. Her heart was full! She was so pleased that Lisette had come to celebrate this momentous occasion with her. Although Lisette had never met Lacey when she was alive, Lisette had a special relationship with Lacey as the holder of her spirit for a while after she died. Sophie had grown close to Lisette during that time, and she was happy when her grandmother Radiance helped Lacey's spirit cross over.

So tonight, Sophie was thrilled when Lisette came striding across the stage to see her before the festivities began.

"How are you doing?" Lisette said, grabbing her arm and pulling her into a warm embrace. "Lacey would love this!" Lisette whispered in her ear, then released her. Sophie spun Lisette around so she could see how spectacular she looked.

Lisette was wearing a long, black dress, simple but elegant. It accentuated all her curves but didn't over advertise any. *The exact opposite effect of how a stripper might dress*, Sophie mused.

"You look fabulous!" Sophie said, smiling at her. "Breathtaking!"

"Thank you! I didn't want to be overdressed. And this is a special outfit, one that Lacey had approved of out of all the ones in my closet for her funeral."

Sophie had to laugh. Anyone else would have thought that maudlin, but Sophie knew how, in Lisette's special way with Lacey, it was a positive thing.

Then Sophie looked up to see Erick coming their way. "I hear that you two have been seeing each other again," Sophie said loudly to Lisette just as Erick came up next to Lisette and wrapped his arm around her. "You two were the talk of the angel investor's lunch on Thursday. They say that sparks were flying!"

Erick's face reddened, but he countered, teasing her. "It wasn't our fault. Somebody was doing a little matchmaking this week, right, Sophie?"

"I would never do that," Sophie said with a laugh. "But I do like it when two people I adore get together."

Suddenly, music blared out of a speaker and then abruptly stopped. "Oh dear!" Sophie exclaimed. "That's not good. It's my job to check on how the music for the program is going. Why don't the two of you move into the VIP area at the back of the stage? The governor should be here any minute. I think you, Ms. Attila the Hunny, and the governor are our top VIPs this evening!"

Sophie felt so full of joy. She hugged Erick first, then Lisette.

She held Lisette an extra moment as she repeated in her ear what Lisette had said to her earlier.

"Lacey would love this!"

CHAPTER TWELVE

Saturday, October 17, 2009

The Arrival

Ambrose was on high alert as cars and limousines drove up to the hotel that evening to attend the Tenth Anniversary Gala. He had several important pieces to pull off tonight, and he didn't want any glitches.

First, his guest of honor should be arriving soon. Not many people tonight would recognize him, but there was one person in the crowd tonight who could pick him out easily. So Ambrose made sure his special guest's appearance would be disguised until it was time for his identity to be revealed before everyone.

Second, he was watching for the governor's car and entourage to make an appearance. He didn't expect Brad tonight, but he was on the watch for any sign that Jenny had any indication that Lisette, Brad's daughter, was in the crowd. He wasn't sure how he might be able to tell that from appearances, but he suspected that Jenny would show something somehow in her exterior. She was not known for having a poker face, and she could be a mean one sometimes. Ambrose should know after incurring her wrath at one point in the not-too-distant past. He wasn't sure she would remember him, but he didn't want to take a chance that she might. He'd watch for her and duck out of sight until she entered the hotel.

Third, of course, was Lisette and her newly proclaimed boy-friend Erick. He was the least worried about them. A few hours ago, he thought things might not keep turning his way when Erick visited him downstairs in the hotel coffee shop with a sour look on his face. Ambrose took the look to mean that Lisette was refusing to sign the paperwork, but he was wrong. He had snagged her into his crazy scheme about pole dancing exercise clubs, and she was dazzled by the shining object he had flashed before her. It was a brand-new, right out of the box, father-daughter relationship with a man who abandoned her almost thirty years ago. She went for it. Go figure!

With that deal in place, Ambrose could now focus on Brad. Yes, he would know who his daughter was by tomorrow for sure, but Ambrose hadn't exactly explained how he would find out. The plan was to publicly expose his daughter as Attila the Hunny tonight in front of his unsuspecting wife, Governor Jenny Jablonski! Too bad Brad had to miss all the excitement, but Ambrose was sure that he would feel its impact tonight when Jenny got home.

It was one of his best schemes, and Ambrose loved it. Of course, it was only foolproof if Wiley could play his part perfectly. Ambrose told Wily he had an opportunity, as the man who once owned the Pussycat Meow's Club, to get his revenge against Lisette tonight, the woman who had so mercilessly taken the club from him last Wednesday.

Yes, this was going to be a great night all around for payback, Ambrose declared. This would be his proudest moment.

If only his son Mark could see him in action now.

❖ ❖ ❖

Lisette was overwhelmed by the number of people who came up to her and thanked her for coming tonight to the Tenth Anniversary Gala. Maybe it was because of her million-dollar donation to Sophie's wonderful organization, or maybe they were just excited to meet Atilla the Hunny in person. So many people at the VIP reception liked the smell of money in the air, loved to be around it, but others just seemed to want to come up to her and talk about how much they enjoyed her pole dancing videos on the club's website.

Lisette was amazed by that. The videos were something she had been wanting to do to encourage women to improve their physical health and stamina, but Todd and the rest of the company management team thought the idea was a little silly. But what did they know? Ambrose, of all people, seemed to get it. Yeah, it was a pretty crazy idea for him to want to invest in a business she hadn't even started yet, but maybe he had something there. If only she didn't have to deal with him. But, as Todd assured her yesterday after reviewing the agreement Ambrose wanted her to sign, any lawyer would be able to find a way for her to wiggle out of it and keep Ambrose and his craziness away from her and the company. Todd told her she'd probably have to pay him a little money to get lost. Still, no matter how much money might come his way in this deal, Lisette knew that a guy like Ambrose would burn a hole through it very fast.

After her initial sense of overwhelm, Lisette was feeling good as she made her way through the crowd at the VIP reception. She was enjoying talking and meeting people. At some point, Erick let her know that Governor Jablonski had arrived and soon would make an entrance into the VIP reception area.

"I know you wanted to meet her, and I'm sure she wants to meet you," Erick said with a laugh. "No one donates a million dollars to a cause that Jenny Jablonski loves without getting some very special attention."

"What are you expecting, some kind of grand entrance from her?" Lisette said teasingly. "You know, she could come flying down one of those ropes hanging from the back of this gigantic stage." She and Erick both looked up.

"That area above the stage actually is called the 'fly space.'" Erick explained. "Did you know that? I bet you've been on a lot of stages in your life. Maybe you've wanted to put a harness on and fly across one of them!"

"No, I've never seen a stage like this. And what is that glass booth up there on the side?" She pointed above them and to one side, but not as high up as the fly space. "I thought I saw someone in there a minute ago."

Erick shook his head. "It doesn't seem like anyone should be up there. Unless it's the governor's security staff. They would pay attention to something like that. They look for any possible breach. Can't be too careful!"

Lisette laughed. "I forgot you worked as a bouncer. Always thinking about security and keeping a place safe!"

He smiled at her, perhaps remembering, Lisette thought, the times he kept her safe at the Pussycat's Meow where they first met. He had hands the size of Texas, and all the dancers wanted him to be the bouncer on duty when they were up on the stage.

Suddenly there was a small commotion in the room, and Erick grabbed her arm. Turning her around, he whispered in her ear, "The Governor has arrived. Now the fun begins!"

❖ ❖ ❖

Ambrose was beside himself.

Everything that he planned was going wrong, so wrong.

It started with Wiley. He showed up late, claiming the limo wasn't on time, but that can't have been true. He must have taken too long putting on his tuxedo, wig, and makeup. They had practiced putting all that on earlier in the week, and Ambrose thought Wiley had it down. Now he wasn't so sure.

Ambrose knew this scheme was a little ambitious for a man like Wiley. He had some admirable qualities in that he ran, quite successfully, for a good many years a very sleazy strip club. Ambrose had frequented that club for years, although there were times he'd been banned from it—like when Lisette was dancing there. But Wiley also had a gripe against Lisette and her Atilla the Hunny franchise for taking away his club when he couldn't keep the banks who held the notes on his loans happy anymore. His business suffered with more sex shows available on internet websites and classier places opening up like Lisette's franchise. And so, Wiley had no choice but to bear the humiliation—his word!—of selling his club to Lisette this past week. She had demanded that she personally deal with him and his lawyers by phone and insisted that she be at the closing of the sale in town.

Hearing of Wiley's agony and anger toward Lisette, Ambrose made a proposition to him Thursday after he found and read Marie's diary and figured out who Lisette's real father was.

"How would you like to do something that would really piss off Lisette and mess her up good?" Ambrose asked Wiley. "She'd never be able to show her face in this town again!"

Wiley's eyes got really big. "That would be great. What do you have in mind?"

Ambrose explained that he had recently acquired some information that Lisette was related to a close relative of the governor.

"You know I'm not a big fan of the governor, and you don't like Lisette for what she did to you," Ambrose continued. "What do you say if we embarrass the hell out of those two bitches by letting people know their connection in a really public way!"

Wiley was excited, and so the plot began. Ambrose got a ticket for Wiley to both the event and the VIP reception before it, convincing him to make a good-sized donation so he'd easily move among those with money. Wiley didn't like the donation part of it, but Ambrose suggested he take it out of the proceeds of the sale. "It will be a nice return on the investment to see Lisette go down in such a public way," Ambrose told him, and finally Wiley agreed.

The plan was that Wiley would be disguised with hair and makeup so Lisette wouldn't recognize him right away. He would arrive early at the VIP reception and get the governor and Lisette together at the right moment to make the big reveal. If that wasn't possible, then Wiley would get a front row seat at the event and rush the stage during the program.

Ambrose had given Wiley a script to read aloud either at the reception or from the stage, whichever he could manage. Bottom line, he had to let the governor and the entire gathering know that Attila the Hunny was the governor's stepdaughter. The more public the announcement, the better—but however it happened, it was sure to cause a commotion and bring the house down!

Ambrose wanted to destroy these people's lives, and he didn't care how. Best of all, they wouldn't know that he had any part in it. He'd never appear at either event, but he still planned to have a bird's eye view of it all. He had staked out the perfect location tonight. He found it yesterday when he was at the hotel to meet with Everett and Brad.

The whole thing was coming together nicely. He already had a signed document from Lisette solidifying a $50,000 investment in her new pole dancing business. He had $500 in cash from Brad and was waiting for the $25,000 from him to be wired to his bank as promised. His bank had told him he'd have it by Monday.

Now the plan was for humiliation and embarrassment to be delivered tonight to all of them.

This was Ambrose's best revenge.

❖ ❖ ❖

Brad never did get to talk to Jenny about coming with her to the hotel for the Tenth Anniversary Gala.

He didn't get a chance to tell her that he used a fake name to get into the event at the last minute including the VIP reception.

He figured he'd need all the time he could get with her to smooth things over.

When he arrived thankfully no one recognized him as he picked up his ticket and entered the backstage area where the VIP reception was being held. Once inside, Brad stood at the door for a moment until he caught Jenny's eye. She glared at him at first, then gave him her steely-eyed look. He watched her excuse herself from the group of people she was talking to and walk slowly but deliberately toward him.

"What the hell are you doing here?" she snarled at him in a loud whisper before Brad had a chance to say a word.

"I tried to get you on the phone all day," he replied. "I wanted to tell you. I didn't want to just show up."

"But you did. I'm not pleased." She looked around quickly. "You've got to get out of here before everyone sees you. Do you understand?" Her voice was high and shrill now.

Brad remained calm. "Look, if you just give me a moment, I'll explain." He paused waiting for her to react, but when she didn't he went on. "I have a chance tonight to meet someone I've wanted to meet for thirty years. It's the most wonderful thing that's ever happened to me." His eyes were shining brightly until he saw the stone-cold look on Jenny's face.

"The most wonderful thing ever?" she spit back at him sarcastically. "What about me? Don't I count as something wonderful in your life?"

"But of course," he said looking intently at her, until something caught his eye across the room.

"Oh my God!" he exclaimed. "This is unbelievable. I knew it was true. I knew I would see her here."

"See who?" Jenny spun around to see what Brad was looking at.

"That girl over there in the long black dress. The stunning one."

"Jesus, Brad! Are you crazy? You're here to pick up that young thing? She's half your age. She could be your daughter."

"Yes," he said simply, looking back at Jenny now, holding her eyes. "Yes, my dear, that's what I'm trying to tell you. That is my daughter!"

❖ ❖ ❖

Lisette looked up at Erick, trying to get his attention, but he was talking intently to a man standing next to him. The crowd around her had dwindled for the moment, and she really wanted another glass of wine. Maybe Erick would walk with her over to the bar. But when she saw the crowd of people around it, she looked around for a waiter she could signal to bring her another drink. Instead, she saw a man talking to the governor, who was staring and pointing directly at her.

Lisette was used to that. The guy might have seen her at some strip club in the past, or maybe he got off on her picture or video on the Internet. But who was he?

Lisette had met the governor a few minutes ago, and it went well, but this man wasn't with her then. Lisette thought Sophie had told her that her husband was not going to be there tonight. Lisette thought the governor was nice; she seemed interested to meet Lisette, but there wasn't a lot of warmth there. She seemed happy to move on and meet someone else. Erick wasn't right about how making a million-dollar donation to Sophie's organization might get her in good with the Governor. But Lisette wasn't surprised. There were a lot of women who didn't ever want to meet her, but their husbands did!

Now she saw the man the governor had been talking to coming quickly across the room toward her and Erick, the governor trailing behind him.

Lisette nudged Erick's arm. "Sorry to interrupt. Erick, do you know who that guy is coming in our direction with the governor?"

Erick looked up and muttered, "That's her husband. His name is Brad. But he's not supposed to be here, I don't understand why..."

Lisette cut in. "Excuse me, his name is what?"

But before anyone could say another word, the guy was in front of her.

"Lisa? Is that you? I thought you'd be here. I had to come."

"What?" Lisette looked at him, and then at the Governor. "You must have me confused with someone else. My name is Lisette." She saw his face change for a moment.

The governor interrupted, "See, I told you, Brad. You have the wrong person here."

"Wait," Lisette said quickly. "Your name is Brad? I *am* Lisa. I was born Lisa. I changed my name after my father Ralph..." her voice trailed off.

"I know Ralph. He's not your father," the man insisted. "I'm your father. I'm Brad Bufford. You are Marie's daughter. You look just like her. I've read her diary. My God, I saw you from across the room in that dress, and I could have sworn it was Marie."

"Who's Marie?" the governor asked sharply, then rambled on. "How do you know Marie? Who is this Ralph?" She pointed at Lisette. "And who is she again? Your daughter? This can't be true. I just met her. She didn't say she was your daughter!"

But Lisette wasn't listening anymore to her or anyone else. She rushed toward Brad and he took her into his arms and held her so tight that Lisette thought she'd break. *This is how it feels to be loved unconditionally,* she thought. *That kind of love. So reliable. Wow!*

She let herself be held like that, until a voice yelled from high above her, screaming out her name. "No, Lisette! NO!"

Then there was a loud crash, a terrible rumble, and lots of people screaming. But all Lisette felt was Brad holding on to her. Then she felt Erick behind her wrapping his arms around her too. She felt protected and shielded from all the craziness. She felt love all around.

It was so powerful and wonderful, she began to cry.

CHAPTER THIRTEEN

Saturday, October 17, 2009

Repercussions

Ambrose was in a rage. How had this thing gone so wrong?

Sure, his scheme was a little hairbrained to start with, but it would have worked if only Wiley had played his part. Ambrose had watched him from up above the stage in the glassed-in booth he found yesterday when he had scouted a location from which to see it all. Wiley was supposed to announce at the VIP reception in front of everyone that Lisette, a.k.a. Atilla the Hunny, who used to dance in his strip club, was the stepdaughter of the governor.

Ambrose didn't expect Wiley to go into all the details of this embarrassing situation—how Marie, Lisette's mother, was Brad's lover years ago, and how he had abandoned Lisette, his daughter, as a child. He'd just let the governor be shocked at hearing the accusation and let her find out the details later.

But Wiley never got to any of that. Ambrose was sure that all those explanations were going on now in the Bufford/Jablonski family as to who was who and what was what and why. But Ambrose was missing all of that. Instead he was being wheeled out to the ambulance waiting at the front of the hotel, and he was furious about that too.

Ambrose had fallen when the door to the glassed-in booth where he was standing burst open and he tumbled down the catwalk to the ground. How all that happened, he wasn't sure, but he thought it might have been due to the fact that when he saw Lisette and Brad actually meeting on the stage below without all the fanfare and attention of the crowd around him, he had pounded on the door of the booth so hard that he caused it to fly open.

His pain was excruciating now, and all he could get from the emergency medical personnel was that he probably had broken his leg in several places. But they and the police were making it sound as if it was more than that. He hadn't fallen directly from the catwalk to the stage which surely would have killed him. Instead he remembered rolling down the catwalk to the stage floor without coming in contact with anyone else in the process. Desperately he tried to remember what happened before the drugs he'd been given for the pain kicked in. Everyone had to understand that this wasn't his fault! He had so many people to blame!

He recalled being up there in that booth, waiting to see the moment when Jenny Jablonski got her due, humiliated in front of everyone by the past actions of her husband who once again failed to let her know what an ass he was. Never could keep his hands off the women, they'd say, and Jenny bore the brunt of it. This time there was a child to prove his depravity.

Instead, what Ambrose saw from high above was Wiley forgetting his part and walking away from the mission at hand. Instead of confronting the governor and Lisette, he was standing by the bar drinking and stuffing appetizers in his mouth as though he hadn't eaten for months. What was he thinking? He'd thrown away his own money and lost a chance to get back at Lisette. From what Ambrose could see, Lisette didn't even know Wiley was there or why.

Ambrose would never have a chance to tell her either. He wouldn't be able to tell her what he saw from up there in that stupid booth—how Brad recognized her from across the room and came right up to her. Did she look that much like Marie? Ambrose did remember Lisette showing her a picture years ago of her and her mother. He might have even remarked at the time, "You look just like your mom."

Why didn't he figure that Brad would recognize her quickly? But Ambrose hadn't expected Brad to show up tonight. How did that happen? Did he tip Brad's hand by something he said to him in their last phone call? Something that made Brad believe Lisette would be at this hotel and at this event?

He wouldn't be able to figure much more of this out right now, and he didn't care anyway. The drugs were great, so much better than being in pain. It was nice to be on such a buzz. He remembered that buzz from the last time Lisette was in town. That day he had burst into that woman's apartment and injured himself, just like tonight.

Now the drugs had brought on, once again, the long, slow easing of his mind.

No worries, no cares.

Why hadn't he remembered how wonderful pure oblivion like this feels?

❖ ❖ ❖

From the moment Lisette saw Brad staring at her across the room to when he called her Lisa and said he was her father to now standing here with him, she couldn't stop crying tears of joy. What her mother had told her on one of those shamanic journeys to the Upper World she had taken years ago with Radiance had come true.

"Ralph is not your father. Believe it when you find out."

She was still trying to believe it. There were so many things to understand, so many thoughts going through her head.

But right now, she was learning more minute by minute about what Ambrose was doing in the rafts of that stage and what he expected to watch happen down below. After he came rolling down that backstage catwalk, he landed in a heap on the floor, screaming, cursing at people and demanding money. It was a nightmare! At the first sound of the disturbance, the governor's security people scooped her up and rushed her out of the area. The governor was gone without a word, leaving Lisette, Brad, Erick, and Sophie just standing there.

Then medical people swarmed into the area behind the stage to deal with injuries from falling debris after Ambrose's stunt, and the police arrived and began asking questions. It seemed that the governor's presence at the time and a rumor being spread by some that Ambrose had been screaming, "Jenny Jablonski, I'm going to get you!" as he came tumbling down to the back of the stage needed to be investigated.

Lisette couldn't believe what a mess this was.

"Are you okay?" Erick asked her, taking her hand and squeezing it. She nodded her head, and they stood together silently, stunned. Then he said to Sophie, "Can't say when we'll be able to leave. Looks like the cops aren't letting anyone go."

"No," Brad interjected, "no one will be allowed to leave the reception area until witness statements have been taken by the police from everyone since the governor is involved."

"What?" Sophie exclaimed. "The Gala has to go on. People are out front in the auditorium waiting for reception to be over and the program to begin. They paid money to hear the governor speak and meet Lisette—Attila the Hunny! They expect a program. What am I going to say to them?"

"I don't know, but it looks like that isn't going to happen," Erick said. Just then a police officer came up to Sophie and asked, "Are you in charge here?"

"Yes, I am, officer. I'm running this event. I'd like to be able to proceed."

"Sorry, ma'am, you can't. It's not safe here back stage and the folks in front of the curtain will have to leave, too. There are security issues. Show's over for the night."

"But this is a fundraiser for my nonprofit! This is important!" Sophie replied with desperation in her voice.

"No, ma'am. This is a crime scene. We have to investigate and see what we have here. Several people may have been injured, and there was a threat to the governor."

"But we didn't see anything," Lisette protested to the cop. "We were all here up front. We don't know what happened back there!"

"Fine," the officer replied firmly. "You didn't see anything. We'll write that in our report." Then he walked away, shouting out the same orders to others in the crowd as he did. Lisette cursed him under her breath, but she knew there was nothing she could do for Sophie. She felt awful.

"But there was no crime!" Sophie insisted to Lisette. "I went to law school. I can't see what Ambrose did except maybe trespass up in the rafters. Is that a crime? And only Ambrose was injured, as far as I can see. People trying to duck falling debris were screaming, but no one was seriously hurt."

Brad shook his head. "Sorry, Sophie. With the governor here, this kind of thing gets cranked up into high gear pretty fast. Trust me, I've lived with being in the governor's entourage for a while now. Every possible threat to the governor is considered a high priority. And it should be that way." He smiled and added, "The governor happens to be my wife!"

"Right!" Sophie muttered. "But now I've got to figure out what to say to all those people out in front who won't want to leave without some kind of show, as well as the ones back here who don't want to stay and be interrogated by the cops."

She turned to Erick and asked, "Can you give me a hand? Most of the people back here are donors and board members. You know them. Let's bring out some wine on the house and any kind of food the hotel can rustle up. See if we can calm things down a bit." Then she added as she and Erick moved away, "I'll go out front and make an announcement. Maybe I should offer them a refund. I don't know."

Then her voice trailed off and Lisette and Brad were alone.

Lisette looked at him and sighed. "This is so crazy. You should go. Be with your wife—make sure she is okay."

Brad shook his head. "She's all right. She has a lot of people taking care of her when they go into this emergency mode. I want to stay here with you. I want to make sure *you're* okay."

"I'm fine. It's just that so much is happening all at once. Tonight is crazy, but since I came to town last Wednesday, my whole world has changed. First, Erick is my boyfriend again, then Ambrose shows up with his crazy scheme, and now I'm meeting you. I can't believe it!"

"And I still can't believe how much you look like your mother," he said, his voice full of surprise. "It's so amazing!"

"But I don't look like you," she said, noticing for the first time that his brown eyes and dark hair were a totally different color than hers.

"I know," he agreed. "But it's all spelled out in your mother's diary. The whole story, how we met, how we fell in love, and how she got pregnant. Right before you were born, she told me Ralph was the father. Like an idiot, I believed her. But in the diary, she admits it was a lie. She only said it because she knew my parents would never approve us getting married. They knew she was a dancer and would never accept her." He heaved a deep sigh. "She was right. This was all my parents' doing, and I let them do it."

Lisette winced, feeling bad she didn't know any of this until she read the diary herself yesterday. "I never read the diary," she said, her voice quivering. "It was too hard."

"I can understand that," Brad said sympathetically. "It would be hard to read about your mother and how she sacrificed so much for you."

"Yeah," Lisette said quickly. "But I have to tell you something else. I didn't read the diary when I had it because it was too hard for me to get through all those words."

"You couldn't read?" Brad's voice was full of surprise. "I don't understand. Why not?"

"I read a little now. I get stuck on the big words, though. It's just that my mom used to take me to the library when I was a little kid and we'd read together. When she died, I was only ten years old, and I think...I know that I just stopped reading then. It was too hard to do it without her." Lisette's voice was shaking now.

"You stopped reading at about a fifth-grade level—is what you are telling me?"

"I guess so. No one's ever described it that way. I can read. I just need someone to help me. Todd, my business manager, does that for me. Like today, when he read the paper Ambrose had me sign before he would give me your full name and tell me how to find you."

"You signed a paper?"

"Yeah, it's some crazy deal Ambrose dreamed up. I have a copy. Ambrose wants me to open up pole dancing clubs, like the Attila the Hunny strip clubs I have. And he wants in as an investor."

"An investor?" Brad laughed. "Ambrose doesn't have a pot to piss in, let alone money to invest! He's basically homeless. He works a little at the Community Center for my friend Pedro."

"You had Ambrose checked out?" Lisette asked, impressed that Brad was so careful.

"Of course. But only because he knew where my daughter was, and I didn't. But now you are here!" His face brightened. "And you are my daughter!"

Lisette smiled. "That's why I signed the paper. I wanted to find out your full name. Before that Ambrose would only give me diary pages with names crossed out. "

Brad looked at her, his eyes tearing up. "You did that for me? You were anxious to find me too, huh?"

She nodded, her eyes full too. "But Todd—he's a lawyer too—told me that I could easily get out of the deal with Ambrose." Then she frowned. "Of course, I don't know what happens to the deal now that all this has happened. Funny, I did like Ambrose's idea about pole dancing clubs, though. Might be something we could add to our strip clubs."

"You own strip clubs?" Brad asked her incredulously. "So you are a dancer, just like your mother was."

"Not anymore. I gave it up ten years ago right after I left here to go back to Los Angeles. I couldn't dance anymore after what happened to Lacey."

"That's the girl who was killed at the college back then, right?' Brad interjected. "You were here in town when that happened?"

"Yeah, I was dancing at a club near the campus. But then I quit and got involved in a business. We franchise strip clubs under my stage name, Atilla the Hunny."

"Your act was based on Attila the Hun?"

"Sure, but we run clean clubs, much better than the ones I used to dance in."

"Jesus, maybe we shouldn't be so hard on Ambrose," Brad said with a laugh. "He had quite a scheme to embarrass Jenny and me tonight—and God knows who else! But still, if it wasn't for him, we might never have found each other!"

"But that's what I don't get. You said you knew my mother was pregnant, but you never tried to find me, not once, not ever, in all these years."

"But everyone, including your mother, convinced me that Ralph was your father. How could I have known differently?"

Lisette didn't know the answer to that question, but suddenly she wanted it to be Brad's fault. She wanted him to feel bad about believing the lies everyone had told him about her mother. It was easier that way. Otherwise, she'd have to wonder why her mother never told her who her father really was. How could she lie to her daughter about something as important as that?

Then her mind raced to where it probably shouldn't have gone. She wondered how different things might have been if Brad had been in their lives. Maybe her mother wouldn't have died, and she wouldn't have had to go live with Ralph. She wouldn't have tried to kill him or get stuck in the system. Maybe she wouldn't have become a stripper and had to dance at crappy clubs like the Pussycat. Maybe all the bad things, that could never be undone, would never have happened to her!

"I know if I had been in your life from the start, maybe things would have been different," Brad said, as if reading her mind. "Look, I really screwed up. I want to make it up to you. Your mother did the right thing years ago. She saved you! Now I want to do the right thing. And then maybe you can forgive me some day."

"What about your wife?" Lisette asked him directly now. "She's got a lot to lose with me as her stepdaughter. Can she accept me, or will she be like your parents with my Mom?"

Just then Erick appeared and grabbed her arm. "You've got to come quick. We've got to get out of here. The police will want to talk to you, but I don't think you want to talk to them right now."

"About what?"

"It's Wiley. He's here. He's in a disguise, wearing a wig and bad makeup. He's telling the cops Ambrose sent him. He has this piece of paper, some statement he was supposed to read. He was supposed to publicly announce in front of everyone that you are

Atilla the Hunny and Brad is your father. To embarrass you, Brad, and the governor, I guess."

Erick took a quick breath and continued. "So this story is about to break, Lisette, and I don't think you or Brad want to be talking to the cops or the press tonight."

"The press is here?" Lisette asked quickly, and she watched Brad's eyes get big.

"Yeah, they weren't invited to the VIP reception, but a few are here for the Gala out front. With all the commotion back here and the governor present, the reporters want to find out what's going on. If Ambrose calculated all this to embarrass the governor, he may still get his wish if someone doesn't get control of this now."

Brad looked worried and upset. "Erick's right," he said. "In the world of politics that I live in—and now you live in, too—everything is done to embarrass or undercut somebody running for office or in office. That's what it's all about. Soon the press will get the story. Maybe not with Wiley's name in it, whoever he is, but certainly with yours and mine and Jenny's. It won't be pretty." Then he sighed. "Welcome to my world!"

He took Lisette's hand. "I'm sorry, I have to go find Jenny and be with her. Her team can get me out of here. I'll tell them what's happening." His voice got softer as he held Lisette's eyes. "I'm sorry. So sorry. I want to stay here and find out more about you and how all this happened to us. But I can't. We'll talk. I promise we will. I'll call you. Give me your cell number. Or I'll give you mine. Whatever."

"Yes, okay," Lisette said, searching in her evening bag for something to write her number on. Flustered when she couldn't find anything, suddenly Erick was there, handing Brad a business card.

"Here. Lisette's cell phone number is on the back."

Brad looked at the front of the card. "Is this your gym?" he asked.

"Yeah. I own it. It's by the Capitol."

"Sure, I know the place. I've been there. Nice job. You do good work."

Then he flipped the card over, looked at the back, and turned to Lisette.

"I'll call you. We'll have lunch or something tomorrow. I'll talk to Jenny. I'll sort everything out." Then he warned her, "Get out of here quick. Don't talk to the press. Neither of you want to get in the middle of this. We'll let Jenny's press office handle it. Don't worry—we will survive."

He looked at Lisette for a long moment, holding her eyes. He grabbed her arm and squeezed it gently. "I'll see you tomorrow. I promise. I'll call."

Of course, Lisette believed him. It was reliable love. That was what she wanted from him.

That's what it felt like she got.

CHAPTER FOURTEEN

Sunday, October 18, 2009

We Are Family

From the moment he found out on Thursday that he had a daughter, Brad had fantasized about what he might say when he first laid eyes on her. But none of those imagined moments came anywhere close to the real thing.

Brad couldn't believe it. Her voice even sounded like Marie's. He never thought he'd hear it again in his lifetime. She was Marie. She was Lisette. She was his daughter.

He had found her at last. It was amazing! Somehow the revelation of finding out that he had a daughter and then actually meeting her tonight changed his life so significantly that he had to believe it was for the better. He felt that so strongly and clearly that nothing or no one could shake it.

Except maybe Jenny.

If only he could convince her that this transformational moment in his life was good for him, for her, and for their marriage and their family.

He wasn't sure how he would do that, but he was going to try!

Jenny sat across from him now at breakfast this morning with that same stony look she had on her face last night as they drove to the governor's mansion in silence. He tried several times to get her to talk to him then and again when they arrived home, but she would have nothing of it.

"I don't want to talk about it," was her one and only repeated response. But she was talking to someone about it because Brad heard her making phone calls from her office until late in the night. No use trying to restore peace with her anymore that night. Brad knew that the silent treatment from Jenny was a sign he was in deep trouble. His only hope was to throw himself at her mercy this morning after a night spent alone on the couch in his office.

"You are right!" he said out of the blue, putting his fork down on his plate and looking at her squarely in the eyes. "I should have told you about Marie years ago." Then he hedged that statement. "But I did tell you that I met someone while I was in college and we had a scare about a pregnancy. You remember me telling you that, right?"

Jenny merely glared at him in stony silence.

"Okay, so I should have told you more about that. Like maybe her name—Marie—and what happened between us and how this guy named Ralph was also involved. Marie told me he was the father, and I just believed it. But I did tell you I wanted her to have the baby. That I remember clearly telling you, and you can read it in the diary pages. Marie said that I told her, 'I don't want you to get rid of this baby.' I can show it to you."

Jenny spoke for the first time now. "You don't have to prove anything to me. I get it. You had a relationship with a woman long before you met me, and things didn't go well. That's not why I'm upset." She stumbled over her next words. "I'm not sure *upset* is the right word. I'm unhappy that you didn't tell me any of this, so I could do one of two things."

Brad could feel the weight of these two things already. Jenny liked to deal with two or three things when she made a list. No more, no less. He just had to hear her out.

"First, let me ask you. Would you say you have been dealing with all this stuff since when? The middle of last week? Not just this latest thing, but the sexual harassment indictment thing too ..."

"You mean the *accusations* of sexual harassment. I wasn't indicted by the feds. Let's be clear about that."

"Sure, fine—accusations. So the feds were threatening to indict you, you were collecting evidence to exonerate yourself, you went to see Pedro to get the evidence, and then you made a deal with the feds." She stopped and looked up at Brad. "I've got that right so far?"

"Yes," Brad agreed. "We talked about all that."

"Right!" she agreed and went on. "Then on Friday afternoon, you met with Everett, who was, as I understand it, your intermediary with Ambrose. He's the guy who wanted to make a deal with you: he would not only identify for you a daughter you have never seen, but also he would find her for you at a fee—a finder's fee of—let me get this right..." She paused to refer to a piece of paper in front of her and then continued. "$50,000. He wanted half of that fee up front, and you agreed to wire $25,000 to his bank account in exchange for copies of the pages of a diary he says belonged to this woman, Marie."

Brad interrupted her. "But I never wired him that money. I did give him five hundred dollars in cash when we met, and subsequently, in a phone call on Saturday morning, I offered him an additional five hundred in cash to find my daughter within a twenty-four-hour period." Brad paused for a moment, then added, "Of course, I found Lisette myself on Saturday night, but then all hell broke loose, and, well, you know the rest of that scene."

"All too well," Jenny said flatly. "Can I go on? Have I gotten the details right so far?"

"Yeah, sure, go on." Brad sighed and put down his fork. No use trying to eat his breakfast when he could already feel indigestion coming on. He hated it when Jenny got her prosecutor-judge hat on, and she was going for it this morning. All he could do was be the audience she wanted him to be. But there was usually a 'gotcha' involved. He sat waiting for it.

"Furthermore," she went on now, "it might have come to your attention that this Ambrose, who currently goes under the name Ambrose August Smith, was arrested ten years ago almost to the exact date in an assault case in which he injured a woman named Ruth in her apartment. Curious to find out that a witness in that case was a young woman, in town for a short period of time, whose name was Lisette LaTour."

That last name rang a bell for Brad, although he hadn't had time last night to ask Lisette what her full name was or how her mother died or even how she liked living in LA. There were so many things he wanted to know about her so he could show her how much he loved her.

"But I believe she has also been known as 'Lisa,' and maybe Lisa Rozniak, the daughter of Ralph Rozniak, her sometimes father as we know him." Jenny stopped and took a breath.

Brad interjected, "I believe you can cross Ralph off the list as her father."

Jenny looked up at him. "Based on what exactly? Something like an actual blood test or DNA?"

"Yes, Lisette says Ralph is not her father. She has a blood test to prove that."

"A blood test! Fabulous! I assume that you've seen this paper, this proof she has of this test?"

"No, she told me over the phone this morning, but I believe her."

"You talked to her on the phone this morning? Is that why you didn't sleep with me last night? So you could call her in the morning?"

Brad could hear the hurt in Jenny's voice. "No," he said gently. "I didn't sleep with you last night—even though I really wanted to—because I didn't want to have this out last night when we were both tired. We'd say things we didn't really mean. It was all so raw, so unreal."

He waited a moment for Jenny to respond, but when she sat quietly, taking it in, he continued. "So I told Lisette I'd call, and I did. That's it. And I just wanted to hear her voice. She has such a lovely voice, don't you think?"

Again, no response. So he went where he thought Jenny wanted to go.

"Look, Jenny. I get it. I was wrong. I should have told you more about all this. But it was happening fast, and I wanted it to happen. I was overwhelmed emotionally. I'm ecstatic that I found Lisette, amazed that she is in my life, and I feel damn guilty for screwing this up years ago. So yes, I screwed up. Let's stipulate that."

"But that's not the point I'm trying to make here," Jenny said. "What this point is—and there is another point too that I'll get to—that if you would have told me or released Everett to let others know, we could've gotten ahead of all this. Because right now we have more than a public relations problem. Frankly, I'm terrified for you, me, and Lisette and what might happen next."

"What do you mean? What did you find in the background check? I know you did one already. I heard you on the phone last night and this morning."

"Under the name Lisa Rozniak, I found that, as a juvenile, she was detained on suspicion that she attempted to kill her father."

Brad looked at her, confused. "But she didn't do that. I'm her father."

"No, I mean Ralph. Ralph Rozniak, her father at that moment. He was, he *is*, listed as her father on her birth certificate. You did know that, right?"

———

225

Brad was taken aback. "No," he said softly. "Not until I read the diary yesterday. It still hurts to hear that." Then he took a breath and added, "You said Lisette tried to kill Ralph. What do you mean? How old was she when this happened?"

"According to the state records I could obtain so far, she was sixteen when she tried to burn down Ralph's bar with him in it."

"I know that bar," Brad said with a laugh. "It should've been burned down."

"This is not funny, Brad!" Jenny shouted. "You don't know anything about this girl. You don't know what she is all about."

"True," he replied. "But I also know something about Ralph. He's a son of a bitch, and if Marie died when Lisette was ten years old like she told me, Ralph was probably the only relative she had. She got stuck with him and…"

"So that justifies what she did?"

"No, Jenny, but there is a story here. Maybe we should ask her to tell us about it before we judge her. I'd like to do that."

"There's something else," Jenny said with a sigh. "This is about me now. And about Ambrose. Actually his legal name is Jeffrey Alexander. He was an attorney…"

"Yeah, I know. He doesn't have a license to practice law anymore. He does some sort of paralegal work at Pedro's legal aid clinic. He's not a practicing attorney."

"I know, but that's not the issue."

"Lisette knows him. She made a deal with him to find out who her father was."

"What kind of a deal? Did she sign something?"

"Yeah, but from what she told me, it doesn't sound like anything enforceable."

"That's not what I'm getting at. It's about me. When I was a County Court judge, I decided a case that took Jeffrey's young son away from him, due to substantial evidence of his inability to take care of the son after a car accident that killed his wife and young daughter."

Jenny took a deep breath and then continued. "He didn't like my decision, and he has held it against me ever since apparently. He and his son were estranged. That's what he's told the police so far. But with the pain medication the doctors are giving him, they say he is fairly out of it—not making a lot of sense about what happened last night."

"So that's why he hates you!" Brad exclaimed. "It was reported that he was screaming 'Jenny Jablonski, I'm going to get you!' as he went flying down the stage catwalk last night. Yeah, that makes sense."

"What makes sense?"

"What you are saying to me. That I should have told you more about this as it was going on so that all this background information could be considered and people could be vetted. Yeah, that makes sense to me. But Jenny, this was about my daughter. Besides marrying you and becoming stepfather to Maryssa, finding out about Lisette is one of the most amazing things that has ever happened to me. I was excited, Jenny! I was ecstatic and overjoyed and..."

Jenny cut in. "I get all that, Brad. But that brings me to my second point."

Yes, he thought. *Jenny did have a second point.*

"And that is..." she went on. "I don't understand why you didn't say anything to me, your wife. Not the governor who might have some political issues here, but your wife. You didn't think I'd want to know what you were going through?"

Brad looked at her, stunned. "Frankly, I didn't know how to tell you. It was hard enough to tell Everett about how I badly screwed up with Lisette."

"You told Everett about this?" Brad could hear the disappointment in Jenny's voice.

"Yeah, but just about the deal, not about my personal stuff with all this. Besides, it was Ambrose who called Everett first. Everett was the link between Ambrose and me to start with. Then at some point Everett knew more than you did, and to speak on Everett's behalf, he told me to tell you everything. Several times. I was the one that screwed that up, not Everett. I don't want you to think that Everett…"

"Trust me, I'm not worried about Everett," Jenny said with a sigh. "But I am worried about you and me. Look, I've said a lot of harsh things to you a few days ago when the feds were breathing down your neck…"

"Yeah," Brad interrupted her, "like 'Clean up this mess, and if nothing else rotten turns up from you past, I won't dump you before the election.' That's what you said to last week about the investigation by the feds. I remember it word for word."

"As I said," Jenny began slowly, "I've said a few harsh things to you recently. That could be one of them. But what I'm trying to say is—here's my point—this hurts! I want to be able to trust the man I love, and I do love you. But to see you ogling that beautiful young woman across the room last night, that hurt!"

She stopped to regain her composure. Brad could see she was getting emotional.

"Now, I understand in the cool light of the morning that you weren't doing that, but in that moment because I didn't know a whole lot of things that were going on, I didn't and couldn't understand. I don't want that to be how our relationship goes here. I want us to share our life together, not just bump into each other every so often and maybe catch up on what's happening in our lives so that one or the other of us doesn't get caught in an emotional trap."

Brad appreciated the warmth and concern in Jenny's voice.

Still he had a point to make too. "I did try to call you yesterday.

I did try to tell you why it was so important for me to attend the gala. I thought I'd see Lisa—Lisette—there. I wanted you to know, to be there with me. But sometimes, Jenny, you cut me off. Not only because of the work you do—and I love and respect that you are the governor—but also because you like to keep a tight control on your emotions."

"I have to," Jenny jumped in. "As a female politician, I can get eaten alive if I show too much feeling. People are just waiting for me to act on something emotionally and then discount me as just a woman who is too emotional and weak."

"I understand that is how you have to act in your political world," Brad countered. "But not in our personal world. Can't you see?"

Jenny was silent for a moment. Brad continued, "Look, I want to see Lisette today. I want to spend some time with her. This is important to me. She's going to leave soon, go back home to LA, and I want to talk with her some more, see what our father/daughter relationship is going to be about."

He stopped for a moment and reached over for Jenny's hand.

"I'd like you to be there," he continued. "But if you think there's too much potential political fallout for you to do that, I'll understand. I can go to her hotel and see her by myself and…"

Jenny interrupted him. "Of course we can do that together. I want to get to know Lisette too. My God, you have a daughter. We have a new member of our family. She can come see us today. Let's have her over for dinner. Call her right now."

Brad was shocked. "Are you sure? Can we pull this off?"

"Of course we can. I was a mother, cook, and hostess long before I was a governor. I'll see what we have in the refrigerator, something quick but filling. Of course we can do dinner for Lisette. Let's see if we can get some of the questions we have for her answered. And invite her boyfriend—Erick is his name, I think.

Nice young man, owns a gym. I talked to him about it last night before everything went crazy. I'll have to go over and see it."

Wow! Brad thought. "You are amazing! Yes, dinner is a great idea. I know you can cook, but mostly I was asking you if we could pull this off emotionally. Look, I don't want this new relationship that I have with Lisette to change or jeopardize anything I have with you. Okay?"

Jenny gave him a warm smile. "Yes, of course not. But there's one more thing you need to know. The article in this morning's paper barely scratches the surface of last night's events. We need to be together on this. As of now, I've decided to not to hold a press conference, but I do want to release this statement today. Sunday is a slow news day, so we'll just get the facts out there and see how it goes. Low-key is the idea."

Jenny handed a sheet of paper across the table to Brad. He took it and read:

Governor Jenny Jablonski and her husband, Brad Bufford, are pleased to announce the addition of a new member to the Jablonski/Bufford family. Brad's daughter, Lisette, has been invited to spend time with the governor and her husband at the Governor's Mansion, their home, and reacquaint herself with the many attractions here in our state. Ms. LaTour is a successful twenty-nine-year-old business woman who recently donated one million dollars to a state nonprofit organization, *Survivor Strong, Thriver Resilient.* This organization was set up ten years ago to honor Lacey Lockhart, a nineteen-year-old college student who was murdered in October 1999 by her ex-boyfriend on campus.

The press statement went on to describe more of the work that had been done by the organization, but Brad had to stop reading. Tears had flooded his eyes.

"This is great, Jenny. I love it." He stopped to wipe the tears away and got more focused. "Of course, we'll have to ask Lisette what she thinks. Can we do that? Is there time?"

"Yes, yes, of course. We'll see what she'd like to add or subtract."

Then his voice got soft and low. "Thanks, Jenny. I appreciate all the work you have done, the research, the background material. I get it. We need to stay on top of this thing. I want us to do this together."

Then he added, his voice clearing, "There is one more thing I wanted to tell you in the interest of full disclosure."

"Okay," Jenny said quickly. "And that is?"

"Lisette and I talked this morning about us doing a blood test. I mean we'd both get a test to make sure that we are in fact father and daughter. I believe she is my daughter, but we thought just to be extra sure."

"That's a great idea," Jenny responded. Then she added, her voice getting soft and low now, "You know this won't be easy. The press knows about the incident last night at the hotel. My press office tried to play it down, something about how details of the nature of the attack on the governor have been 'withheld pending further investigation in order to ensure the safety of the governor and her family.'"

Brad had to smile. "Nice, Jenny. First you pull out the 'family needs to be protected and secure' stuff and the next thing, you add Lisette to the family and put her under the shield."

"But it's going to get worse before it settles down. We can manage this, though, if we keep working together. Nice work with the idea of getting the blood test. It's good to be certain and have some proof."

"Thanks, Jenny." Brad smiled. "You know that you are the best, my dear!" He leaned over and planted a kiss on her face.

"Hey," she said sharply, getting up from the table and walking over to him. "I think I should get a major hug for all that work."

Brad stood up, took her in his arms, and embraced her. "Yes! You do," he agreed.

"But much as I'd like to snuggle with you all day, we need to get busy here. You need to call your daughter. Lisette must be waiting for you to call her back. Tell her to come for dinner at 5:00 p.m. and tell her that her boyfriend is welcome too." She paused and then added, "And oh, Brad..."

"Yes?" he said with a lilt in his voice that matched Jenny's.

"Let me talk to her myself before you hang up."

❖ ❖ ❖

Sunday morning, Lisette woke up to the sound of a buzzing she thought might be Brad calling her again this morning on her cell phone. He had called her earlier, waking her up, but Lisette didn't mind. She took her phone into the other room so as not to disturb Erick. When she was done chatting with Brad, she came back to bed and fell sound asleep again.

Now it was the buzzer on Erick's phone that she heard. She turned over in bed and saw that he had already gotten up. She knew he used his phone as a timer when he cooked, so she imagined him out there cooking her another gigantic breakfast this morning. She loved it!

She pulled on her robe and walked from the bedroom into the outer room of the hotel suite. Erick was there in the tiny kitchen, and so was Sophie, laughing and talking with him over a cup of coffee that smelled terrific to Lisette.

Both Erick and Sophie looked up as she entered the room.

"Good morning!" they both called out and Sophie held out a hot cup of coffee in her hands. "Straight from my favorite coffee shop down the street!" she said with a laugh. "My contribution to breakfast! Hard to make a good café latte in this kitchen."

"Thanks, Sophie," Lisette said coming over to her and taking the cup from her. Then she moved toward Erick, put her hand on his back, and stood on her tippy toes to give him a kiss. Then she added with a smile, "Good morning to you, chef! And what incredible thing are you cooking for us today?" She turned to Sophie, "I don't know that I have ever met a man who could cook a breakfast like Erick. He is a treasure!"

"Yes, I'd hold on to this one for sure," Sophie replied.

"And he has other good qualities too!" Lisette added.

They both laughed, and Erick looked embarrassed.

Lisette mercifully changed the subject. "How are you doing after last night, Sophie? That was quite the evening, huh? I'm so sorry that your event got ruined."

"Thanks," Sophie replied. "But there is some good news this morning. I brought you the Sunday paper." She pointed to a newspaper sitting on the counter between them. "The front-page article is all about the governor being whisked away last night due to a threat to her safety, and it continues by stating that 'an investigation is pending by the state police.' More details to follow!"

"That's good, you're right," Lisette said hopefully. "At least my face and a story about me being the governor's stepdaughter hasn't been sprayed all over yet. At least Ambrose didn't get what he wanted about that."

"Yeah, but don't expect it to stay that way. The governor managed to keep those details under wraps for now, but the media is a hungry beast that loves to feed on salacious details of nasty facts and unproven suppositions. Your time will come!"

"Wow!" Lisette was impressed. "I don't know what all those words mean, but for now, I think we're safe."

"I am happy about you finding your dad, Lisette. You must be thrilled! It's so amazing that it's Brad Bufford. Have you heard from him or the governor this morning yet?"

"Yeah, Brad and I talked a little bit this morning." Then she turned to Erick. I took the call out here so you could sleep."

Erick nodded and smiled at her. Then he asked, "What did you two talk about?"

"Mostly about Ralph. And he wanted to know how my mom died."

"How did that go?" Sophie jumped in.

"It was good. I think it made him sad about Marie. He wanted to know about her, but it was hard. We were both crying by the end of it."

"Sounds like you got through that okay."

"Yeah, but I'm still trying to believe that all this is really happening. Finding that you have a dad when you didn't think you had one is pretty crazy. But finding out that he's married to the governor is really wild. Now I'm in the middle of all this political stuff Brad was trying to explain to me last night. I mean, I know Ambrose was pissed off at me because I wouldn't do the performance art thing with him ten years ago. But I did sign the agreement with him Saturday morning about the pole dancing, so he shouldn't be pissed at me anymore, right? So what was going on with him last night? He was up there in the rafters of the stage screaming my name out at the top of his lungs. And what was Wiley doing there? Has anyone figured that out yet?"

"What I heard last night as the cops were talking to Wiley," Erick offered, "is that he was working with Ambrose to embarrass both you and the governor last night. He was going to make the announcement publicly that you were Brad's daughter and that you had danced at his club as Atilla the Hunny."

"So Wiley was mad at me for buying his club? But we paid him good money for that hellhole. He was lucky to find a buyer at all."

"But maybe he didn't like you coming into town personally and taking it away from him," Erick offered. "Maybe he didn't like that suddenly you were in charge and he wasn't."

"That's pathetic," Lisette said. "So that means Ambrose was furious because Brad and I met almost by accident at the event without Wiley being able to embarrass all of us in public, including the governor."

"Yeah something like that. Ambrose beat on that door to the glass booth so hard that it broke and he went skidding down the backstage catwalk to the ground. All the other noise was things falling from the catwalk as he slid and people screamed. Thank God he didn't kill himself or injure anyone else with his stunt. Or else we'd all be on the front page of the newspaper."

"But why was Ambrose out to get the governor? What did she ever do to him?"

"That's where I come in," Sophie said, pulling a piece of paper out of her briefcase. "Remember when we first met, Lisette? You came to the college looking for someone to read a newspaper story to you. Do you remember what that story was about?"

Lisette looked at her curiously. "It was about Ambrose and his son. I don't remember all the details."

"I thought you might not. I didn't either. I looked the article up on the internet this morning, and I found it!" Sophie waved a paper in her hand. "I think this is the reason Ambrose was mad at the governor."

Sophie summarized the article quickly, reminding Lisette that after the car accident that killed his wife and daughter, Ambrose was accused of abusing his son who had survived the accident. He went to court to fight for custody of the son, but the court hearing went badly.

"Do you remember who the judge in the case was?" Sophie asked Lisette.

"No, but I remember the grandmother got custody. Her name was Abigail. I can't remember her last name. But I met her on the steps out in front of the library. She's the one that gave me the article to read. She hated Ambrose! Called him by his real name, Jeffrey, and told me he was a liar."

"Yeah, that's about right. Her name was Abigail Durocher and she won custody of her grandson back then. He was only six years old."

"Years later Ambrose told me she wouldn't let him see his son at all, not even for his birthday. But what does all this have to do with the governor?"

"That's the part I forgot or didn't even realize back when first read this article over cheeseburgers at the diner. Jenny Jablonski was a judge before she became lieutenant governor and then governor. So guess who was the judge in this custody case?"

"Jenny Jablonski!" Lisette and Erick said out loud almost simultaneously.

"The governor has to know this, right?" Sophie asked them now. "If she didn't remember last night, she has to have figured it out this morning. The cops were all over Ambrose last night because he also was yelling as he slid down that catwalk, 'Jenny Jablonski, I'm going to get you.'"

"Right!" Erick interjected. "That's what escalated the whole situation into a security breach for the governor and why the show couldn't go on."

"Wow," Lisette said, sighing. "What a mess!"

"So you've got to think this through, Lisette," Sophie was advising her now. "Does the governor have any plans to issue a press release or hold a press conference about this? She's got to get out in front of it. You do still want to be part of this family now, right?"

"What do you mean?" Lisette asked.

"You know, will you be publicly acknowledged? I mean, will Brad and the governor include you in family events in the future? The governor's daughter is included at times. No big deal, but she is part of the family and shows up for holidays and other events."

"The governor has a daughter? I didn't know that." Then she thought for a moment. "Brad didn't say anything about that. Of course, we didn't have a lot of time to talk about everything last night or this morning."

"She does have a daughter. Her name is Maryssa. She's about the same age as us." Sophie paused for a moment. "That's why she's always been interested in what happened to Lacey. It could have been her daughter."

"Really," Lisette said soberly. "I had no idea. There is so much to know, to learn. How will I ever do this?"

At that moment, Lisette's cell rang. It was there on the desk where she had left it after talking to Brad earlier. She walked over to it, switched it on and checked the caller ID.

"It's Brad again. What should I tell him about dinner? What am I doing here?"

"You're answering the phone," Sophie said, her voice calm and steady. "You can do this."

Yes, of course, I can, Lisette thought.

She just had to answer the phone.

❖ ❖ ❖

Lisette was so nervous about going to see Jenny and Brad that she almost threw up two times on the way to the governor's mansion that afternoon. Brad had a car sent to pick them up and all the way there, Lisette couldn't believe this was really happening!

When Brad first called her early on that Sunday morning, he told her he hadn't talked to Jenny yet but that he'd call back to confirm dinner plans for that evening. Lisette didn't think Brad would be able pull it off so soon. She thought Brad would have a lot of explaining to do and it would take some time for Jenny to come around.

But when Brad called her the second time this morning, Jenny insisted on talking to her.

"Yes," Jenny said to her. "Come see us for supper at 5:00 p.m. tonight. I'll make something nice for you and your boyfriend, Erick. And tell him I'll come see his gym soon."

She sounded so nice, but still Lisette was in a panic. What was she going to wear? What was she going to say? How did someone like her talk to someone as important as the governor? She had no idea, and now she was terrified.

Lisette realized that while she might be the ferocious Atilla the Hunny on stage, that didn't mean anything to Jenny. Thank God Erick was coming with her. She wanted Sophie to come too, but she begged off.

"This is your big opportunity. Go and enjoy your time with your dad!"

Wow, Lisette liked the sound of that—spending time with her dad.

"At least help me pick out something to wear," she begged Sophie before she left. Sophie also helped Erick and her leave the hotel without being spotted by any enterprising reporters who might have figured out who Lisette was, where she was staying, and who she was going to see. Sophie talked to the hotel people about having the car being sent to pick up Lisette and Erick drive around the back of the hotel to the service entrance just in case.

When Lisette and Erick arrived at the governor's mansion, Brad was there to greet them. When he opened the car door and Lisette emerged, he stood looking at her for a moment before enveloping her in a big bear hug.

"Wow!" he said as he held her tight. "You look terrific."

She was puzzled. She looked down at her outfit. She wasn't wearing anything particularly exciting, but something that seemed easy and not too—what was the word Sophie used?– provocative. But she realized that Brad wasn't talking about what she was wearing because then he added, "It's terrific to see you, my lovely daughter."

When he released her from his arms, he gripped Erick's hand in greeting and they walked up to the door of the mansion and into a small hallway. Brad took their coats and then brought out a huge bouquet of flowers.

"These are for you," he said putting them in her hands. "I wasn't sure what kind you liked, so I had them throw a whole bunch of different kinds together."

She smiled and took the flowers from him, cradling them in her arms.

"They're beautiful," she said with a sigh. "Thank you. They smell wonderful. But you didn't have to give me flowers."

"I wanted to do something special for you."

"Flowers are great, and candy too," Lisette said, sounding like a kid.

"Oh no! I should've brought you candy too. Why didn't I think of that?"

"Don't worry," she said. "This made me forget how nervous I am."

Brad put his arm around her. "Don't be nervous. Jenny has been cooking up a storm for you two all day. She is going to love you."

Lisette was surprised. "Do you think so? I've been nervous about what to say to her. I even wrote something down on a paper. Erick helped me with it this afternoon. When I met her at the gala last night before you came in, we did talk a little. But I was telling Erick, this is all different now. I hope she's not mad at me for what happened last night at the event. I had no idea Ambrose was going to do any of that."

"Of course she doesn't blame you for anything. Look, Jenny and I have sorted this all out. It was my fault. I should have told her about you and Marie years ago. But Jenny and I talked. Not to worry."

Lisette decided not to and she giggled. "Coming here is like living my happily ever after in a fairy tale!" Then she remembered that Erick was with her. "You're part of that too," she said softly to him. "My knight in shining armor!"

It was true, she thought. If there was ever a guy a girl could take to meet a governor, Erick was it. He made her feel happy and relaxed. He was her guy, and she loved it.

She had got it right this time.

Thank God! She had finally gotten it right.

CHAPTER FIFTEEN

Sunday, October 18, 2009

Unbounded Love

After dinner was over, Jenny looked over and flashed Lisette a smile that made her feel like a million bucks.

All through dinner, Jenny was so funny and so nice to everyone, especially to Lisette. Jenny made her feel special, as though she were the only person in the room, the one she loved the best. Lisette hadn't felt that way since her mother died, and she tried hard not to be taken in too easily by Jenny. She wanted to like her. She was her stepmother now, and Lisette wanted to be able to trust her. But Lisette knew after spending part of her childhood with Ralph, a guy she could never trust, that being able to trust others was a big deal for her.

"So, what do you say, Lisette?" Jenny said as she stood up and gestured for her to follow. "How about if you and I sneak off? We need some girl-talk time."

"Sure," Lisette said, but inside she was in a panic. As she had told Brad earlier, she had the notes on what she wanted to say to Jenny in her pocket. There hadn't been time at dinner to say what she wanted. But she and Jenny, Brad and Erick had had so much fun together while they ate, there didn't seem to be time for serious talk. But now Jenny wanted to speak to her alone, and Lisette guessed this was her moment. But she was terrified. She had never talked to a governor before and being in the governor's mansion was very intimidating.

She looked over at Brad and Erick to see what they thought she should do. Erick just smiled at her and Brad said, "Go ahead, Lisette. We'll do some boy talk here. We can entertain ourselves."

So Lisette got up and followed Jenny out of the dining room and into the kitchen. At first, she thought they'd sit there at the kitchen table, like she and her mother used to do, but Jenny breezed right by it. Lisette followed her, noticing the pots and pans stacked up in the sink.

"Who's going to do the dishes?" she asked.

"Not me. That's one good thing about being the governor."

"When I was little, I helped my mom cook and clean up afterward," Lisette said wistfully. "But I don't cook much anymore."

"Too bad. Maybe that's something you could change," Jenny said with a smile.

Oh God! Lisette thought. *Here she goes, trying to fix me already.* It was going to be tough holding her own with someone like Jenny. Why had she left Erick behind? She was going to be tortured by Jenny somewhere in the back room of the governor's mansion and she'd never find her way back to him. By then, they had gone down several hallways, and Lisette was lost. She was trapped alone with Jenny, and she should have seen it coming.

Finally, Jenny came to a room at the end of the hallway and walked in. Lisette came up behind her and peeked in. She couldn't believe it. It was the bedroom she had dreamed of her whole life. She stepped inside and could see it was a big and airy room with a large bed against one wall and a canopy over it. Against the other wall was a giant chest of drawers and a vanity table with a mirror and a stool. Finally, there was a fireplace between two large bay windows on the far wall, and in front of it were two comfortable-looking armchairs covered in a bright floral pattern that matched the pale yellow of the walls. There were other chairs in the room, but these two were placed before a blazing fire that brightened up the whole room. Lisette could tell, though, that even during the day with sunlight streaming through the wide windows, the room would look just as grand.

It was a fabulous room, and she loved it.

"The wife of our last governor decorated this room," Jenny said, as she motioned for Lisette to sit down in one of the chairs in front of the fireplace. "She did a great job, didn't she?"

Lisette nodded and settled into one chair, while Jenny sat in the other one.

"The rest of the mansion was like a tomb when I got here," Jenny went on. "I changed everything but this room. It's kind of girly and cute. It feels like home."

Lisette smiled at Jenny in agreement. She felt wonderful in this room.

Jenny continued, "After I got elected, a woman who worked on my campaign came to see me with her daughter. I brought them here and sat in these same chairs. Her daughter piped up and said, 'I like it here, Mommy. I'm going to be governor, too, when I grow up.' Only six years old, and she already knew what she wanted to be."

Jenny stopped for a moment, took a deep breath. "That was the day I knew why I was elected the first woman governor of this state," she continued. "Now girls know that they can be anything they want to be and all they ever dreamed of. What I've done is only the beginning."

Jenny paused again and then turned in her chair toward Lisette. "So that brings us to you," she said.

"It does?" Lisette murmured, not sure how she meant that.

"You're a businesswoman and a good one, so I've heard," Jenny began. " You've made a lot of money. Sophie tells me you donated one million dollars to her organization. That's a lot of money to give away. You make your money owning strip clubs, right?"

"I don't own them exactly. I just license my stage name to them and do a little training with the new girls."

"Do you like that kind of work?"

"It's something I fell into. My mother was a stripper, and so was I until ten years ago when I was last here in town. Something changed back then, and I stopped dancing. I liked moving into the business side. I liked how we upgraded the places. When I was dancing, I worked in some really seedy places. It makes me feel good when we can make the places better and safer for the girls."

"Really? There must be something else you've dreamed of doing."

Lisette looked at Jenny. "To tell you the truth, I've gotten this new idea since I've been in town. I don't know. That guy, Ambrose, gave it to me. He says I should open up pole dancing clubs for women and men. He says it is good exercise and everyone loves the pole dancing video I did on my website. That it would help other women get fit and stay healthy."

"So that's your dream?" Jenny said. "Are you sure?"

"It's part of it," Lisette said. "I love the work that Sophie is doing. She's so smart and so brave. I don't know if I could do what she does, but I'd love to try."

Then she got quiet. "But one thing I have learned this week is that I want something I haven't had in my life for a long time."

"Really?" Jenny looked at her with wide eyes. "What's that?"

"It's called 'unconditional love,' something Erick and I have been talking about. He calls it 'reliable love.' I like those words. It means something to me." She paused for a moment and then added softly, "I had that with my mom. She was the best mom a girl could ever have. I don't think I really appreciated her when she was alive. But she gave me that 'reliable' kind of love. No matter what, she was there for me. She gave it to me every day I was with her, and I've missed it so much."

Jenny was quiet for a moment. "I like what you said about your mom. She sounds wonderful. You know, I'm a mom too. Did Brad tell you? I have a daughter, Maryssa. She's just about your age. I love being her mom. I've been in politics for many years now as a legislator, lieutenant governor, and now governor. I have the highest approval rating of any sitting governor in the last two decades, but that's not my highest achievement. Don't get me wrong, I love being involved in politics and helping people. That hasn't been what makes me really happy, though."

"What is that happy place for you?"

"Exactly what you said. Giving and receiving unconditional love as a mom, a wife, and a friend. It's that kind of love that fuels us all and allows us keep doing whatever we have dreamed of being or doing. It's that 'we can do it!' spirit, no matter what!"

Lisette smiled. "You've got that right. When I was a kid, there was a time after my mother died when I was a 'ward of the state.' That sucked. No one was there for me."

"You were in foster care?" Jenny asked.

Lisette nodded and went on. "Only for a while until I was seventeen, and then I got emancipated. Best thing that ever happened to me. Ever since then, I've been on my own."

"That's one of the things I wanted to talk to you about, Lisette. It's something Brad and I would like you to do for us."

"Is it something that I have to read or write? I'm not so good at that."

Jenny sighed. "I didn't know about the reading and writing. Does Brad?"

"I have told him a little about that. But I don't want to keep going on about the messed up things in my life before finding him. It might make him feel guilty for not being there when I was growing up. But I didn't want him to think I'm stupid either about my reading and writing."

"There may be a lot of things people could say about you, Lisette, but stupid is not one of them. But we do need to hear from you about something in your past. Something that may be hard for you to talk about. It's something we need to know more about before the press gets a hold of it. It may seem as if it's to protect me more than you, but I think we both have something to lose here."

Just as Jenny was finishing her sentence, Brad and Erick came into the room. "Are we interrupting, or is this a good time to come into the conversation?"

Jenny nodded. "Yeah, Brad. I was just about to ask Lisette to tell us…"

"They want to know about Ralph," Erick cut in. "Sorry, I told your dad about you and Ralph. He asked me just now. He and Jenny need to hear the whole story you told me the other night. It explains so much, Lisette. I think it will help."

Lisette flashed a look of panic at Jenny for a moment, then at Brad before she asked, "Can Erick and I talk out in the hall for a moment? Just a minute."

"Sure," Brad said, pulling up a chair from the other side of the room and sitting down next to Jenny near the fireplace. "Take all the time you need."

"Okay, we'll be right back."

Lisette grabbed Erick's arm and pulled him out into the hall.

❖ ❖ ❖

Erick knew Lisette wasn't going to be happy with him, so as they moved into a room down the hall from where Jenny and Brad sat waiting for them, Erick had his arguments all ready.

"Look," he said to her. "You want Brad and Jenny to love you unconditionally, right? Then they have to know the conditions under which you are asking them to love you. They need to know what you did to Ralph and how that all turned out."

Lisette looked skeptical, but Erick continued.

"If that is the worst you've ever done and ever expect to do, then they need to know that. They need to know you will never go there again, but that they have to love you in spite of it. That's unconditional love! Someone that loves you without conditions, remember?" Then he added, "You told me this whole story the other night, and I still love you, right?"

"Yeah but you're not them. She's the governor. He's her husband. They are important people. I don't know."

"You won't know unless you try. And if you don't tell them now and they find it out from someone else, just think about how that will feel. For both of them and for you."

Lisette still didn't look convinced. Erick tried another tact.

"Look, you know my mother died when I was six, and my father too. They were both killed in a car crash. My grandmother raised me until she died last year."

"Yeah," Lisette said looking at him with wide eyes. "You grew up hard too. You're one of those—what do they call it when both of your parents are dead?" she asked.

"Orphan. Yes, that's me, but I've never let it get in my way. My grandmother always told me, 'People won't care where you came from if they like where you are going.' So that's what I try to do, keep going to a better place."

"But you don't understand," Lisette whined.

"But I do," Erick interjected. "Just because you had a tough break as a kid doesn't mean that is who you are now. There are people who love you and want to love you just as you are. Two of them are sitting in that room back there, just waiting to love you unconditionally."

Lisette said with a whimper. "Okay, but you'll be there with me when I tell them, won't you?"

"Of course, I will. You know how I feel about you. I have loved you from the first day I saw you dancing up on that stage in that fuzzy white jacket and Attila the Hunny hat. It just took us a while to get this right."

"You have! You are the best." She reached up to kiss him, and he kissed her back. "I want Brad to love me to the moon like my mom did. Do you think he can?"

"Let's go back in there and find out. You can do this, right?"

She nodded, and Erick kissed her, long and hard. Then they went back into the room where Brad and Jenny were waiting for them.

❖ ❖ ❖

She told Brad and Jenny the story the way she remembered it and what she had been able to piece together over the years.

Lisette had found out from Diedre, her lawyer, that even when Ralph was barely conscious in the burn unit of the hospital, he asked for Lisa. He drove the nurses crazy about it until one of them called the police to see what could be done. The police had already tried to question him about what happened that night, but he wouldn't say a word. Now he insisted upon seeing Lisa.

"Mr. Rozniak, this is Detective Charbonneau. I talked to you earlier. Is there something else you want to say to me?"

"Lisa. See Lisa. Lisa," Ralph repeated, sounding almost delirious.

"Yes, Lisa. She's your daughter. What do you want to tell me about her?"

"See Lisa," he said again, but more insistently.

"Mr. Rozniak, I can't bring Lisa here to see you. She is in detention. She is being held pending a decision by the judge as to whether—well, to be frank with you—as to whether she tried to kill you, sir."

"No," he grew quite agitated. "Not Lisa." He was almost incoherent.

"Not what about Lisa?"

"She didn't. Me."

"Are you telling me that Lisa didn't do this to you? You did this to yourself." The officer was incredulous as he looked at the bandages covering the burns on Ralph's face, hands, and chest."

"Yes, yes!" His voice was agitated, and he sounded like he was in agony. "Please. Please."

"Calm down now, Mr. Rozniak. I understand what you are trying to say."

"Help her. Help her please." His voice faded now, and he passed from consciousness. The nurse came to his side.

"You're not going to get much more out of him now. He fades in and out of consciousness from the pain and the medication." She looked squarely at the detective. "Did you get what he wanted to tell you about Lisa?"

"Yes. Yes, I did. Thank you for calling me. This is very helpful."

"He just seemed to be in such agony about Lisa. Is she his wife?"

"No, his daughter."

"Oh, she's the one who's in all the papers. Poor girl. She must have really hated this guy to do this to him."

"He says she didn't do it. That's what he's been trying to say."

She looked down at the man lying in the bed. "Jesus, either he's a hero or a good liar. But after all, he is her father. Wouldn't you want your father to do that for you?"

❖ ❖ ❖

It was Sandy, Lisette's social worker until she was emancipated at seventeen years of age, who made her go see Ralph. Sandy had some crazy idea that if Lisette would go see him, it would heal her. Lisette didn't believe that, but Sandy wouldn't support her emancipation unless she went to see Ralph, so she went.

She was terrified.

Lisette walked behind Sandy as they entered the small, clean room where Ralph was living on the second floor of a large old house that had been converted to a rest home for patients with special nursing needs. That's how Sandy described it to Lisette when she asked Sandy where exactly they were going to see Ralph. The nurse had escorted the two visitors up a staircase and down the quiet, deserted hallway that led to Ralph's room, the last one at the far end.

Entering the room, Lisette remembered being blinded by the sunlight streaming in through the window to the right of Ralph's bed. At first, she only saw a white lump of bandages in the bed covered with white sheets. It took her eyes a while to focus as she stood in the doorway. Sandy immediately walked across the room to Ralph's bed.

"Good morning, Mr. Rozniak," she said, extending her right hand to him. "I'm Sandy Curry from the Susan B. Anthony Home for Girls. I've been working with your daughter, Lisette."

Lisette watched Ralph look angrily at Sandy as if she should have noticed that both of his hands were heavily bandaged and he couldn't shake hers. When she did, she dropped her hand awkwardly at her side, but then added cheerfully, "I'm glad to meet you."

"Her name is Lisa," Ralph said in a flat, hoarse voice. "I don't know a Lisette."

"All right," Sandy said carefully. "I'm sure that your daughter can respond to whatever name you're most comfortable with." She turned to Lisette still hovering in the doorway. "Can't you now, Lisa?"

"Sure. Whatever," Lisette mumbled.

Ralph growled and strained his body up from the bed a bit so that he could see Lisette. "That doesn't sound like the Lisa I know. Willing to please her dad?" He spoke with an edge in his voice. "Isn't that special?"

Lisette fidgeted with her hands as she watched Sandy turn and walk toward her. Sandy took her hand and pulled her reluctantly into the room. Standing now at the bed holding Sandy's hand, Lisette heard Sandy go on. "Maybe you don't know her as well as you thought you did, Mr. Rozniak."

"Oh, call me Ralph, why don't you?" he snarled, his voice thick-coated with phlegm. He wheezed and coughed for a minute from deep down in his chest. Lisette's eyes grew wide and she gripped Sandy's hand tighter as her father struggled to breathe.

"Damn lungs," he said gruffly, still addressing Sandy. "It's from the smoke I inhaled. Can't get a clear path." He hacked some more and then reached over in an attempt to get a paper cup full of water sitting on the tray table near his bed. But with his hands so heavily bandaged, he almost knocked the cup over onto the floor.

"Here," Sandy said, lunging toward the cup and grabbing it. "Let me help you with that, Ralph." She also spotted a straw on the table and asked, "Do you want the straw too?"

"Yeah. Just put it in the cup," he replied.

Sandy did that and, drawing the straw up to his mouth, she held the cup in front of him as he sipped at the liquid. The slurping sound he made with his lips as the water went into his mouth drew Lisette's attention to his face and she saw the burns there for the first time. Unlike those on his hands, these burns were no longer bandaged. They looked raw and purplish and the skin over them was healing tightly across his cheeks and forehead. *God,* Lisette thought, *if this is how it looks now, what must it have been like right after the fire?* But she didn't turn her eyes away. She knew this was the punishment she deserved—to look into her father's face and see what she had done to him.

Sandy voice interrupted her thoughts. "Why don't you pull up some chairs for us by this side of the bed? The light from the window won't be in our eyes and we can hear Ralph better. Okay?"

Lisette nodded without speaking, welcoming the idea of doing something, anything rather than look at her father's face any longer from this angle. She found two chairs against the wall and carried them over to the side of Ralph's bed. She sat down in one just as Ralph finished sipping on the straw and waved the cup of water away. Sandy put the cup back on the tray table and sat down next to Lisette.

Ralph cleared his throat. "So, are they treating you okay in that place?" he asked, speaking directly to Lisette for the first time.

Lisette looked at him and found her voice now that from where she sat she couldn't see the burns on his face so well.

"Yes, I like it very much. I'm learning a lot of things, you know, stuff that's helping me a lot."

Sandy interjected, "The home—SBA, as we call it—is specially designed for girls like Lisa who need help in finding a focus for their lives. We try to build on the things that are good about them so they can become even better."

"Yeah," Ralph said disinterestedly. But then he added, "Have you found anything good yet in Lisa? I'd sure like to know."

The edge was back again in Ralph's voice, and Lisette reacted to it almost immediately. Her body went stiff and she sensed Ralph signal that he had fighting with her in mind. But Sandy continued talking casually with him.

"Well, if you don't mind, maybe you could help me with that. You see, I'd like to know what you think Lisa's strengths are. You've known her since birth, after all."

"I don't know if I'm the one to ask."

"Surely you can help me here, can't you?" Sandy insisted. "Just take a stab at it for me. What *do* you admire most about Lisa?"

Ralph squirmed for a moment, and Lisette stole a glance at Sandy sitting with her hands in her lap and patiently waiting for his response. A small, tight smile had come over her face. Lisette decided it was almost a smirk so Ralph might think Sandy was putting him on, but it was also enough of a look to let him know that she meant business.

Ralph fussed with the bandage on his hands. Then he spoke in a hoarse whisper that Lisette couldn't hear.

"Excuse me," Sandy said, leaning toward Ralph. "I couldn't hear that."

"I said 'persistent.' She's persistent. Stubborn as a mule, in fact. Never seen anyone like it except maybe her mother, God rest her soul."

Lisette's jaw dropped. What was this shit about her mother's soul? Ralph had never said anything like that before. Suddenly she wanted to say something, but Sandy spoke first.

"All right. So, she's not a quitter. I'd agree with that. What else?"

Ralph reacted with a jerk of his body. "What is this—twenty questions? You asked me, and I told you. Can't we move along?"

"Move along to what?"

"To whatever is that you and *her*," pointing his gnarled bandaged hand at Lisette, "want from me. If I never see her again, I'll be a happy man." He gasped for a quick breath and then folded his bandaged hands over his chest.

"I don't believe that," Sandy shot back. "If you didn't want to see us, you could've said no."

"Right!" he snapped. "Do you know what they do to 'uncooperative' patients around here? Already everyone is fussing over my body and picking at my mind. Those damn shrinks say I should forgive her for what she did to me."

Lisette's heart leaped as the word *forgive* came out of Ralph's mouth. Why hadn't she thought of asking him to forgive her? Not that she wanted it if he didn't want to give it to her, but if she could bargain with him, then yes, she wanted that.

"What did she do to you?" Sandy sounded puzzled.

"Why, the bitch tried to kill me! And still I don't even know why."

"Wait a minute," Sandy said, quickly fixing her eyes on Ralph's. "What do you mean she tried to kill you? That's not what you told the police officer; that's not what he reported in court."

Suddenly Ralph went silent. He hacked for a moment but did not speak. Sandy turned to Lisette, who sat rigid in the chair next to her, her eyes downcast and her hands twisting wildly in her lap.

"What's he talking about?" Sandy demanded of her.

"How am I supposed to know?" Lisette whined. "He'd being paranoid. It's his delusional behavior. I can't account for it."

"What are you talking about?" Sandy screamed at her. "You don't know what those words mean." Then she blurted out, "You can't even read, can you?"

"I *can* read," Lisette insisted with a quiver in her voice. "And why are you yelling at me? Yell at him!" Her eyes were filled with tears. "Why does he always get to win?"

"I'm talking about what went on that night in the bar," Sandy said, looking first at Ralph and then back at Lisette. "I want the truth!" The panicked sound of her voice boomed around the small room.

"The truth?" Ralph finally croaked hoarsely. "Why do *you* need to know that?"

"I have to know what kind of people I am dealing with here," Sandy said, clenching her teeth. "What *did* go on between you two? Jake testified at the trial that you were *selling* your *own* daughter to him for sex. Is that true?"

"No!" Ralph shot back.

"You're lying!" Lisette cried out now unable to be silent any longer. "You sold me like a prostitute, and you *know* it." Her voice trembled, and she turned to Sandy. "He's lying!"

"Do you understand what you are saying?" Sandy's eyes were

wild now. "If you tell me that Lisa tried to kill you, then you committed perjury before the court and so did your daughter. That a crime, a serious one."

Ralph shifted his body in the bed and looked coldly at the woman.

"All I'm saying is that the bitch tried to hurt me. I'm lying here because of her and my business is ruined. Who's going to give me back my life? Who?"

"What, that ratty old bar?" Lisette interjected before Sandy could reply. "*That's* what you lost? What about me? Don't you care about what you did to me?"

Suddenly Ralph was silent.

Lisette waited and then said with a shrug, "Fine. You don't have to come out and say it. I already know the truth. What I want to know is why. Why would a father do that to his own daughter?"

"I didn't do that!" Ralph exploded. "Jake is lying. If you really want to know, I was giving *him* a little money—you know, to take you out, for a good time. He got pissed off when I wouldn't bankroll a birthday party for you," he said almost proudly.

"He wanted to do that for my birthday?" Suddenly Lisette was surprised and touched.

"Yeah, I guess," Ralph said offhandedly. "And when I told him no, I didn't have the money that week, he told you his lies."

"That *he* didn't have the money to pay *you*?"

"Whatever he told you," Ralph growled, waving his bandaged hands. "I was sinking all my money then into the business. I had big plans to expand. All legitimate stuff. I was lining up all the permits and licenses I needed from the city. That's why I stopped paying him."

"And you're sure that he wasn't paying you?" Lisette's voice quivered.

"Yes! It was too risky to sell sex, and I could have made good money with other stuff I was planning to do. It was all legal. That was my dream—until this. Look at what you did!" He pulled down the sheet over his chest to show her the burns there too.

"I didn't do that!" Lisette turned away, her eyes stinging with tears. "You did it to yourself. You're a selfish, greedy, disgusting man, and I hate you!"

She sobbed and fell into Sandy's lap, who had been listening to the father-daughter battle from her seat ringside. As Sandy wrapped her arms around the girl's shoulders and gently stroked her hair, she looked at Ralph and spoke in a steady voice.

"So, what *did* you say to the psychiatrists who wanted you to forgive Lisa?"

"What?" Ralph seemed distracted by the question. He had been watching Lisette's shoulder's heave up and down in Sandy's lap.

"The shrinks," Sandy demanded. "What did you tell them about letting go of this?"

"I told them I didn't want to let *her* off the hook so easy." Ralph thrust a bandaged hand in Lisette's direction. "But she was driving me crazy with all that emancipation shit. Hell, I should have let her go and starve out in the real world. Why should I care?"

"Oh, I think you care a great deal, Mr. Rozniak. In my experience, when people like you and Lisa," she stroked the girl's head and pulled the long blonde hair from her face, "spend a lot of time telling me how you hate each other, it usually means you don't."

Suddenly Lisette sat up, tears running down her face, and pointed toward Ralph. "I want the police to prosecute *him* for selling me to Jake." She turned and screamed back at Sandy, "I can do that, you know. I'll get him."

"Oh, you'd better be careful," Sandy said sharply. "He's accused you of trying to kill him, and you want to charge him with taking money for sex. Two wrongs don't make a right, now do they? I thought your mother would have taught you that."

"She taught me *not* to take any *shit* from an asshole even if he was my father. And what are you screaming at me for?" Lisette pointed furiously at Ralph. "He's the one that hasn't told us yet why he did it." Lisette turned on him. "Did you really think I wouldn't find out? Jake told me."

"Jake told a lot of people a lot of things. He came to see me in the hospital after the accident, you know. He told me he had made videotapes of you and him having sex."

"What tapes?" Lisette's eyes flared. "What are you talking about?"

"I didn't know about them until then. I told him he couldn't sell them."

"Why?" Lisette snorted. "Did you want to sell them yourself? That would be just like you, wouldn't it?"

Lisette threw herself back down into Sandy's lap and sobbed.

Sandy spoke in a calm but firm voice to Ralph. "So, you aren't going to forgive Lisa for what she did to you, are you? And you're going to keep provoking her even more with talk about videotapes. What are you so angry about anyway?"

"God, you're nosey, aren't you? First, you want to know about that 'forgiveness' crap and now you want to know why I'm angry. Well, I'm angry because I'm angry and it's none of your damn business why. Except that that child sniffling in your lap has something to do with it, and if you haven't figured that out yet, then you are stupider than I think you are," Ralph sputtered at her. "Get off my back, would you?"

"I feel sorry for you, Ralph," Sandy continued in the same calm voice. "After all of this, I still don't know what to believe—are you telling the truth or is Lisette? I have to wonder why Jake would make up such a story if it wasn't true. But then I figure we're all missing the point here."

"And what *is* the point?"

"How's Lisette supposed to know if you or Jake ever really cared about her? Did you lie to the court because you loved her or to cover up the real reason why Lisette wanted to kill you in the first place? Maybe you have some shame after all."

"I *am* telling the truth! Jake never cared about her. He only wanted my money."

"How do you know that?" Lisette interjected, jumping up from Sandy's lap. "He wanted to give me a birthday party. You didn't even remember my birthday!"

"I remembered all right," Ralph shot back. "But I knew you were going to start again on that emancipation shit, and I was sick of it. You wanted too much from me. I'm not your mother, you know. She wanted you. I didn't."

"You're disgusting!" Lisette sputtered. "As if I couldn't figure it out for myself, but you just had to tell me, didn't you? You never came to see me after I was born. But don't worry. I never really thought of you as my father anyway."

"I gave you a roof over your head and food to eat when Marie was gone. What more did you want?"

"I wanted a life!"

"Why should *you* have one? I had one with your mother, but you spoiled that. You weren't even..." His voice trailed off and his breathing slowed.

"I wasn't even what?" Lisette sobbed. "I am your flesh and blood. You should want *everything* for me. But it's always about you, isn't it?" She pushed herself into Sandy's arms again and glared up at her father.

"You're the sperm that got away," Ralph spewed his words at Lisette. "Christ! Why don't you both just leave. I'm tired of this," he moaned.

"Oh, we'll be going soon," Sandy said. "The truth of the matter is, Ralph, I was wrong. I convinced Lisette to come here to see you because I thought it would help her get through a horrible time in her life. I told her that if she did, I'd help her get emancipated by the judge. I told her that if you'd care enough about your daughter, you'd want to help her get better. But you did things to her I didn't think a father could do to his daughter."

"She's a liar!" Ralph hissed. "Can't you see that?"

"Frankly, I do believe her. I think you are incapable of knowing what the truth is. It's whatever you want it to be, so you can get your way. That's what pathological liars do. Right now, you'd destroy this girl with your lies because she's something you'll never be. Despite your worst efforts, she's a pretty normal human being, and you can't stand it."

Sandy stood up with Lisette cradled close to her body. "I can tell you right now, I will do whatever I have to do for this girl so she never has to see or be with you again. If it's emancipation she wants, I'll go for that. In my mind, you have forfeited any right that you have to be a father."

Ralph groaned and shifted in his bed.

"Oh, don't worry," Sandy went on with contempt in her voice. "I'm not a judge, so I can't stand here and take away your parental rights. But I'll tell any judge what I just told you. You don't intimidate me. You always counted on the fact that everyone would be so afraid of you that they'd never do anything about your outrageous behavior. But I'm not afraid of you, and neither is Lisette. Are you, honey?"

Lisette looked up at Sandy and nodded her head vigorously.

Then Sandy turned to Ralph again. "If you ever come near this girl again, you'll have me to deal with first. Do you understand?"

He looked at them both for a moment, then turned his body and head away from them. He lay motionless as if he was dead. Then when his breathing came in short, wheezy spurts, he hacked away to clear his throat.

Somehow, in that moment Lisette knew that it was the last time she would see her father. She knew she'd never forget the smell of Ralph rotting away in that room or the roar of Sandy's voice fighting for her. As they walked out of his room, she felt a great weight lift from her shoulders. It was the weight of needing her father's forgiveness for what she had done. She walked in the room not even knowing that she wanted it and walked out understanding that it wouldn't have meant anything to her if she had gotten it.

Now she only had to find a way to forgive herself.

Somehow, she thought that would be easier than what she had just been through.

❖ ❖ ❖

Everyone was quiet in the room when Lisette finished.

They sat there together in tight circle of chairs around the fireplace. Lisette was crying, and so was Brad. Jenny was dabbing her eyes, too, with a tissue.

Erick sat next to Lisette, holding her hand. He spoke first. "You did good."

"You were so brave to go and see Ralph," Brad said with admiration in his voice. "I only met him once years ago, and he was a pretty intimidating guy." Then Brad added, "You were never convicted of trying to kill Ralph, were you? He saved you, didn't he?"

"Yeah, he did. I still don't understand why."

"That's an amazing story, Lisette," Jenny finally said. Then she asked, "Is he still alive?"

"As far as I know he is. I don't think he's gotten any better. I don't know. I try not to think about it most days."

Erick squeezed her hand again. "You don't have to Lisette. Not any longer."

"Your record doesn't reflect this as a crime," Jenny said. "Actually, you were more the victim, depending how you look at it."

"Thanks again for telling us," Brad said quietly.

"Erick said I had to. He said if I wanted you to love me unconditionally, I had to give you all the conditions of my life, and then you could decide."

Suddenly Brad was on his knees in front of her in a second. "Of course, I love you, Lisette, no matter what. I loved you from the first moment your mom told me she was pregnant. I wanted you to be my baby so much. I'm sorry I missed that part of your life, but now you have this part to share with me. And with Jenny and Maryssa." Then he paused. "And Erick too! We are all family now!"

"I'm so amazed," Lisette replied. "I don't know what to say."

"Just say yes!" Jenny exclaimed. "Come join our family. We're a pretty motley crew as it is."

"But I don't live here now. Most of the time I live in Los Angeles. That's where my business is. I could come stay here for a time, though—do my business long distance. I'd have to see what Todd thinks."

"Whose Todd?" Jenny and Brad ask almost together.

"He's my business manager. He was sort of my boyfriend." She looked over at Erick. "But he's not anymore. I have a new one." She smiled at him. "I have a great one!"

"Okay," Brad said carefully. "Jenny and I have talked this over, and we want to offer you a place to stay here. What did you call it, Jenny?"

"'A Room of Her Own,' just like Virginia Woolf!" Jenny said.

"Who is she?" Lisette asked.

"A famous female author who decided she needed her own space. You do, too—here with us! No strings attached!" Then Jenny added, "Your father and I talked this afternoon while he was helping me with dinner. We thought this would be a good room for you. It's away from all the craziness that goes on in the mansion, and you'd have your own side entrance. There's even a little kitchenette back there. You could cook your own food. Have friends over. Special friends! What do you think? You can come stay with us whenever you like."

"I don't know what to say." Lisette was truly overwhelmed. She turned to Brad and, in her excitement, blurted out, "Dad, what do you think?"

Brad gave her a look of amazement. She hadn't meant to call him Dad. It just slipped out, but Lisette could tell it made him happy.

He had a big grin on his face when he replied, "I can't think of a better way for us to get to know each other better. Welcome to our house!"

She hadn't expected this; she hadn't even thought about it. It was too much.

"Just say yes," Jenny said gleefully, "and I'll arrange everything." Then she added, "I know you don't want Brad and me butting into your life. Kids hate that. Maryssa hates it when I do that. But we can help you. You're not alone. You have us."

Oh my God, Lisette thought. *This is like a dream.* For the first time in a very long time, she felt hope. Her life was going to get better. Sure, she had money from her business, but now she'd have something even more important. With the kind of love Brad and Jenny were offering her, she knew that anything was possible.

This was so unexpected. Suddenly, there were all these people— Sophie and Brad and Jenny and Erick—who wanted to help her, take care of her, and love her. So many people had let her down. It was easy to walk away from them, go find another town to dance in, and keep on feeling miserable. Now there were people who cared about her, and with them, she'd have the family she always wanted, people she could trust. This was real, not fake.

"For years I've told myself that if I had a chance to make my life better, I'd take it, and now here it is. I'd be a fool to say no."

Brad was ecstatic. "That's fabulous. Welcome to our family!"

He stood up, pulled her out of her chair and hugged her. Then Jenny was hugging her too, and so was Erick.

"Okay!" Jenny finally, putting her arm around Brad. "Why don't you two young people sit here for a few minutes and take in this great room? Then come back to the dining room and join Brad and me for dessert. We have strawberry shortcake that is to die for."

Lisette nodded and smiled, as Brad and Jenny left the room hand in hand. She and Erick sat back down next to each other.

"Wow!" he exclaimed. "It's been quite the day. You came here afraid the governor and her husband wouldn't even like you. Look what you've done! You've charmed them into loving you, and now you'll be living in the governor's mansion. Not bad! You did it, Lisette. You were great!"

"I couldn't have done it without you, Erick."

"I was glad to help. You have a lot of other people now who can help you whenever you need them. Brad and Jenny, and Sophie too. Sophie will be so excited when she hears your news."

"And don't forget Lacey," Lisette added with a sigh. "You know, she told me once when I was on that shamanic journey with her in the Upper World before she crossed over that I had to find my own power. I think she was talking about the power of love, and today I really feel that. This is living well, and it's my best revenge—just like Lacey said."

Erick smiled. "Lacey would be so proud of you. Maybe finding your real father was the sign you were waiting for. Remember, he came to find you. He didn't have to do that. He loves you that much."

Lisette gave Erick a look of pure surprise and replied, "You're right about that."

Then she sighed with relief as she realized that what Lacey had told her was true. She did have the power to love and to change her life. It was only going to get better.

Thank you, Lacey, and thank you, Mom.

❖ ❖ ❖

Not long after Lisette and Erick left the governor's mansion that night, Jenny's phone buzzed with an emergency alert as she and Brad sat in upstairs in the living room of the residence.

Brad was familiar with alerts like this. They usually came from the state police and provided critical law enforcement information to the governor first before the press, if possible, and they might have information the press may not be privy to.

This one came as Brad and Jenny were sitting next to each other on the couch with the television on. Their Sunday night ritual was watching *60 Minutes* together, but by the time Erick and Lisette left, Brad and Jenny had missed that program that night. Now with some other program on, neither one of them was watching intently. Instead they were reading the Sunday paper, trading sections back and forth between them, and commenting on anything they found interesting as they went along.

Brad noticed that this alert was more alarming than most to Jenny. She sat up quickly, and while she didn't usually share much of this top-level information with him, this time she did.

Her voice was altered but calm as she turned to him and said, "There's been a shooting at the mall. Police say one of the shooters is down. They have a tentative ID on him. Not sure if there are others." Then as she read more, her voice shifted. "I can't believe this. I know this kid. This can't be happening!"

Brad looked at her squarely. "What's happening? What mall?"

Please don't let it be Westingham, he thought, waiting for her response. He had worked on the Westingham Mall expansion project for three years. With the mall's current setup, someone with a gun would come in and open fire into spaces where a lot of people could get hurt. That was scheduled to change as the mall was renovated and expanded.

"It's Westingham," she said quickly, and Brad's heart sank.

They didn't get to the expansion fast enough. The nightmare had begun. Then she added, "There's an email now from Jerry."

Brad knew Jerry as Lt. Jerry Stanton, the commander of the governor's Security Unit, the guy who would immediately feed to the governor all the law enforcement details she needed.

Jenny read aloud from her phone. "'Police are responding to multiple shots in the mall. Unknown how many shot or killed.'" Then she stopped reading and asked Brad frantically. "What were you and Lisette saying at dinner about Ambrose and his son? Something about how he told you in the coffee shop that his son had changed his name so he wouldn't have his father's last name anymore."

Brad looked at her blankly for a moment. "You mean Mark? Yes, Ambrose was very angry about not seeing his son for years. Mark had changed his last name to Durocher to spite his father. At dinner, Lisette said Durocher was his grandmother's last name."

"Yes," Jenny exclaimed. "Oh God! His grandmother's name was Abigail— Abigail Durocher. I remember her from the custody case. I gave her custody of Mark over Ambrose." Then she thrust her cell phone in Brad's face. "Look. Right here. That's the name of the shooter—Mark Durocher!"

Brad looked at her, then at her phone. The name was there in the text of the email.

Jenny was on her feet now, pacing the floor. "Now this will be on me too!" she shouted. "Why? What's Mark's problem? He's got to be in his twenties now! I haven't seen him since he was a kid. But someone's going to figure out who this kid is to me. It won't take long. What Ambrose did yesterday and the whole story about how I was the judge in his custody case was in the local Sunday paper today. Just wait until the national press gets this story."

"But even if they do, you could say that you did try to help

Mark when he was a kid. It was something else that set him off today. You can't be held responsible for that."

Before Brad could say anything more to ease Jenny's anxiety, he noticed a "National News Alert" sign flashing on the television set in front of them. The national network had the story.

The announcer said: "There has been a shooting at a mall, and the suspect who shot and killed at least four people has been tied to Governor Jenny Jablonski…"

Brad looked at Jenny and saw that all the color had drained from her face.

The announcer droned on.

"Jablonski is a very popular governor in her state. Until now, her name has been mentioned as a potential vice-presidential candidate in the coming election. More details are coming in. Let's go to our reporter on the scene of the shooting…"

Oh God! Brad thought. *Where does this go from here? No place good. It's already a nightmare for those killed and injured in the mall and their families. But now there is my family.*

Brad's mind raced. Just when he and Jenny had worked out a way to embrace Lisette as his daughter and avoid having to answer embarrassing questions or endure endless public interest in a story that was really a family matter, this happened.

If Ambrose was back in the news along with his son, it wasn't that much of a leap for some enterprising reporter to find out how Ambrose, Mark, Jenny, Brad, and Lisette were all connected together.

"I love you to the moon, Lisette," Brad muttered to himself, echoing something that he had said to Marie years ago about his feelings for her. Then he added cautiously to his daughter.

"Hang on for the ride. It's going to a be rocky one!"

October 17, 2019

The Anniversary

Sophie got Lisette thinking about the twentieth anniversary of Lacey's death almost from the first day she came on board full-time to work with *Survivor Strong, Thriver Resilient,* Sophie's non-profit organization.

The two women were inspired by the rise of the #MeToo move-ment two years ago when the hashtag #MeToo had been posted online millions of times, some with an accompanying personal story of sexual harassment or sexual assault. They reveled in the fact that #MeToo spread so virally on social media that it raised the awareness in the United States and around the world of how widespread and prevalent sexual assault, domestic violence, and sexual harassment still was. It also created greater empathy for the victims—mostly female—and the impact of these crimes on them physically, financially, and emotionally.

Sophie liked to think that empathy was the ability to stand in someone else's shoes. That's how she got an idea for the Twentieth Anniversary Gala. She wanted to be sure that milestone would be marked in a bigger and better way than the tenth-year anniversa-ry one, but also that this time, the event would come off without a hitch. They had no plans to repeat the disastrous Tenth Anni-versary Gala when everything came crashing down.

But it wasn't lost on either Sophie or Lisette that the event ten years ago illustrated another issue that the #MeToo movement put in the spotlight, that of "toxic masculinity." To them, that was masculinity gone wild. It was the view that to be a "real man," men always had to be strong and never show their emotions because that was a sign of weakness. "Real men" are allowed, of course, to show anger, and violence is always the answer when anger builds to a peak and needs to be released. Finally, "real men" solve their problems through violence and with violence, and they expect that such actions will not be punished or condemned by society. In fact, they expect them to be celebrated as the true essence of how men are supposed to be.

Sophie recognized that such toxic masculinity was part of Ambrose's actions at the Tenth Anniversary Gala. He was so furious with Lisette and Governor Jenny Jablonski for all his real and imagined grievances that he aggressively plotted against them and disrupted the event when he didn't get his way. But the actions of his son, Mark Durocher, a day later at a local shopping mall that killed ten people, were fueled by even more violent rage, and the ramifications of his son's actions were still being played out ten years later. It was easy to say "like father, like son" with Ambrose and Mark, but Sophie knew that the way men are socialized had a lot to do with it. She was determined that neither of these men or their actions would destroy the event she was planning this year for the anniversary. But longer term, she and Lisette had added working with men and male offenders to their mission.

While they had much to celebrate in their work, they had also reached some important milestones in their personal lives. With both of them approaching their fortieth birthdays, they also had changed their names. Sophie got married and added a hyphenated name to her last name, one that she and her spouse now shared. Lisette had changed her name almost ten years ago to the day for another reason. After she discovered that Brad Bufford was her real father and in honor of her mother, Marie Patterson, she legally became Lisette Patterson Bufford. The blending of the family of Jenny Jablonski and Brad Bufford had gone a little less smoothly, but Sophie was sure things would get better.

Ultimately, what Sophie and Lisette most wanted to celebrate at the Twentieth Anniversary Gala was their initial work to transform the services at the college for students who experienced violence against them into trauma-informed, survivor-centered programs. That meant the services had to be designed and delivered in a way that prioritized the rights, needs, and wishes of the survivor and treated the trauma experienced without re-traumatizing the survivor.

To achieve that kind of transformation along with all the other work they had taken on, Sophie needed to find some new sources of money. Over the years Lisette's donation of a good portion of the money from her Attila the Hunny strip clubs to the organization meant that both she and Sophie could work full-time along with other staff. But with the #MeToo movement's spotlight on the sexual exploitation of women, it became harder for Sophie to accept such tainted money. In addition, with the political fortune of Jenny Jablonski, her stepmother, heating up as the 2020 presidential election was coming near, Lisette found it almost impossible to stay in that business. Eventually she and Erick had struck out on their own to support themselves, but new sources of funding had to be found for the nonprofit organization.

Sophie put on her attorney hat and got this crazy idea to try to duplicate the success of New York's groundbreaking 2018 "Enough Is Enough" law in their own state. That state law required that all colleges and universities adopt a set of comprehensive procedures and guidelines related to domestic violence, dating violence, stalking, and sexual assault to ensure the safety of all students attending colleges in the state. Sophie believed that she and Lisette could convince a certain female governor to push to do the same in their state and increase state funding to their organization. They could also find corporate sponsors as they expanded into programs that would foster economic empowerment for women on and off campus. They planned to work with businesses and colleges to provide more resources and encourage women to move into careers in science, engineering, and math as well as entrepreneurship to start and manage their own businesses.

So as the year of the Twentieth Anniversary Gala rolled around, Sophie and Lisette had much to add to Lacey's legacy and so for the Gala they decided to go big or go home. They made a list of celebrities and famous people to invite and started in January asking each one of them if they'd join them in October. By June they had invited and booked the best of the best.

And now the party was ready to begin! No one was going to spoil it this time. Neither Ambrose nor his son, Mark, had that power. Whatever challenges they would face, Sophie and Lisette were ready to face them.

This year, 2019, was their time to change the world!

The Resistance was on!

THE END

DISCUSSION QUESTIONS
A Reader's Guide
For Individuals and Groups

❖ ❖ ❖

Awaken, the first book in *The Best Revenge Series™,* is a novel about two young women, Lacey and Lisette, who are on a healing journey from victim to survivor to "thriver." In the second book, *Emerge,* the story continues and focuses on Lisette's journey to find the kind of love and support she'll need to move forward with her life and thrive!

Watch for *Thrive,* the third book in *The Best Revenge Series™* coming soon!

1. What are some of the ways that Lisette was impacted by the traumas of her life? These traumas include her mother dying when she was very young, going to live with Ralph and not finishing school or learning to read well as a child.

2. How has Lisette been able to deal with some of these impacts in her life? In this story, who came to help her and who hindered her in this healing process?

3. What did you learn about the healing process from this book that has been most helpful to you?

4. In the book, Lisette talks about "unconditional love" as "reliable love." What does it mean for Lisette to lose unconditional love when her mother dies and regain it again when she finds a new family with Jenny and Brad?

5. How do you think Brad will be as a father to Lisette? She has forgiven him for not finding her sooner, but can he step up now and be the father she's never had? What does Brad have to do to show that he is interested and involved in her life?

6. What are some of the instances in the story where characters, such as Gerald and Shirley, Erick's gym clients, need to be more aware of the *Warning Signs of an Unhealthy, Abusive Relationship* listed on the next few pages? How could Shirley keep herself safer in her marriage? Or should she leave the marriage?

7. Has anything ever happened to you in one of your relationship that might be described as unhealthy or abusive? How did you deal with this or how might you react now that you have more knowledge of the dangerous dynamics in such a relationship?

8. What would be the best way for Sophie and Lisette to remember Lacey and give her a lasting legacy on that campus? How could a community such as Lacey's college work to prevent dating violence?

9. What are some of the changes for women that have taken place since 1979 when Marie was a dancer in a strip club and pregnant out of wedlock? What are some of the ways violence against women has been addressed since 1999 when Lacey was killed on a college campus? How has the #MeToo movement impacted the lives of men and women in this country?

10. How have the political aspirations of women changed since 1979? Are women faring better as governors, members of Congress, and potential presidential candidates than Jenny Jablonski did in 2009?

11. Who was your favorite character in the story and why?

12. What would you like to see next for this character as they continue to grow, change and heal?

WARNING SIGNS OF AN UNHEALTHY, ABUSIVE RELATIONSHIP

❖ ❖ ❖

He is controlling, possessive and overly demanding of her time and attention. He appears at times to be two different people: one, charming, loving, and kind; the other, abusive, vicious, and mean. He has what is called a "Dr. Jekyll and Mr. Hyde" dual personality. He keeps her on edge, not knowing who he'll be at any moment. He manipulates what she feels for him and makes her feel bad about herself.

He will at times be sorry for what he has said and done and will promise never to do it again, but he will also deny, minimize, or blame others for his behavior. She will feel it is her fault, that *if only* she had done something else, pleased him more, been more compliant, she would not be treated this way by him.

EMOTIONAL
- He insults her, calls her names and belittles her in private and in public with her family and friends.
- He isolates her from family and friends, forbidding her to see them or limiting her access to them.
- He is jealous of her contact with others, particularly with other men. He exaggerates her relationships with other men, accusing her unfairly of having affairs outside of their relationship.
- He wants to know where she is at all times, calling or texting her to find out who she is with. He invades her privacy by checking her cell phone, viewing her email, or monitoring her Web pages.
- He refuses to accept when she ends the relationship and may stalk her long afterward.

PHYSICAL
- He yells, screams, and loses his temper easily, sometimes disproportionately over unimportant things.
- He destroys her things, kicks, or breaks other property, making her fear that he could hurt her, too.
- He intimidates her, making her afraid of him by his looks, actions, and gestures.
- He grabs her, kicks her, slaps her, punches her, strangles her, draws a gun or weapon, and threatens to kill her. He harms her pets or threatens to hurt or harm her family or friends.
- He stalks her with unwanted phone calls, visits to her house or job, and secretly monitors her actions.

ECONOMIC
- He controls her access to money, even her own money or money she has earned herself.
- He refuses to pay bills or let her know about family income, investments, or property.
- He keeps her from getting or keeping a job, and he refuses to support their family or children.
- He makes all the big decisions, using male privilege to get his way and insisting on rigid gender roles.

PSYCHOLOGICAL
- She feels like she is going crazy, that his view of the world is not reasonable, but she will have little chance of convincing him otherwise, and he demands her absolute loyalty to his way of thinking.
- He says he can't live without her or will kill himself if she leaves, so she fears ending the relationship.
- He pushes the relationship too far, too fast, and is obsessed with her and wants her for himself.
- He has unrealistic expectations and demands, and she feels it is her fault he's not happy.

SEXUAL

- He demands to have sex forcibly without her consent with him or with others.
- He withdraws sex from her or makes it conditional on her compliance to his demands.
- He calls her crude names, implying she is promiscuous and unfaithful sexually to him.

Signs of a Healthy Relationship

In a healthy relationship, two people are on an equal footing, and they respect, trust, and support each other. They are honest with each other and take responsibility for their actions. They are good parents, sharing responsibility in raising their kids. They have an economic partnership in which the best interests of both are considered, and they communicate, negotiate, and treat each other fairly.

Reprinted from
Entering the Thriver Zone: A Seven-Step Guide to Thriving After Abuse
by Susan M. Omilian, JD
For more information on Susan and her work, visit *thriverzone.com.*

RESOURCES

❖ ❖ ❖

As you read this book, you might find a need for the resources below. It is important to view violence and abuse seriously in a relationship and take care. Stay safe!

Crisis Intervention
For immediate crisis intervention services in your local community, contact:

- The National Domestic Violence Hotline 1-800-799-SAFE (7233) **www.thehotline.org**

- National Sexual Assault Hotline at 1-800-656-HOPE (4673) **www.rainn.org**

- National Center for Victims of Crime **www.victimsofcrime.org/help-for-crime-victims**

- Office for Victims of Crime, U.S. Department of Justice **www.ovc.gov**

Dating Violence and Stalking

- Break the Cycle: Empowering Youth to End Dating Violence **www.breakthecycle.org**

- Love Is Respect – National Teen Dating Abuse Help Line 1-866-331-9474 **www.loveisrespect.org**

- Stalking Resource Center **www.victimsofcrime.org/our-programs/stalking-resource-center** has a mission is to enhance the ability of professionals, organizations, and systems to effectively respond to stalking. It also offers resources on stalking to victims, how to identify stalking and deal with it through an online support group

- Women's Law.org **www.womenslaw.org** is a project of the National Network to End Domestic Violence, providing legal information and support to victims of domestic violence, stalking, and sexual assault.

Domestic Violence

- National Network to End Domestic Violence (NNEDV) **www.nnedv.org** offers support to victims of domestic violence who are escaping abusive relationships and empowers survivors to build new lives.

- National Coalition Against Domestic Violence (NCADV) **www.ncadv.org** works closely with battered women's advocates around the country to identify the issues and develop a legislative agenda.

- **www.domesticshelters.org** Free, online, searchable database of domestic violence shelter programs nationally.

- National Resource Center on Domestic Violence (NRCDV) **www.nrcdv.org** is a source of information for those wanting to educate themselves and help others on the many issues related to domestic violence.

Sexual Assault

- RAINN — Rape, Abuse & Incest National Network **www.rainn.org** operates the National Sexual Assault Hotline and has programs to prevent sexual assault, help Victims, and ensure they receive justice.

- National Sexual Violence Resource Center **www.nsvrc.org** provides leadership in preventing and responding to sexual violence through creating resources and promoting research.

- The Victim Rights Law Center **www.victimrights.org** is dedicated solely to serving the legal needs of sexual assault victims. It provides training, technical assistance, and in some cases, free legal assistance in civil cases to sexual assault victims in certain parts of the country.

Child Abuse

- Childhelp USA National Child Abuse **www.childhelp.org** directly serves abused and neglected children through the National Child Abuse Hotline, 1-800-4-A-CHILD® and other programs.

Post-Traumatic Stress

See information listed at National Institute of Mental Health website, **www.nimh.nih.gov**

BOOKS BY SUSAN M. OMILIAN, JD

THE THRIVER ZONE SERIES™

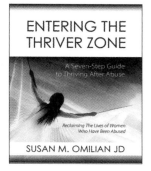

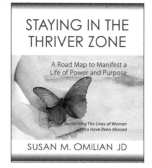

Entering the Thriver Zone
*A Seven-Step Guide to
Thriving After Abuse*

Staying in the Thriver Zone
*A Road Map to Manifest
a Life of Power and Purpose*

NEXT - *Living in the Thriver Zone*
A Celebration of Living Well as the Best Revenge

THE BEST REVENGE SERIES™

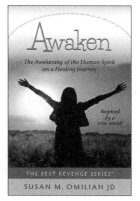

AWAKEN:
The Awakening of the Human Spirit on a Healing Journey

NEXT – THRIVE!

For updates please visit www.ThriverZone.com

ABOUT THE AUTHOR

An attorney, author, and motivational speaker, Susan Omilian has worked extensively as an advocate to end violence against women for the past four decades. In the 1970s, she founded a rape crisis center and represented battered women in divorce proceedings in the early 1980s. She also litigated sex discrimination cases including helping to articulate the legal concept that made sexual harassment illegal in the 1990s.

Since her nineteen-year-old niece Maggie was shot and killed by her ex-boyfriend in 1999, Susan has worked extensively with hundreds of women who have experienced abuse helping them take the journey from victim to survivor to "thriver."

A recognized national expert on the process of recovery after violence and abuse, Susan is the author of two book series, *The Thriver Zone* and *The Best Revenge*.

**For more about Susan, her books and further resources,
visit thriverzone.com.**